Responsible Economics

Frontiers of Business Ethics

Series Editor
LÁSZLÓ ZSOLNAI
Business Ethics Center
Corvinus University of Budapest

VOLUME 11

PETER LANG

Oxford · Bern · Berlin · Bruxelles · Frankfurt am Main · New York · Wien

Responsible Economics

E.F. Schumacher and His Legacy for the 21st Century

edited by

HENDRIK OPDEBEECK

PETER LANG

Oxford · Bern · Berlin · Bruxelles · Frankfurt am Main · New York · Wien

Bibliographic information published by Die Deutsche Nationalbibliothek
Die Deutsche Nationalbibliothek lists this publication in the Deutsche National-
bibliografie; detailed bibliographic data is available on the Internet at
http://dnb.d-nb.de.

A catalogue record for this book is available from the British Library.

Library of Congress Control Number: 2013944467

Cover design: Judit Kovacs, Createch Ltd, Hungary

ISSN 1661-4844
ISBN 978-3-0343-1707-8

© Peter Lang AG, International Academic Publishers, Bern 2013
Hochfeldstrasse 32, CH-3012 Bern, Switzerland
info@peterlang.com, www.peterlang.com, www.peterlang.net

This publication has been peer reviewed.

Printed in Germany

Contents

viii

x

BARBARA WOOD-SCHUMACHER

Preface

If a prediction comes true, one says it is a success but if a prophesy is fulfilled it is considered as a failure. This is because prophets are there to warn us to change our ways in order to avert disaster. Many people have said that my father's voice was prophetic. However, what he warned us of has come about. Does this mean he was a failure? You would not expect me to answer yes to this question. And I don't because as long as some people are still listening his voice is still being heard and there is hope. There is no doubt that many still hear his voice in *Small is Beautiful*. Unfortunately few look to *A Guide for the Perplexed*. The role of the prophet is first to read the signs of the times, to look at what is going on and see where it is leading. My father was not born with that ability. He had to learn how to read the signs of the times and how to interpret them correctly. This meant learning to see reality in all its fullness. *Small is Beautiful* and *A Guide for the Perplexed* belong together because in different ways they present us with that reality in its fullness: material and spiritual.

What I want to do in this preface is to look at a few key times in his life which gave him a new perspective on reality and made it possible for him to develop the ideas contained in his two books. I believe this is important because if we understand how people like him came to think as they did it might help us to learn to think more clearly about what is going on now and make the right decisions about what to do about it. It is also important because what he wanted above all is that we should learn to think clearly ourselves. His books are not so much guides as to how to act but rather how to think so that we make the right decisions about how to respond to the challenges of life.

The *first* moment concerns Nazi Germany. My father left Germany for Oxford in 1930 to study economics and then went to Columbia University in New York. During this time Hitler came to power. My father was a patriotic German who loved his country. He had experienced the economic chaos of post world war I Germany and felt the humiliation of the punitive conditions the allies had imposed on Germany. He did not support the Nazis but he felt that Germany needed a strong leader. When he heard the reports that were coming out of Germany he decided to go back to see for himself what was going on. This was 1934. He was horrified by what he saw and shocked that whenever he tried to discuss this with others he was always dismissed with the same answer: 'Where there is planing (as in planing a piece of wood) there are shavings'. In other words: Hitler is doing a good job getting the economy going and restoring Germany's strength so we have to put up with a few unfortunate side effects. This response taught him an important lesson. He saw that you can't leave out some aspects of reality if they are inconvenient. You have to take everything into account if you want to understand what is going on so that you can make a proper judgement and decide what to do about it. Dismiss something as an unfortunate but inevitable 'side effect' and you might miss the whole point of what is really going on.

For a long time we have put up with the unfortunate side effects of economic growth in the west: pollution, waste, depletion of the world resources, mind numbing work, global warming and of course millions who live in poverty. He observed those so called 'side effects' and took them seriously and then had the courage to speak out before most people even recognised their existence. So the first lesson is: observe everything – even 'inconvenient truths'. The side effects may be more significant than that which everyone else thinks is the main point.

The *second* period that was important in shaping his thinking was the Second World War. In 1937 he left Germany and returned to England because he could no longer bear to live in Hitler's Germany. It was not easy to be a German in England especially once war broke out and he was classed as an enemy alien. He could no longer work as an economist and was lucky to get a job as a farm labourer. This was quite a shock to his system. After all he was an intellectual – a thinker – not a manual worker. That shock was followed another. He was arrested and interned along with an extraordinary mixture of other Germans – refugees, anti-Nazis, Nazis and Communists. My father always claimed that this wartime experience

– working as a farm labourer and then living in the internment camp – was where he received his real education. On the farm he had to count the cows every day. One day he found that one cow had died. The farmer was furious and shouted at him: 'Why didn't you tell me that that cow was not well?' My father was shocked. He had just counted and not looked at the condition of the cows.

In the internment camp he had to look beyond the different types of prisoners and work to weld them into a mutually supporting community. He took the motto 'I never met a man I didn't like'. He never forgot that lesson: That reality has an inner dimension. That there are more important things that numbers and the exterior of things. It made him see that if he wanted to make a difference he would have to see people differently – not as people in the abstract but as real flesh and blood – who they are, their context, their needs, their way of doing things. Thus far he was a scientific rationalist and a convinced atheist. He had no time for the 'mumbo jumbo' of religion. But his wartime experience and then the shock of returning to Germany after the war began to make him question everything he thought he believed. He found that he could not answer the question of why the country that had produced the sublime works of people like Bach and Beethoven and Goethe had gone so wrong. Reason and science was inadequate. It was as if he had to start learning everything all over again. He said he felt like Dante in the Divine Comedy who says:

> Midway along the journey of our life
> I woke to find myself in a dark wood,
> For I had wandered off from the straight path.

He started to ask new questions: What is man? and What is the purpose of life? and How does economics help in fulfilling that purpose? These were not easy questions for him to answer. For the first half of his life he had dismissed such philosophical questions as irrational and unscientific. Honesty now required that he gave them attention.

The *final* moment I want to mention is his visit to Burma in 1955 as an economic adviser with the UN. Again he observed carefully and reflected on what he saw and experienced. The Burmese seemed to be so happy. It was a very different place from the Burma of the generals today. There he saw that western economics was not adding to the happiness of the Burmese but rather the reverse. It was making them want things they did not need. It dawned upon him that economics was not a science independent of values: what the economist believes to be the meaning and purpose of life is also relevant. He wrote: 'Economics means a certain ordering of life according to the philosophy inherent and implicit in economics. The science of economics does not stand on its own feet: it is derived from a view of the meaning and purpose of life – whether the economist himself knows this or not'.[1]

Burma brought into focus the spiritual side of life and was the beginning of a spiritual journey which eventually led my father into Christianity. He said: 'I came to Burma a thirsty wanderer and there I found living water'. Burma was where economics met the spiritual and from then on he wove the two inextricably together. At the end of *Small is Beautiful* there is a brief epilogue which refers to the Christian teaching of the Four Cardinal Virtues: prudence, temperance, fortitude and justice. He writes: 'there is perhaps no body of teaching which is more relevant and appropriate to the modern predicament [...]. Prudence implies a translation of the knowledge of truth into decisions corresponding to reality. What, therefore, could be of greater importance today than the study and cultivation of prudence, which would almost inevitably lead to a real understanding of the three other cardinal virtues, all of which are indispensable for the survival of civilisation?'[2] The Cardinal virtue of prudence is the rigorously truthful apprehension of reality followed by the courage to act appropriately. Prudence requires absolute honesty in the way we look at reality. In the words of Joseph Pieper, it requires 'the kind of open-mindedness which recognises the true variety of things and situations to be experienced and does not cage itself in any presumption of deceptive knowledge. [...]. A closed mind and know-it-allness are fundamentally forms of resistance to the truth of real things'.[3]

---

1   *Buddhist Economics*: Report to Burmese Government 1955
2   *Small is Beautiful*, 251. Here Schumacher is drawing on two works of Joseph Pieper: *Prudence*, London: Faber & Faber 1959 and *Fortitude and Temperance*, London: Faber and Faber 1955.
3   Pieper 1959.

The thinking contained in my father's publications was how he saw reality in the most rigorous and truthful way possible and its purpose was to inspire his readers to action. This is why they belong together. Together they give a picture of reality, as it were from the outside and the inside. *Small is Beautiful* is a book that inspires people to take action. It is not prescriptive. It is prophetic because it describes the reality of the situation the world is in and leaves people to make their own decisions about how to respond. That is why it is so liberating and empowering. *A Guide for the Perplexed* is an essential companion because it helps us to think about what we are aiming for as we work to make the world a better place for all who inhabit it. It teaches us how to think.

Often people ask me what I think my father would say about this or that happening in the world today. Well, I haven't got his expertise, wisdom and insight to answer those questions but I hope that by having given a few examples from his life, I have thrown a bit of light on how he thought and was able to have such insight. He did not subscribe to any ideology but thought for himself. He took all the facts into account, even those that others thought ridiculous, and never left out anything that was inconvenient. He believed that, however small and insignificant people are, they matter and are beautiful. He believed in facing reality in its fullness and then taking appropriate action. In all this he was a prudent man.

All that remains is for all of us to learn from him and continue his work.

Acknowledgements

We are grateful for the financial support we received from the Leopold Mayer Foundation to publish this book. The main objective of the Leopold Mayer Foundation for Human Progress is to support the emergence of a world community. It aims to engage not only the academic world but every kind of social and occupational group. The Foundation defines itself as a 'human adventure' developed over the long term in co-operation with public and private partners on the various continents. Furthermore, on the one hand, it considers itself to be a learning organization within which the management of memory plays an essential role, which it combines with the development of a co-ordinated strategy. The Foundation regards particular initiative as a value in itself, but above all believes that true meaning emerges from the synergies which occur through interlinking with other initiatives. So its broad aim is through donations or loans to finance research projects and initiatives which are involved in 'a significant and innovative way with the progress of mankind'. For more information on its mission and activities like the promotion of a *Charter of Universal Responsibilities*, see www.fph.ch and the appendix of this publication. We hope that this publication will contribute to the realization of this mission.

— HENDRIK OPDEBEECK

HENDRIK OPDEBEECK
UNIVERSITY OF ANTWERP

1   Introduction: A Utopian Economic Paradigm?

The centenary of E.F. Schumacher's birth (1911–77) offers an interesting opportunity to revisit his work and life. From the perspective of the crisis at the beginning of this twenty-first century, reconsidering Schumacher's *Small is Beautiful* paradigm makes clear that advances in responsible economics more than ever are becoming a priority. This book contains the proceedings of the international conference on *Responsibility in Economics: the legacy of E.F. Schumacher*. This seventh annual *European SPES Forum* conference was organized in September 2011 by the Center for Ethics of the University of Antwerp in collaboration with the Business Ethics Center of Budapest, to celebrate the 100th anniversary of E.F. Schumacher's birth and to confront Schumacher's vision with the need for responsibility in current economics and business.

The first part of this book reconsiders economics from the perspective of E.F. Schumacher's *Economics as if People Mattered*. In the next chapter Walter Moss gives a survey of Schumacher's wisdom-centered life and work with a view to summarizing the essence of his philosophy and economics. In the third chapter Laszlo Zsolnai confronts the assumptions of mainstream economics with what is called alternative meta-economics like Schumacher's frugality- and responsibility-based theories. For Gábor Kovács in chapter 4 the history of Buddhist Economics reveals how Schumacher's work contributes to rediscovering Buddhist economics as a field of scholarship. Chapter 5 by Roy Varghese interprets Schumacher from both a Gandhian and an Aristotelian perspective. Authentic development in a frugality-based economy asks for responsibility for oneself, the other and the environment. In chapter 6 Zubin Mulla explains how Schumacher's legacy can be considered a current application of Karma-Yoga, the Indian philosophy of work. Gerrit De Vylder in chapter 7 interprets the East as a practical and spiritual basis for economics through which the West rediscovers its own sources of dealing with economics. Philip Bruce in chapter 8 concludes this first part on economics reconsidered, describing *Scott Bader* today. It was Schumacher who sixty years ago inspired this company to review its structures as if people mattered.

Part two of the book reconsiders responsibility from the perspective of E.F. Schumacher's frugality- and responsibility-based economics. In chapter 9 Christian Arnsperger gives a critical reappraisal of Schumacher. It becomes apparent how a further articulation of responsibility beyond responsiveness is a *conditio sine qua non*. Like Arnsperger also Carlos Hoevel and Michal Michalski in respectively chapter 10 and 11 rediscover in Schumacher's *Guide for the Perplexed* the importance of Schumacher's call for responsibility towards work, family life, property, credit and consumption. A broader (business) education appeals. Ludo Abicht demonstrates in chapter 12 how not only a more Christian interpretation of the *Guide for the Perplexed* like the one of Hoevel and Michalski is possible, but that more than ever also an atheist interpretation presents itself. However, his analysis does not prevent Abicht from ending his paper with the remarkable conclusion that neither frugality nor responsibility are possible without religious or secular spirituality. Simon Trace in chapter 13 concludes this second part, describing responsibility in technology as integrated in the international NGO *Practical Action*. This NGO formerly was known as the *Intermediate Technology Development Group*, founded by Fritz Schumacher in 1966.

Part three finally reconsiders responsibility in economics. In chapter 14 Luk Bouckaert further elaborates the concept of responsibility as a spiritual commitment for real economics. He rediscovers the importance of democratic entrepreneurship. In chapter 15 Paul Jorion focuses on financial economics starting from Schumacher's questions on profit and Aristotle's view on price formation. In the next chapters the authors work out what responsibility in economics means for concrete situations in rich and poor countries all over the world. Knut Ims and Ove Jakobsen explore in chapter 16 how in Norway a continuation of articulating responsibility requires initiating an open research system based on creativity and interdisciplinarity. In chapter 17 Alexis Versele, Barbara Wauman and Hilde

Breesch apply Schumacher's theories on energy, ownership and poverty to a Belgian sustainable housing project. Chapter 18 demonstrates how in Africa responsible economics of permanence can be regained in the modern economic era. Joel Thompson demonstrates here how to change the way money functions, through incentivizing economic behavior which promotes the common good. In chapter 19 Bennie Callebaut and Luigino Bruni explain how the initiative of the *Economy of Communion* launched in Brazil implements responsibility in economics by discovering the importance of sharing. Stewart Wallis in chapter 20 concludes this third part on responsibility in economics reconsidered. He describes the *New Economics Foundation*, a British think-tank founded in 1986 by the leaders of The Other Economic Summit (TOES). The central aim of NEF is to work for a new model of wealth creation, based on equality, diversity and economic stability, in essence inspired by the legacy of E.F. Schumacher.

In the concluding chapter of the book, Hendrik Opdebeeck summarizes Schumacher's frugality- and responsibility-based economics, not as a utopian but as what he calls an emerging 'u-globian' economic paradigm. The answers presented here to the crisis of the beginning of the twenty-first century prove that the legacy of an economist and philosopher like Schumacher no longer belongs just to a utopian economic paradigm. A utopian economic paradigm is concerned with creating a number of particular, unique utopias. Schumacher reconsidered today makes clear that society needs *uglobian* economics investing in the sustainability of the globe, right now.

PART I

Economics

WALTER MOSS
EASTERN MICHIGAN UNIVERSITY

2   Schumacher's Wisdom-Centered Economics[1]

1   The Nature of Wisdom

E.F. Schumacher (1911–77) believed that wisdom should be like the sun, lighting up (*enlightening*) all aspects of our lives, including our science, technology, economics, politics, and personal lives. In his most popular book, *Small is Beautiful*, which first appeared in 1973, he wrote that 'more education can help us only if it produces more wisdom' (Schumacher 1975: 82).

2   How Can Wisdom Be Achieved?

As we have seen, Schumacher believed that education should help us become wiser, but too often it was not much help. In his most philosophical work, *A Guide for the Perplexed*, he wrote: 'All through school and university I had been given maps of life and knowledge on which there was hardly a trace of many of the things that I most cared about and that seemed to me to be of the greatest possible importance to the conduct of my life. I remembered that for many years my perplexity had been complete' (Schumacher 1977: 1). But if his formal education did not help much in his quest for wisdom, there was the more informal, self-educational path available to him and other wisdom seekers.

1   Most of the material in this paper first appeared in my essay 'The Wisdom of E.F. Schumacher', at http://www.wisdompage.com/SchumacherEssay.pdf.

Born in Germany in 1911, he received his primary and secondary education there before spending the early years of the Great Depression (1929–33)
mainly in England and the United States, studying economics at Oxford
and Columbia. In 1934, a year after Hitler had come to power, he returned
to Germany, where he soon married Anna Maria Petersen (Muschi to her
friends). But he discovered that many of Hitler's policies, including his per-
secution of the Jews, were abhorrent to him. He later told family members
that there was not room for him and Hitler in the same country, and that
one of them had to go. Thus, in 1937, he left Germany to settle in England,
where he and his wife raised four children – two years after her death from
cancer in 1960, he remarried and had four more children with his second
wife. From 1937 to 1945 he held several different jobs including being an
investment adviser, farm worker, and employee of the Oxford Institute of
Statistics. After England had gone to war with Germany in 1939, however,
he was interred for several months in 1940, along with other Germans, in
a barbed-wire camp.

But seeker after wisdom that he was, he came to view the camp as a
great educational opportunity. One of his fellow internees was a German
Marxist, and during his camp months and afterwards, in leisure hours
after performing farm work, he delved deeply into Marx's ideas. Not only
Marxian economics, but economic failures, especially a failed global trade
and exchange system, that helped lead to war, were much on his mind. In
December 1941 England's leading economist, John Maynard Keynes, invited
him for a visit to discuss a proposal Schumacher had developed to establish
an international clearing office to facilitate postwar multilateral trade. The
two economists spent several hours discussing this and other economic ideas.

Shortly after Germany's surrender in the summer of 1945, Schumacher
found himself back in his native land, where he mainly remained until
1950, acting as an economic adviser to the British Control Commission
and later to a more united Western Allied occupation authority. In 1950
he returned to England, where he served as the Chief Economic Adviser
to the National Coal Board (NCB). Although he had gone through an
atheistic phase during the Second World War, in the early 1950s he read
many works on Asian religions and philosophy, Gandhi's ideas, and various books dealing with mysticism and the occult, especially by and about

G.I. Gurdjieff (d. 1949) and his one-time pupil P.D. Ouspensky (1878–1947). Schumacher indicated the impact these ideas were having on him in a letter to his parents: 'Through this contact with Indian and Chinese philosophy and religion, my whole way of thinking has come into motion. New possibilities of knowledge (and experience) have been opened to me of whose existence I had no inkling. [...] I have the feeling that I will look back to my forty-first year as a turning point for the rest of my life'. And later, in April 1953, concerning Gurdjieff's ideas: 'The crux of the matter – and that of all other "schools of wisdom" is the method of allowing a deep inner stillness and calmness to enter, – a stillness not only of the body, but also of thoughts and feelings. Through this one gains an extraordinary strength and happiness' (quoted in Wood 1984: 230 and 232).

In 1955, on leave from the NCB and in Burma giving economic advice to its newly-independent government, Schumacher displayed effects of his new 'wisdom thinking' on his economic ideas. In a paper on 'Economics in a Buddhist Country' he indicated his belief that Gandhi's economic ideas might be more appropriate for Burma to follow than Western models. While there he spent many weekends at one of Burma's best Buddhist monasteries, receiving meditation instructions and training. After returning from Burma, he told one of his friends that he had become a Buddhist, but he soon began emphasizing that all the great religions had comparable contemplative and mystical traditions. And he decided to read more of the Christian mystics and leading Western religious thinkers such as Thomas Aquinas. His interest in religious thinking would continue for the rest of his life, and in September 1971 he followed the example of his second wife (Vreni) and his oldest daughter (Barbara) and became a Catholic.

3 Schumacher's Thoughts on Religion and Wisdom

During his last few decades, Schumacher continually emphasized the traditional values taught by the great world religions. He also emphasized that although the 'essence of education [...] is the transmission of values', they had to be internalized, sifted through, made one's own, keeping the good and jettisoning the bad. Education for wisdom, however, still had to help an individual accomplish one more task – 'dying to oneself [...] to all one's egocentric preoccupations'. He went on to say that to be wise there were three things that people 'most need to do and education ought to prepare them for these things: To act as spiritual beings, that is to say, to act in accordance with their moral impulses. [...] To act as neighbors, to render service [... and] to act as persons, as autonomous centers of power and responsibility' (Schumacher 1975: 82; Schumacher 1979: 115–16).

Although he thought Catholicism the religion most appropriate for him to adopt in 1971, he recognized the essential similarity of the values taught by all the major religions. In his personal library he possessed several books reflecting the ecumenical ideas and tolerance of the Russian philosopher Vladimir Soloviev (Solovyev), and his own thinking reflected an open-minded spirituality. He concluded 'it may conceivably be possible to live without churches; but it is not possible to live without religion, that is, without systematic work to keep in contact with, and develop toward, Higher Levels' (Schumacher 1977: 139). For him such 'systematic work' included contemplation, meditation, and attempting to overcome egoism. Those efforts, plus spiritual values like love, compassion, humility, and tolerance, would enable us to make wiser judgments.

His viewpoint was similar to one more recently expressed by one of America's leading wisdom scholars, psychologist Robert Sternberg, who has written that 'teaching for wisdom recognizes that there are certain values – honesty, sincerity, doing toward others as you would have them do toward you – that are shared the world over by the great ethical systems of many cultures'. But like Schumacher, who thought that people had to internalize such values and 'render service', Sternberg has stated that such teaching should not be propagandizing but rather helping people 'develop positive values of their own that promote social welfare' (Sternberg 2002).

4 Wisdom and Economics

Schumacher believed that the dominant economics of modern times, whether capitalist or communist, was not guided by wisdom. Rather than wisdom being the guiding force, it was technology. What was technologically possible was done. Whether it was good or not was not even considered. Not only was Western economics contrary to what Schumacher thought a Buddhist economics might entail, but it also clashed with certain basic Christian principles. He believed that modern Western economics reflected a materialist approach. With its emphasis on rapid change, economic growth, and increasing Gross National Product (GNP), it failed to adequately consider 'the availability of basic resources and, alternatively or additionally, the capacity of the environment to cope with the degree of interference implied'. By advertising and marketing, it also encouraged a 'frenzy of greed and [...] an orgy of envy'. And he wrote that 'the cultivation and expansion of needs is the antithesis of wisdom' (Schumacher 1975: 30–3). The basic aim of modern industrialism, increasing productivity, also exacerbated the alienation of labour, ecological damage, and the over-crowding of cities.

In *Small is Beautiful* Schumacher wrote: 'The exclusion of wisdom from economics, science, and technology was something which we could perhaps get away with for a little while, as long as we were relatively unsuccessful; but now that we have become very successful, the problem of spiritual and moral truth moves into the central position. [...] Wisdom demands a new orientation of science and technology towards the organic, the gentle, the nonviolent, the elegant and beautiful' (Schumacher 1975: 33–4).

A wisdom-centered economics would emphasize well-being rather than consumption, and meaningful and rewarding employment rather than productivity. Land use, he thought, should 'be primarily orientated towards three goals – health, beauty, and permanence'. Agriculture should also 'keep man in touch with living nature' and humanize his 'wider habitat' (Schumacher 1975: 112–13).

He accepted the principle of subsidiarity that taught that bigger organizations should not do what smaller ones could do better. Since he believed it likely that large organizations would not go away, he emphasized the importance of establishing some of the virtues of smallness within large organizations. He was also sympathetic with the distributism of his English predecessors G.K. Chesterton and Hilaire Belloc – its key tenet being that the ownership of the means of production should be as widespread as possible.

Schumacher was sympathetic with a type of socialism perhaps best described in his daughter's biography of him: 'A socialism which did away with the concentrations of economic power, a socialism which gave people work that allowed them to be fully human. [...] Small-scale technology, small-scale enterprise, workshops and small factories serving a community and served by a community; that was real socialism in action' (Wood 1984: 342). His goal was to structure private enterprise so that it operated more for public gain without discouraging individual initiative and innovation. He wished to further communitarianism without sacrificing freedom. Although, like the British Labour Party, he supported nationalization of some industries, he also wrote: 'I am convinced that, in normal circumstances, nothing would be gained and a great deal lost if a "public hand" were to interfere with or restrict the freedom of action and the fullness of responsibility of the existing business managements' (Schumacher 1975: 287).

Although the economic ends he sought could be considered radical, the means he recommended for achieving them were pragmatic and gradual. As he said about one of his ideas, he was for restructuring 'large-scale ownership without revolution, expropriation, centralisation, or the substitution of bureaucratic ponderousness for private flexibility. It could be introduced in an experimental and evolutionary manner – by starting with the biggest enterprises and gradually working down the scale, until it was felt that the public interest had been given sufficient weight in the citadels of business enterprise. All the indications are that the present structure of large-scale industrial enterprise, in spite of heavy taxation and an endless proliferation of legislation, is not conducive to the public welfare' (Schumacher 1975: 292).

To find the best means he encouraged small-scale experiments like the Scott Bader Commonwealth and the Intermediate Technology Development Group (ITDG). The first organization, still in existence today, was a plastics and polymers company, where Schumacher served first as a trustee and then board member in the 1960s and 1970s. Its founder, Ernest Bader, had transformed his employees into partners who could not be fired except for 'gross personal misconduct'. This Commonwealth had the power to 'confirm or withdraw the appointment of directors and also to agree to their level of remuneration'. And its members agreed that pay levels should 'not vary, as between the lowest paid and the highest paid, irrespective of age, sex, function or experience, beyond a range of 1: 7, before tax'. They also stipulated that 'the firm shall remain an undertaking of limited size, so that every person in it can embrace it in his mind and imagination. It shall not grow beyond 350 persons or thereabouts'. Schumacher pointed out that 'Bader set out to make "revolutionary changes" in his firm, but *"to do this by ways and means that could be generally acceptable to the private sector of industry"*. His revolution has been bloodless; no one has come to grief, not even Mr Bader or his family; with plenty of strikes all around them, the Scott Bader people can proudly claim: "We have no strikes" (Schumacher 1975: 276 and 282).

Schumacher thought that 'in small-scale enterprise, private ownership is natural, fruitful, and just', but in medium and large enterprises such ownership was more complex and often unjust. He believed the Bader Commonwealth was an example of a just medium-size enterprise, and he quoted the Quaker Ernest Bader, who stated that 'the experience gained during many years of effort to establish the Christian way of life in our business has been a great encouragement; it has brought us good results in our relations with one another as well as in the quality and quantity of our production' (Schumacher 1975: 266 and 282).

The second organization, ITDG, reflecting Schumacher's experimental and pragmatic thinking, also still exists, but has changed its name to Practical Action. In 1965, as the organization's web site indicates:

Schumacher had an article published in the *Observer*. In it he pointed out the inadequacies of conventional aid policies based, as they were then, on the transfer of modern, capital-intensive and large-scale technologies to developing countries which

did not have the financial resources, technical skills or mass markets to accommodate
them. He argued that there should be a shift in emphasis towards 'intermediate technologies' based on the needs and skills possessed by the people of developing countries. The article aroused considerable interest at home and abroad from academics,
politicians and the development community. Encouraged by this Schumacher and
a few of his associates [...] decided to create an 'advisory centre' to promote the use
of efficient labour-intensive techniques and in 1966 the Intermediate Technology
Development Group (ITDG) – now known as Practical Action – was born.[2]

This concept of Intermediate (or Appropriate) Technology was his chief
response to the excesses and harmful effects of modern technology, and he
is often referred to as the 'founder of the Intermediate Technology movement' (Gasper 2004: 17). Developing this type of technology was also, he
believed, the best way to improve society in general – 'I know of no better
way of changing the "system" than by putting into the world a *new type* of
technology – technologies by which small people can make themselves
productive and relatively independent' (Schumacher 1979: 43).

Since he thought technology had taken four wrong directions – 'ever-
bigger size, ever-bigger complexity, ever-bigger capital intensity, and ever-
bigger violence' – he envisioned intermediate technology taking steps
in the opposite direction, toward a smaller, simpler, less capital intensive
and violent technology. 'We need methods and equipment which are
cheap enough so that they are accessible to virtually everyone; suitable
for small-scale application; and compatible with man's need for creativity. Out of these three characteristics is born non-violence and a relationship of man to nature which guarantees permanence. If only one of these
three is neglected, things are bound to go wrong' (Schumacher 1979: 54;
Schumacher 1975: 34).

Again, he elaborated on these basic ideas. In regard to violent technology, for example, he wrote that 'nonviolence, in this context, refers
to modes of production which respect ecological principles and strive to
work with nature instead of attempting to force their way through natural
systems' (Schumacher 1979: 57).

2   See Practical Action, at http://practicalaction.org/history, for this quote.

He arrived at his ideas primarily as a result of his trips to Third World countries. His trip to India in 1962 was especially crucial. He traveled around the country including its rural areas and told its economic planners that the main question they should ask themselves is 'What is the appropriate technology for rural India?' His answer was 'an intermediate technology, something much better than the hoe and much cheaper and easier to maintain than the tractor plow'. He thought that 'the appropriate technology at the intermediate level will be simple enough that you don't have to have [...] specialists' like specially trained managers and engineers. Big projects in major urban areas usually required extensive infrastructure like roads, worker housing, schools, hospitals, and experts. 'But if you have small-scale it doesn't require an elaborate infrastructure and you can become productive quickly and then perhaps later you will have the wealth to make the infrastructure a bit more elaborate' (Schumacher 1979: 130–2).

To understand what would work best for people in poorer countries, Schumacher believed the advisers from rich countries had to try to put themselves in the minds of poorer peoples and ask themselves what type of technology would really help them the most. If such technology did not yet exist, ITDG attempted to adapt existing technology for use by poorer people or even invent new technology appropriate to their needs. In the final speech he gave before his death, he said the following:

> When I asked myself this question, 'What would be the appropriate technology for rural India or rural Latin America or maybe the city slums?' I came to a very simple provisional answer. That technology would indeed be really much more intelligent, efficient, scientific if you like, than the very low level technology employed. But it should be very, very much simpler, very much cheaper, very much easier to maintain, than the highly sophisticated technology of the modern West. In other words it would be an intermediate technology, somewhere in between.[3]

Schumacher realized that 'the applicability of intermediate technology is, of course, not universal', especially in advanced industrialized societies.

---

3   This cited material and other extracts from the speech are available at http://real-talkworld.com/2009/04/25/caring-for-real-ef-schumacher.

There are products which are themselves the typical outcome of highly sophisticated modern industry and cannot be produced except by such an industry. These products, at the same time, are not normally an urgent need of the poor. What the poor need most of all is simple things – building materials, clothing, household goods, agricultural implements – and a better return for their agricultural products. They also most urgently need in many places: trees, water, and crop storage facilities. Most agricultural populations would be helped immensely if they could themselves do the first stages of processing their products. All these are ideal fields for intermediate technology. (Schumacher 1975: 186)

Even in countries like England, however, he thought that some small steps could be taken away from the dominant trend toward technological gigantism. One such step was the Scott Bader Commonwealth. Another example he gave was the following:

One can convince, if not the organizations, at least people in the organizations, that something, some reorientation, is necessary and that they have the resources and they can do it without any strain.

My formula for this is a lifeboat. I have persuaded some big farmers in England to have a lifeboat, to separate out a bit of their land, which they don't need for making a living – they make their living on 95 percent of their land, and take 5 percent and run this as an organic unit or experimental unit to try to minimize their dependence on a very sophisticated and vulnerable industrial system. Well, after some persuasion this is actually happening. They are hard up as to who is going to manage this, because we haven't trained any people in non-chemical methods of farming. And of course it is harder now than it was fifty years ago, because the standardized farming, the chemicals, virtually irrespective of the quality of the soil, has lost us the traditional knowledge. [...] of how really to cooperate with the soil. [... but] it has to be regained. (Schumacher 1979: 62–3)

5   The Environment and Economic Sustainability

In *Small is Beautiful* Schumacher wrote 'ecology, indeed, ought to be a compulsory subject for all economists' (Schumacher 1975: 134). But already in the 1950s – years ahead of the establishment of the U.S. Environmental

Protection Agency and the first Earth Day, both in 1970 – he was emphasizing the economic and overall importance of environmentalism. He did so in his private life, practicing organic gardening and having solar panels on the roof of his house, and he did so in his talks and writings.

We see this in his presentation 'Population in Relation to the Development of Energy from Coal' at the World Population Conference in Rome in 1954 and in his 1955 paper 'Economics in a Buddhist Country'. In his Rome talk he indicated the connection between global population growth and increasing energy demands. In his 1955 paper he stated that 'a civilization built on renewable resources, such as the products of forestry and agriculture, is by this fact alone superior to one built on non-renewable resources, such as oil, coal, metal, etc. This is because the former can last, while the latter cannot last. The former cooperates with nature, while the latter robs nature. The former bears the sign of life, while the latter bears the sign of death' (quoted in Wood 1984: 248).

By this point in his life, he already realized what the two major factors affecting the twentieth-century global environment would be: population growth and economic activities, especially industrialization and increased consumption. And he recognized that scientific and technological developments were the driving forces behind these increases that would put growing pressure on non-renewable resources and increase urbanization, pollution, and other threats to the environment.

To realize how farsighted he was, we should note that 'from 1900 to 1950, world population increased from 1.6 billion to 2.5 billion, and then reached 6 billion in 1999. [...] By the 1990s the world was using twice as much cropland, 9 times as much freshwater, and 16 times as much energy as in the 1890s. [...] During the century the world's forests [...] decreased by about one-fifth, mainly due to increased demand for timber and conversion of forest lands to farmlands'. And whereas only about one-sixth of the world's population lived in urban areas in 1900, around half did in 1999. By then slum dwellers comprised about one-third of the overall global urban population (Moss 2008: 155–7, 158 and 166).

In *Small is Beautiful* he devoted a whole section to 'Resources', including separate chapters on 'The Proper Use of Land', 'Resources for Industry' and 'Nuclear Energy'. In these chapters, as well as in scattered other portions of his book, he dealt with one of his main concerns for many years – the consequences of the accelerating use and rapid depletion of the world's energy and other primary resources.

He paid special attention to the gobbling up of world resources by the United States. 'For the 5.6 per cent of the world population which live in the United States require something of the order of forty per cent of the world's primary resources to keep going'. Such a rapacious consumption he thought 'could be called efficient only if it obtained strikingly success-ful results in terms of human happiness, well-being, culture, peace, and harmony'. But, he added, it had failed to do so. He also called attention to the 'ever-increasing dependence of the United States economy on raw material and fuel supplies from outside the country' – a problem that only increased in the decades after his death (Schumacher 1975: 119).This increasing dependence had implications far beyond environmental ones, as did his prediction that most non-renewable resources would become more costly and more a source of global contention.

In his chapter on land use in *Small is Beautiful*, Schumacher furnished a long quote from a 1955 book on ecology that observed that throughout much of history 'man usually changed or despoiled his environment'.

> How did civilised man despoil this favourable environment? He did it mainly by depleting or destroying the natural resources. He cut down or burned most of the usable timber from forested hillsides and valleys. He overgrazed and denuded the grasslands that fed his livestock. He killed most of the wildlife and much of the fish and other water life. He permitted erosion to rob his farm land of its productive topsoil. He allowed eroded soil to clog the streams and fill his reservoirs, irrigation canals, and harbours with silt. In many cases, he used and wasted most of the easily mined metals or other needed minerals. Then his civilisation declined amidst the despoliation of his own creation or he moved to new land.

In 1977, during the last summer of his life, Schumacher narrated a forty-three-minute film in an Australian forest. It dealt with the devastating con-sequences of deforestation and was called 'On the Edge of the Forest'. In it he stands amidst trees, waters, and singing birds – but also walks to areas of cut-down trees, bulldozers, and abandoned logging equipment. His mes-sage is the same as he had delivered for years: humans must respect nature and live in harmony with it.[4] Although in the 1970s neither Schumacher nor most other environmentalists yet considered global warming a major threat, his criticism of consumption-driven accelerated energy use and irresponsible deforestation both attacked problems that would later be identified as chief causes of global warming.

Unlike many others in the 1950s, he did not believe that atomic energy was a panacea. Although nuclear energy could be expanded to meet growing energy demands, 'this would just shift the energy shortage problem to a different level', one that produced 'environmental hazards of an unprecedented kind'. And he believed that 'of all the changes introduced by man into the household of nature, large-scale nuclear fission is undoubtedly the most dangerous and profound'. He concluded that 'no degree of prosperity could justify the accumulation of large amounts of highly toxic substances [nuclear materials] which nobody knows how to make "safe" and which remain an incalculable danger to the whole of creation for historical or even geological ages' (Schumacher 1975: 29, 135 and 145).

Although nuclear pollution was perhaps his greatest pollution fear, he was well aware of other types. He was familiar with Rachel Carson's thinking as described in her groundbreaking 1962 study, *Silent Spring*, which helped to launch the environmental movement of the late twentieth century: 'The pollution entering our waterways [that] comes from many sources: radioactive wastes from reactors, laboratories, and hospitals; fallout from nuclear explosions; domestic wastes from cities and towns; chemical wastes from factories. [...] chemical sprays applied to croplands and gardens, forests and fields' (Carson 1964: 44).

In *Small is Beautiful* Schumacher identified some of the causes of the pollution about which Carson wrote. 'Scientists and technologists have learned to compound substances unknown to nature. Against many of them, nature is virtually defenceless. There are no natural agents to attack and break them down. [...] These substances, unknown to nature, owe their almost magical effectiveness precisely to nature's defencelessness – and that

4   As of January 2012, the film was still available at http://www.littlepaperboats.com/ fivetotwelve.html.

accounts also for their dangerous ecological impact. It is only in the last twenty years or so that they have made their appearance *in bulk*. Because they have no natural enemies, they tend to accumulate, and the long-term consequences of this accumulation are in many cases known to be extremely dangerous, and in other cases totally unpredictable' (Schumacher 1975: 18).

In his Epilogue to *Small is Beautiful*, Schumacher summed up the connections he saw between wisdom, economics, and the environment. He paraphrased the conclusion of a 1972 report by noting that 'pollution must be brought under control and mankind's population and consumption of resources must be steered towards a permanent and sustainable equilibrium'. He then quoted directly from it, 'Unless this is done, sooner or later – and some believe that there is little time left – the downfall of civilisation will not be a matter of science fiction. It will be the experience of our children and grandchildren'. And he ended his book with his own words: 'The guidance we need for this work cannot be found in science or technology, the value of which utterly depends on the ends they serve; but it can still be found in the traditional wisdom of mankind' (Schumacher 1975: 295–7).

References

Aquinas, T. (2008). *Summa Theologica*, <http://www.newadvent.org/summa/2057. htm> accessed 15 July 2011.

Carson, R. (1964). *Silent Spring.* Greenwich: CN, Fawcett Crest Book.

Gasper, D. (2004). *The Ethics of Development.* Edinburg: Edinburgh University Press.

Moss, W.G. (2008). *An Age of Progress?: Clashing Twentieth-century Global Forces.* London: Anthem Press.

Schumacher, E.F. (1975). *Small is Beautiful: Economics as if People Mattered.* New York: Harper Perennial.

Schumacher, E.F. (1977). *A Guide for the Perplexed.* New York: Harper & Row.

Schumacher, E.F. (1979). *Good Work*. New York: Harper & Row.

Sternberg, R. (2002). 'It's Not What You Know, but How You Use It: Teaching for Wisdom', *Chronicle of Higher Education*, 28 June 2002, <http://www.wisdom-page.com/SternbergArticle01.html> accessed 15 July 2011.

Wood, B. (1984). *E.F. Schumacher. His Life and Thought*. New York: Harper & Row.

LASZLO ZSOLNAI

CORVINUS UNIVERSITY BUDAPEST

3   The Importance of Meta-economics

1   The Metasystems Approach

The term *meta* stems from Greek where its original meaning is 'after'. Metaphysics starts where physics ends. Nowadays, however, *meta* is mostly used in the meaning of 'above'. 'A system is defined as a set of elements and relationships between the elements. As long as one deals with these elements and relationships – the objects of the system – the considerations on the system are at object level. When this level is exceeded, the considerations are at metasystemic level' (Kickert and VanGigch 1979: 1218).

Ian Mitroff summarizes the function of a meta-theory as follows: 'the goals of a meta-theory are to advise us (1) at the global level, on how to choose that problem we ought to be solving, (2) at the detailed level, on how to specify the detailed structure of the problem we have chosen to solve, and (3) on which criteria to accept or reject a proposed solution' (Mitroff and Betz 1972: 11–12).

The metasystem approach can be used in illuminating the current 'mess' produced by economics. Schumacher observes: 'economics is a "derived" science which accepts instructions from [...] meta-economics. As the instructions are changed, so changes the content of economics' (Schumacher 1973). Figure 1 shows a hierarchy where economic systems are at the bottom. Economics is in the middle. Finally, meta-economics is at the top. Economics provides direction for economic systems and rates its solutions. Meta-economics directs and judges economics itself. The truth of economics is guaranteed by the adequacy of meta-economics. If meta-economics is wrong then economics becomes misguided and dysfunctional.

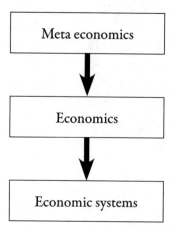

Figure 1 *Meta-economics, Economics, and Economic Systems*

Meta-economic choices concern three basic questions: What is the *subject matter* of economics? Which *value-commitment* is right for economics? And what is the appropriate *methodology* of economics?

2   Erroneous Assumptions of Mainstream Economics

Mainstream economics continuously produces environmental and social failures. Its instruments are blunted. Its directions are confused. The broad economic consensus has evaporated. The experts are in doubt and the public opinion is skeptical and bewildered. The failures of mainstream economics come from its inadequate meta-economic choices.

Mainstream economics defines its subject matter as the *monetary economy*, that is, the monetary sphere of the society. Only those processes and assets are relevant for mainstream economics which are measured and traded on the market. The remaining part, because it does not create marketable values, is qualified as economically 'non-productive' and consequently negligible and worthless.

However, the monetary economy is only a minor part, a small fraction of the whole 'economic iceberg' which is the total interaction between society and nature. There are other layers below the monetary sphere, namely the social economy (including household works and community activities) and Mother Earth which provides natural resources and services and absorbs (or does not absorb) the externalities produced by the functioning of humans and their organizations. (Figure 2)

Figure 2 *The Whole Economic Iceberg*

Andrew Brody notes that 'about 50 percent of the population of the more advanced countries is gainfully employed – and only their work is covered in the usual accounts of the national income. In less developed countries this share is still less'. Considering leisure and other non-working activities 'in advanced countries not more than 14 percent of the total disposable time is reckoned, and when total and partial unemployment is also considered then it will be less than 10 percent' (Brody 1985: 57–8).

Most of the value-creation of nature is disregarded in mainstream economics. According to the calculation by Robert Constanza and his colleagues the *ecosystem services* and *natural capital stocks* of the Earth exceeds about two times the GNP of the global economy. They have estimated the economic value of seventeen ecosystem services for sixteen biomes, based on published studies and a few original calculations. For the entire biosphere, the value (most of which is outside the market) is estimated to be in the range of US $16–54 trillion per year, with an average of US $33 trillion per year. Because of the nature of the uncertainties, this must be considered a minimum estimate. Global gross national product total is around US $18 trillion per year (Constanza et al. 1997).

The monetized sphere of society represents not more than a tiny fraction of the total economic process. By focusing on the monetized activities mainstream economics commits the error of the *pars pro toto* because it neglects the non-monetized social economy and the life-supporting functioning of nature. It is known from systems theory that if only a part of a greater system is considered and optimized then the whole system will be misunderstood and destroyed.

The basic value commitment of mainstream economics can be labeled as *materialistic hedonism*. According to mainstream economics the principal task of the economy is to attain the maximum fulfillment of the unlimited wants of people.

Psychological research shows that materialistic hedonism cannot lead to human well-being and happiness but actually destroys them. Psychologist Tim Kasser writes that

> materialistic values reflect the priority that individuals give to goals such as money, possessions, image, and status. Empirical research shows that the more that people focus on materialistic goals, the less they tend to care about spiritual goals. Further, [...] numerous studies document that the more people prioritize materialistic goals, the lower their personal well-being and the more likely they are to engage in manipulative, competitive, and ecologically degrading behaviors. (Kasser 2011: 204)

Schumacher argues that hedonism is in conflict with the permanence of nature.

> An attitude to life which seeks fulfillment in the single-minded pursuit of wealth [...] does not fit into this world, because it contains within itself no limiting principle while the environment in which it is place is strictly limited. [...] We find the unlimited economic growth, more and more until everybody is saturated with wealth, needs to be seriously questioned on at least two counts: the availability of basic resources, and [...] the capacity of the environment to cope with the degree of interference implied. (Schumacher 1973: 26)

In the contemporary 'full world economy' (Daly 1996) materialistic hedonism as a value orientation is dangerous. It necessarily leads to the destruction of natural ecosystems, biodiversity losses and climate change while producing 'welfare malaise' and increasing social inequality.

The epistemology of mainstream economics is *positivism*. A popular economics textbook writes: 'In studying any problem or segment of the economy, the economists must first gather the relevant facts. These facts must then be systematically arranged, interpreted and generalized upon. These generalizations are useful not only in explaining economic behavior, but also predicting and therefore controlling future events' (McConnell 1984: 3).

By drawing a strict demarcation line between facts and values mainstream economics tries to discover economic laws similar to the laws of natural sciences. It is an impossible mission because economic regularities are always conditional, that is, influenced by the environmental, social and cultural context within which economic actors are functioning.

Positivism as a methodology is not fruitful for economics because economic agents are not physical object but conscious beings and their behaviour cannot be adequately treated by the methods of natural sciences.

As a summary we can say that monetary economy as subject matter, material hedonism as basic value-commitment and positivism as methodology are *erroneous meta-economic choices* for economics. Deeply concerned about the failures of mainstream economics, Andrew Brody resignedly writes the following: 'We are not entitled to claim to have discharged the function assigned to us by our fellow men in our capacity as economists, and it is also very doubtful whether we set ourselves at the task in the right way' (Brody 1985: 9).

3   The Promise of Alternative Economics

Alternative economics is a response to the ecological and human crisis of our age. Its aim is to re-orient and reform economic activities in order to transform modern economies into less counter-ecological and more human forms. Alternative economics employs other meta-economics assumptions than mainstream economics.

The subject-matter of alternative economics can be defined as the *total economic process* which consists of the multiple interactions among natural ecosystems, economic organizations and human persons. (Figure 3) Natural ecosystems provide humans with life-supporting ecological services and produce natural resources for economic organizations. Economic organizations (firms, households and community institutions) produce goods and services for humans and influence the functioning of the ecosystems. Finally, humans take part in the activities of economic organizations and contribute to their own livelihoods.

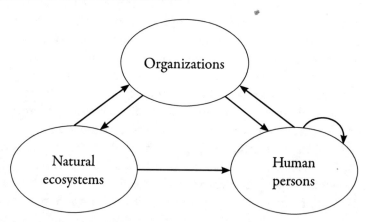

Figure 3 *The Total Economic Process*

The basic value-commitment of alternative economics is *sustainable livelihood*. It implies an engagement in ecological sustainability, respect for future generations, and human development. Sustainable livelihood requires that α) Economic activities may not harm nature or allow others to come to harm.

β) Economic activities must respect the freedom of future generations

γ) Economic activities must serve the well-being of people.

Economic organizations and humans should use natural ecosystems in such a way that the structural and functional properties of the ecosystems remain invariant. Economic organizations should serve the whole person, that is, the material, psychological and spiritual needs of people. Humans should develop ways of life which are consistent with the permanence of nature and the well-being of other people including the prospect of future generations. Ecological sustainability and human development are complementary tasks. If natural ecosystems are damaged and destroyed then the lives of people cannot be healthy. Inversely, deprived people are not able to regenerate destroyed ecosystems.

Alternative economics uses *constructive methodology*. Constructive research is based on the hope that we can transform the actual world into a possible world which is better. Constructive methodology means that we search for new ways things could be and make practical efforts to realize these possibilities.

Action research and evaluation research are instructive for alternative economics. *Action research* represents a circular process. The departure point is an action-oriented theory. In the light of such a theory researchers produce a diagnosis of the problematic situation. The next step is to develop a plan of intervention, that is, a series of actions for the betterment of the situation. Then the implementation of the plan comes. In the final step researchers evaluate the intervention and feed back the lessons learnt to the action-oriented theory and the plan of action. The circular process ends when the results are satisfactory both for the researchers and the stakeholders. Action research is a participatory process: stakeholders are actively involved in all steps of the inquiry. The dialogue between the researchers and the stakeholders is vital in creating usable knowledge and practical solutions.

Evaluation research breaks with the value-neutral ideal of social sciences. Value neutrality is impossible in economics because all concepts and methods used in economic research are unavoidably infected by values (Zsolnai

1992). Evaluation research explicitly evaluates processes and states of affairs. Its basic rules include (i) all the relevant value dimensions should be considered, (ii) both positive and negative values should be taken into account, (iii) present, past and future values should be carefully examined, and (iv) intrinsic values, use values, and contributory values should be distinguished.

4   The Future of Economics

Table 1 shows the meta-economic assumptions of mainstream and alternative economics (Zsolnai 1991).

Table 1 *Mainstream Economics versus Alternative Economics*

	Mainstream Economics	Alternative Economics
subject matter	monetized processes	the total economic process
value-orientation	materialistic hedonism	sustainable livelihood
methodology	positivist	constructive

Centuries ago Galileo rejected Aristotelian physics because of its inadequacy. In that time he did not yet have any complete construction of a new physics. The incompleteness of alternative economics is not an argument for keeping erroneous mainstream economics alive. If economics will not become a reliable and useful tool for the ecological and human reconstruction it risks losing its position in the academic world as well as in the policy arena.

References

Constanza, R. et al. (1997). 'The value of the world's ecosystem services and natural capital', *Nature* 387, 15 May 1997, 253–60.

Daly, H. (1996). *Beyond Growth. The Economics of Sustainable Development*. Boston: Beacon Press.

Brody, A. (1985). *Slowdown*. Beverly Hills, Calif.: Sage.

Kasser, T. (2011). 'Materialistic Value Orientation'. In L. Bouckaert and L. Zsolnai (eds), *Handbook of Spirituality and Business*, pp. 204–11. Houndmills Basingstoke: Palgrave-Macmillan.

Kickert, W.J.M. and VanGigch, J.P. (1979). 'A metasystems approach to organizational decision-making', *Management Science*, 25 (12), 1217–31.

McConnell, C.B. (1984). *Economics*. New York: McGrow Hills.

Mitroff, I.I. and Betz, F. (1972). 'Dialectical decision theory: a metatheory of decision-making', *Management Science*, 19 (1), 1–24.

Schumacher, E.F. (1973). *Small is Beautiful*. London: Abacus.

Zsolnai, L. (1991). 'Meta-economic Choices', *Human Economy*, 6 (June), 6–7.

Zsolnai, L. (1992). 'Beyond Positivism and Normativism', *Journal of Interdisciplinary Economics*, 2 (4), 137–44.

GÁBOR KÓVACS
CORVINUS UNIVERSITY BUDAPEST

4 Buddhist Economics

1 Introduction

From the beginning of the twentieth century there has been a tendency amongst economists to question the relevance, efficiency and validity of neo-classical economics. Some economists do not accept the blind faith in the science of economics, and suggest various alternative approaches to transform its practice. One of these is Buddhist economics, which at first glance seems self-contradictory (Payutto 1994, Daniels 2006), but in spite of this ever since Ernst Friedrich Schumacher mentioned Buddhist economics, it has become a significant and popular approach amongst alternative-minded economists.

This paper explores the history of Buddhist economics theory. It examines various major and minor ideas, notions and interpretations of numerous Western and Eastern scholars and Buddhist thinkers, concentrating especially on the subject of microeconomics.[1] But first of all it presents the basic teachings of Buddhism, which is necessary to understand the notions of this alternative economic approach. After this it explains Ernst Friedrich Schumacher's philosophy and his interpretations of Buddhist economics according to his experiences gathered as an economic advisor in South-East Asia. Furthermore the paper explores the development of theories and interpretations of numerous Western scholars and several Eastern Buddhist

---

[1]   Its aim is to present every viewpoint by a subjective emphasis on them, and the author apologizes in advance if he forgot to include some well- or lesser-known approaches to the subject.

thinkers. It demonstrates that Buddhist economics is not only relevant for Buddhist countries but can help Western countries as well in solving the problems of overconsumption, welfare malaise and destruction of nature. In the 1980s and 1990s more and more alternative-minded Western economists and social scientists had turned to study Buddhist economics, which has become a major alternative to the Western economic mindset. Finally a sketch of Buddhist macroeconomics and the interdisciplinarity of Buddhist economics is presented.

2   The Basic Teachings of the Buddha

Buddhism originates from India in the fifth century BC. *Gotama Siddhattha*, the Buddha, had been teaching his doctrines for more than forty years after he realized *bodhi* – awakening. His philosophical, religious and practical instructions and advice were enunciated for the realization of one supreme goal – the alleviation and the final cessation of suffering. The basic doctrines of Buddhism can be interpreted from the *Pali Canon*, the collection of the sacred scriptures.

The central doctrine of Buddhism is the Four Noble Truths. The first is that every phenomenon is inadequate, unsatisfactory and results in suffering. The second states that this suffering has its origin in a general human characteristic, the ignorance-led, unchecked craving for ephemeral phenomena of the impermanent world. The Third Noble Truth declares that suffering can end. It leads to the Fourth Noble Truth, which enunciates that The Noble Eightfold path is the right way to eradicate suffering. This path, which some may know as the Middle Way, avoids two extremes: (i) asceticism, which is distress; and (ii) hedonism, which is idle and low-graded. The Noble Eightfold path is a lifestyle advice, which refers to right behaviour that leads to the full cessation of suffering. These eight divisions can be grouped into three parts: (i) wisdom, which includes Right View and Right Decision (the first two pieces of the path); (ii) virtue, which includes Right Speech, Right Action and Right Livelihood (the third, fourth and fifth pieces of the path); (iii) and concentration, which is Right Effort, Right Mindfulness and Right Concentration (the last three parts of the path).[2] The Buddhist lifestyle aims to improve these three synergistic abilities to perfection by ongoing practice. The practice of virtue helps the meditation practice, which results in wisdom that leads to the further perfection of virtues. The central notion of 'rightness' according to virtues was contributing to the articulation of the Five Precepts, which are guidelines for Buddhist followers on what to avoid and what to do. These are: (i) refraining from doing harm, but acting with compassion and sympathy; (ii) refraining from taking what is not given, but practising generosity; (iii) refraining from sexual misconduct, but acting with devout conduct and contentment; (iv) refraining from false speech, but acting with the truth; and (v) refraining from taking intoxicants, but acting with an ongoing practice of mindfulness. Another distinguishing feature which differentiates Buddhism from other spiritual traditions is the teaching of non-self (*anattā*) – another crucial notion for Buddhist economics as well. It is the consequence of impermanence: the ongoing change which pervades all phenomena of the world. It implicates that a soul-like, permanent, unchanging essence of human beings does not exist in itself.[3]

Besides, but based on these basic teachings, the Buddha was instructing also his lay followers about right behaviour and right lifestyle. From a modern perspective we could say that these texts constitute the Buddha's economic and social views. They are also recorded in the Pali Canon,[4] and anybody could weave a vibrant theory of economics and society from them (Wee 2001: 102). Nevertheless these theories belong to the field of history and philology rather than to social sciences, because the structure

---

2   It was formulated in the first sermon of the Buddha, which is 'The Discourse on the Setting in Motion of the Wheel of the Teachings' (SN 56.11).

3   It was formulated in the second discourse of the Buddha, which is 'The Discourse on the Not-Self Characteristic' (SN 22.59).

4   These scriptures can be found scattered in the Pali Canon. The most famous and central texts on this subject are: Sigalovada Sutta (DN 31), Kutadanta Sutta (DN 5), Agganna Sutta (DN 27) and Dighajanu Sutta (AN 8.54).

of modern society and the impact of modern economy differs from ancient social and economic circumstances. Yet a strong spiritual aim accompanied by strict ethical guidelines forms a steady basis for Buddhism's usefulness for today's economics, providing economic practices and instruments for the cessation of suffering.

3 The Birth of Buddhist economics

The phrase 'Buddhist economics' was first articulated in the early 1970s. This was an era when most people believed in excessive economic growth. Humankind thought it was able to alter and rule nature without negative consequences. Still some people were able to look behind the scenes and saw the seamy side of limitless economic growth.[5] Amongst those, who did not think as mainstream economic thinkers did, Ernst Friedrich Schumacher was one of the most influential. He was a German-born English economist, but his career shows us that he was a multifaceted person: he was a writer, an economic thinker and a philosopher. He articulated his world view in his famous book *A Guide for the Perplexed* (Schumacher 1978), which shows significant similarity to Buddhist philosophy. He also emphasized the central role of non-knowledge (Schumacher 1979: 83), which is the cause of suffering in Buddhism. From Schumacher's viewpoint, modern sciences represent wrong-knowledge, because they tend to explain only the lifeless, inanimate level of the world (1978: 101–21). Economics has a central role in modern society and pervades every aspect of today's life,

---

5   In the beginning of the 1960s an American writer, Rachel Carson, revealed the nega-
     tive effects of chemicals used in large-scale agriculture, and warned against the fatal
     environmental destruction caused by the excessive use of fertilizers (Carson 1962).
     In 1972 the illusion of infinite growth was ruined by the 'Limits to Growth' report
     (Meadows et al. 1972). The third major event of the early 1970s was the first oil crisis.
     These signs indicated that excessive economic growth cannot be sustained anymore
     without significant environmental and social consequences.

but neoclassical economists, the 'priests' of materialism, are 'unaware of the fact that there are boundaries to the applicability of the economic calculus' (Schumacher 1973: 27), so they destroy and distort human values based on ignorance, which stems from metaphysical blindness. To solve this deficiency, Schumacher turned to the spiritual tradition of Buddhism to substitute Western materialism and got back to the metaphysical foundation of economics,[6] but he emphasized that 'The choice of Buddhism for this purpose is purely incidental; the teachings of Christianity, Islam, or Judaism could have been used just as well as those of any other of the great Eastern traditions' (1973: 32).

4 Buddhist Economics in Schumacher's Interpretation

Ernst Friedrich Schumacher had already articulated his ideas about Buddhist economics before he first published them in his book *Small is Beautiful* in 1973. He made the most evident statement that could be drawn from the basic teachings of Buddhism to connect this tradition with the secular discipline of economics: '"Right Livelihood" is one of the requirements of the Buddha's Noble Eightfold Path. It is clear, therefore, that there must be such a thing as Buddhist economics' (Schumacher 1973: 32). This statement implies that economics alone does not constitute Right Lifestyle, but there are seven more factors above that – all of them as important as Right Livelihood.

Schumacher's notion of Buddhist economics encompasses four major areas – all of them were Western conceptions contrasted with their Buddhist interpretations. Firstly he examined the role and the content of work, and identified its threefold function: (i) to utilize and develop human faculties; (ii) to overcome human ego-centredness by working together

6   In spite of his Catholic convictions, which were emphasized especially in *Good Work*, and also, but not as much, in *A Guide for the Perplexed*.

with others; and (iii) to produce necessary goods and services for human life (Schumacher 1970: 33). Secondly he defined the main characteristics of Buddhist economics. According to him, these are simplicity and non-violence – both of which stem from non-attachment and non-craving for worldly possessions. Simplicity also implies that people want and consume less from the scarce resources of their environment. The additional importance of these two principles appears in the notion of localization, which means to restrict 'production from local resources for local needs' (1973: 36–7), and avoiding exports. Thirdly he emphasized that Buddhism does not accept man's superiority to other species and nature: rather it considers man equal with them, and proposes the behaviour of responsibility and compassion towards them. Fourthly Schumacher had preceded his age as he recommended the distinction between renewable and non-renewable materials, and proposed the use of renewable resources as much as possible, but also with the greatest care, not to exploit and destroy them by overusing (1973: 37–9). From Schumacher's viewpoint, the implementation of Buddhist economics is an inseparable part of realising the Middle Way, and 'not a question of choosing between "modern growth" and "traditional stagnation". It is a question of finding the right path of development' (1973: 39).

5   The Development of Buddhist Economics

5.1 Classic Works and Basic Notions Based on the Holy Scriptures

The first articles in the development of Buddhist economics can be regarded as classic works, because they were written in the early years of the history of Buddhist economics, but more importantly all of them went to the original teachings of the Buddha and encompassed the analysis of the Pali Canon to unfold the corresponding principles of Buddhist economics.

Frederic Pryor was the most prominent scholar of the subject in the beginning of the 1990s. He published two articles about the Buddhist economic system. In his first paper 'A Buddhist Economic System – in Principle' (Pryor 1990) he aims to explore the primary and secondary canonical sources to set up an economic system based upon them.[7] Nevertheless – as he declares – he does not want to give further advice and draw conclusions for today's modern society. His first work is rather a historical retrospection into the economic and ethical teachings of the Buddha. Pryor's second paper deals with more practical subjects, based on his assumption that the canonical sources of Buddhism are proper for modern times (1991: 30). A cornerstone of his article is the enunciation of radiation theory, that is: virtuous actions of individuals lead to radiation that shines through society and moves the economy on to a virtuous path. It is in contrast with the notion of Adam Smith, who wrote that economic prosperity could be achieved only by following self-interest limited by moral constraints (Pryor 1991: 18–19). Pryor draws attention to the distinction between economic needs and wants, and mentions the necessity of satisfying four basic requisites of life: (i) food; (ii) clothing; (iii) shelter; and (iv) medicines (Pryor 1991: 26).

Another early paper is Glen Alexandrin's 'Elements of Buddhist Economics' (1993). According to him these element are: (i) the definition of the actor; (ii) the used operators; (iii) values of economic actions; (iv) the world view; and (v) economic behaviour. In his interpretation the economic actor is a *Bodhisattva* rather than a *homo oeconomicus*.[8] The operators are the realization of the Middle Way, co-determination and optimization rather than rationality and maximization. The values used to describe the results of economic affairs are generosity, patience, compassion, impartiality and mindfulness rather than utility, profit, costs, consumption and investment. The view employed by economics rests on impermanence rather than on the Euclidian one-pointed perspective. Finally Buddhist economics implies the behaviour of co-operation rather than competition (Alexandrin 1993: 8–11).

---

7 The body of commentary on the Buddhist scriptures is considered to be the secondary canonical source.
8 A being strives for enlightenment and the final cessation of suffering.

The most cited and most influential author of the early 1990s was Venerable P.A. Payutto, a Thai Buddhist monk who published *Buddhist Economics: A Middle Way for the Market Place* (1994). The starting points of his discussion are the problems that stem from the separation of economics from other disciplines, which are narrowness and self-centeredness (Payutto 1994). It is concordant with Schumacher's words, as he also emphasized the necessity of an interconnected scientific view for solving the problems of our modern age (1979: 112–24). Payutto continues with the considera- tion of how ethics – rather the lack of ethics – conditions economics. He recommends the extension of responsibility to the three levels of existence: (i) individual; (ii) social; and (iii) environmental. Human beings have to be responsible for their actions on all planes, and economics must make harmony between these three levels. The validity of economic activities can be revealed by investigating their motivation, whether they are associated with craving (negative desire) or aspiration (positive desire) (Payutto 1994).

Payutto's most influential innovation is the articulation of numerous new, and the reinterpretation of other well-known Western economic conceptions from a Buddhist perspective. His most profound notions are moderation, contentment, non-consumption and over-consumption on the consumer side of economics, and non-production regarding the per- formance of economic activities. He goes against the basic Western notion of 'more is more' with moderation, contentment and over-consumption, because these conceptions pertain to the 'rightness' of the Middle Way in consumption. Payutto highlights two major characteristics of Buddhist economics: (i) the realization of true well-being; and (ii) non-harming of oneself and others. The former means the satisfaction of basic needs by employment of optimal economic solutions,[9] plus the reduction of people's desires above this level by their own Buddhist practices (Payutto 1994).

---

9   These are: (i) food, (ii) clothing, (iii) shelter, and (iv) medicine, as was mentioned above, but the author suggests complementing this list with the concept of basic education, which was the Dhamma, the teaching of the Buddha, at this time. As his followers took their refuge, among other things, to the Dhamma, basic education became part of their daily life.

The Thai Buddhist monk, Venerable Phadet Dattajeevo, also deals with the subject from a monastic point of view. His starting point is the same as that of the former author: the lack of ethics in economics (2010). The absence of ethical issues results in exploitation, violence, and could even culminate in armed conflicts. Phadet Dattajeevo is aware of his limits. The method by which the subject is dealt with consists of the analysis and interpretation of the Pali Canon. He covers the deficiencies of economic indicators, and the importance of mental well-being besides material well-being. He emphasizes the central role of the Buddhist virtue of contentment, just as Payutto mentioned its importance at an earlier stage. Dattajeevo comes back to Schumacher's notion of simplicity, and expands it with the dangers of attachment to wealth, which is the source of various kind of exploitation. He has a specific view on competition, as he states that positive competition is conceivable, if participants race in virtue – which is in agreement with Frederic Pryor's view on the positive outcomes of radiation (2010).

5.2 Further Development in the History of Buddhist Economics

In the next stage of the development of Buddhist economics scholars go back to Schumacher's and the above-mentioned authors' notions. They can be characterized by the formulation of new statements, and the reorganization of the already articulated thoughts to get useful notions for today's economics.

In his first paper 'The Practice of Buddhist Economics?' Simon Zadek examines a contemporary initiative, the Sarvodaya Movement of Sri Lanka, which can be regarded as the modern fulfilment of Buddhist economics (Zadek 1993). As he states, he is leaning on Frederic Pryor's contributions, but wants to present the subject from a practical viewpoint, because he recognizes the limitations of the former approach, i.e. that the 'Texts (even "original" ones) are produced in a particular social, political and economic context' (Zadek 1993: 433–4). The major characteristics of Sarvodaya Movement are: (i) the spiritual transformation of rural communities; (ii) the pursuit of bringing forward compassion and wisdom in people's social relationships; (iii) participative decision-making; (iv) and economic development towards the satisfaction of people's real needs (Zadek 1993: 435–9).[10] Furthermore, Zadek stresses the macroeconomics of today's Buddhist societies, and draws attention to the fact that the relations between monks, the laity and national economics are more complex than described by Pryor, as in numerous South-East Asian countries the monastic order makes significant contributions to social services, such as health care and education (Zadek 1993: 439–42). In his second paper, 'Towards a Progressive Buddhist Economics', Zadek sometimes opposes Schumacher's ideas, and lists some possible questions, and employment areas in which Buddhist economics could engage (1997). He is very critical about 'Schumacher's utopia' and with the basic way in which Schumacher expresses it, but he concludes that 'The question is not merely whether there is or is not a Buddhist Economics. The question is more subtle, and I believe more important than this. It is whether we can conceive of an economics that embodies the values that we espouse and try to live by' (Zadek 1997: 244).

What Zadek analyses as the practical fulfilments of Buddhist economics are the economics of a Himalayan monastery, the work of the Intermediate Technology Development Group founded by Schumacher, and the movement of Sarvodaya. None of them 'reflect a mechanical enforcement of a set of guiding principles set out in the canonical texts. Rather, they illustrate how such principles can be, and are, interpreted' (Zadek 1997: 246). He sees the challenges of Buddhist economics, questioning whether they can be a practice relevant for everybody, or just for those who are excluded from the mainstream; and whether they can penetrate modern economy to prevent it from driving us to unsustainability (Zadek 1997: 250–5).

In his short but rather significant paper 'Economics of Sangha. Are Bhikkhus Good for Business?',[11] Colin Ash stresses the role of the Buddhist

---

10 Sarvodaya has its critics and opponents. They criticize the function, the institution and the operations of the movement. This subject is however beyond the scope of this article.

11 The Sangha is the Buddhist Monastic Community. Bhikkhus and bhikkhunis are the members of the community, namely Buddhist monks and Buddhist nuns.

community in economic affairs (2000). He affirms that the Monastic Order has always been contributing in social affairs in most of the countries where Buddhism has spread.[12] Furthermore, he emphasizes two more important contributions, which heighten economic growth: (i) the reduction of worldly people's material desires by their teaching activities; and (ii) lowering transaction costs in business affairs by re-establishing trust in the economy, which is the paramount virtue of social prosperity (and similar to the above-mentioned radiation, based on virtue) (Ash 2000: 182–3).

5.3 Buddhist Economics as a Scholarship

The third stage of the development of Buddhist economics can be considered as a breakthrough. Approaching the new millennium, science has finally and unquestionably recognized and proved man's disastrous impact on the planet. Global climate change, the impacts of deforestation, ecological breakdowns, etc. have been proven to be consequences of human activities. In line with this numerous scholars advocate spirituality as a potential solution for the ever growing problems. Hence Buddhist teachings and Buddhist economics are no longer an exotic doctrine, but an opportunity to alter neo-classical economics.

The first cornerstone was the publication of *Business within Limits: Deep Ecology and Buddhist Economics* in 2006, in which numerous essays were collected from the field of Buddhist economics and deep ecology, written by acknowledged Western scholars (Zsolnai and Ims 2006).

In his paper 'Tackling Greed and Achieving Sustainable Development' Richard Welford comes to a conclusion about the causes of this crisis similar to the Buddha's conclusions about the causes of suffering, namely a narrow mindset or 'simplistic thinking' which results in greed (Welford 2006: 25). It is scientific materialism – a self-centred, anthropocentric view. The most conspicuous forms of simplistic thinking are: (i) a tendency for people to offer simple solutions to complex problems; (ii) many of

12   In Chan and Zen Buddhism, monasteries do not often take part in social engagements.

society's institutions; (iii) the myth that 'we are here to be happy'; (iv) the concept of unlimited growth; and (v) the pursuit of more and more money and material possessions to achieve greater happiness (Welford 2006: 27–8). A Buddhist world view (the realization of Right View) can be the cure for simplistic thinking, because of their different core values. In Welford's interpretation the main characteristics of Buddhist economics are (i) moderation in consumption; and (ii) creativity or the positive utilization of human mind (Welford 2006: 40–2). Furthermore, Welford uses a new interpretation of happiness, which is the ratio between wealth and desire. Capitalism is successful in increasing levels of wealth and therefore increasing happiness, but it also increases people's desires. The result is that both the dividend and the divisor are increased, so it hardly produces greater overall happiness. Contrary to the Western approach, Buddhist economics aims to reduce desires, which results in greater happiness at the maintenance of a given level of wealth by the reduction of the divisor (Welford 2006: 44).

Peter Daniels in his paper 'Reducing Society's Metabolism' stresses that the approaches of material flow analysis (MFA), which refer to the reduction of material and energy flows of the economy, are consistent with the aims of Buddhist economics (Daniels 2006). MFA is a systematic analysis of the impact of human economy in a given society and environment. It is an important methodology for eco-restructuring to achieve sustainable material flows with the reduction of the socioeconomic metabolism for preservation and sustainability (Daniels 2006: 107–11). Daniel's paper describes the common features of and the differences between MFA and Buddhist economics: both aim at the reduction of the metabolism of human economies; share a deep respect for nature; share a co-operative spirit and a sense of collective welfare. The most important difference between them stems from the fact that Buddhism envisages clear limits to welfare, derived from material objects and suggests a structural shift toward spiritual development (Daniels 2006: 126–39).

In her paper 'The Relational Firm: A Buddhist and Feminist Analysis' Julie Nelson examines the existential interpretations of firms and economic institutions (Nelson 2006). She contrasts Western substantivism with the Buddhist conception of relationality. Her basic notion is that small is not always beautiful, big is not always nasty. These statements conflict with Buddhist thought, and represent a Western substantivist ontology, which interprets every phenomenon as a solid, substantive thing, and looks at the world as if it were an ethically and emotionally neutral machine. This non-relational approach to economic institutions results in prejudgments about them. She argues, furthermore, that there is a better understanding of firms in terms of relations, which also is the approach of Buddhism and deep ecology. It is relational ontology, the philosophy of the Middle Way in which nothing is existent in itself, uprooted from its environment. The world consists of interdependent, relational, non-substantive things which are interpreted by their relations. In it every phenomenon has its own place and function in a symmetric mutuality (Nelson 2006: 198–208). By the analysis of economic institutions' inner relations namely the way they manage their employees according to their abilities, and by the analysis of firms' outer relations with other economic agents, relationality is the right interpretation of their existence and performance.

The second cornerstone is the establishment of the *Buddhist Economics Research Platform*, which aims 'to connect people and institutes engaged in developing Buddhist economic theory and practice and to spread ideas and working models of Buddhist Economics to the general public' (http://buddhist-economics.info/whoarewe.html). The Buddhist Economics Research Platform held its first conference in 2007 in Hungary,[13] and held its second conference in 2009 in Thailand.[14] This initiative plays a major role in the dialogue between Eastern and Western scholars, and contributed to the widespread permeation of the notions of Buddhist economics.

Joel C. Magnuson, a Zen-Buddhist practitioner, presented his paper 'Pathways to a Mindful Economy' at the first conference of the Buddhist Economics Research Platform (Magnuson 2007a).[15] He described a

---

13   The title of the first conference was 'Economics with a Buddhist face' which aimed to formulate the basic concepts of Buddhist economics. The conference-papers that are mentioned were published in a special issue of the *Journal of Society and Economics* in 2007 (vol. 29, issue 2).

14   The subject of the second conference was mainly consumption-efficiency.

15   Furthermore, Joel Magnuson wrote a book *Mindful Economics*, in which he describes the above-mentioned subjects in more detail. This book contains an analysis of

systemic change by which the Western economic system can be transformed to a mindful economic system where mindfulness is the core value – and the cure for the pathological systems' condition of environmental destruction, social injustice and inequality, economic instability, and a harmful habit of thoughts (Magnuson 2007a: 254–74). Mindfulness is the key, which has to be loaded as a positive program into the core of the system. He interprets it in accordance with Buddhism as mindfulness. It 'is a state of mind in which people become aware of their thoughts and actions and are fully occupied in the present moment' (Magnuson 2007a: 275). With the cultivation of mindfulness and the Buddhist path, the dispersed economic initiatives will evolve into a new Mindful Economy which has the following characteristics: (i) intrinsically democratic, equitable and just; (ii) based on respect; and (iii) stable (Magnuson 2007a: 279–81).

In his fundamental paper 'Western Economics versus Buddhist Economics', László Zsolnai describes the problem of the self and the strategy of Buddhist economics (Zsolnai 2007). He emphasizes the importance of an up to this point lesser-mentioned conception of the Buddhist basic teaching of no-self, which is confirmed by modern neurosciences (Zsolnai 2007: 145–6). Furthermore, Zsolnai describes Buddhist economics in terms of five distinguishing principles: (i) minimising suffering, (ii) simplifying desires, (iii) practising non-violence, (iv) genuine care, and (v) generosity (Zsolnai 2007: 147–51). Furthermore, in his later paper, 'Buddhist Economic Strategy' Zsolnai stresses the importance of the fact that Buddhist economics is a strategy rather than a system (2008). It implies the notion that 'one needn't be a Buddhist or an economist to practise Buddhist economics' (Payutto 1994). In fact every Eastern or Western initiative, which is in accordance with these five principles can be seen as a Buddhist economic initiative.[16]

---

the economy of the USA, and the detailed description of *The Mindful Economic Movement* (2007b).

16   To mention a few Eastern initiatives: (i) the Sufficiency Economy of Thailand, (ii) the Santi Asoke Movement of Thailand, and (iii) the Sarvodaya Movement of Sri Lanka. Western initiatives are: (i) The Slow Movement, (ii) Community-supported Agriculture, (iii) eco-tourism, (iv) ethical fashion, and (iv) ethical banking.

The central subject of Apichai Puntasen's paper 'Buddhist Economics as a New Paradigm towards Happiness' is the interpretation of happiness from a Buddhist point of view,[17] and the functions of the corresponding economic system. Puntasen shows us how the notion of well-being changed through the ages from an ancient noble meaning through a utilitarian interpretation until today's instrumental economic index of GDP. According to Buddhism well-being is identical to the lack of suffering – and its tradition is about the end of suffering, not about the realization of any kind of happiness (Puntasen 2007: 182–5). Emerging well-being is a by-product of the decreasing suffering. As Puntasen stresses, Buddhism is an appropriate mind-based science to substitute Western capitalist thinking with its interdisciplinary approach, and ensures an adverse motivation behind economic processes to Western motivation of profit-maximization. Buddhist economics is thus defined as 'the subject explaining economic activities with the aim for both individuals and society to achieve peace and tranquillity under resource constraint' (Puntasen 2004 and Puntasen 2007: 190). As wisdom is the key factor and the modus operandi of the economics, Puntasen labelled his system as *paññaism*, from the Pali word wisdom (*paññā*). He stresses what Schumacher and Richard Welford already mentioned: 'Brainpower – knowledge, reasoning and creativity – is the best resource among all other factors of production. The more the brain is used, the more the value added' (Puntasen 2007: 196).

In his paper 'Happiness and Economics: A Buddhist Perspective' Colin Ash stresses the connection between the science of economics and happiness (Ash 2007). He draws attention to 'Easterlin's Paradox', which says that in spite of raising incomes, people do not feel better in the Western world. The reasons are: (i) adaptation; and (ii) social comparison. Both of them are sources of individual unhappiness (Ash 2007: 203–8). Buddhist practice is crucial at this stage as it 'provide[s] skilful means for the mind to control the mood' (Ash 2007: 202) towards the realization of real well-being and towards the happiness which stems from the tranquillity of liberation (Ash 2007: 212).

17 Apichai Puntasen also published a book *Buddhist Economics: Evolution, Theories and Its Application to Various Economic Subjects* in which he analyses the above-mentioned concepts in more detail.

In 2009 His Holiness the Dalai Lama published a book with Laurens van den Muyzenberg about economics. Its central subject is the role of Right View and Right Action in the decision-making procedure,[18] and the role of leaders in the realization of well-being. They stress that the leaders of global companies make decisions that affect millions of people around the world. Therefore right decisions are important, and incompetent decisions could lead to disastrous effects. Right View depends on the calmness and concentratedness of the leader's mind. In the interpretation of the Dalai Lama 'the main tasks of a leader: clarifying purpose, defining values, building faith and making right decisions' (Dalai Lama and Muyzenberg 2009: 76). Furthermore, the authors emphasize the importance of trust as it is 'the most valuable immaterial asset that any organization possesses' (Dalai Lama and Muyzenberg 2009: 172) which agrees with Colin Ash's notions.

The development of Buddhist economics is an ongoing process. The popularity of the subject shows its importance and relevance for the possible solutions for today's economic problems. The next section summarizes the notions of Buddhist economics which have not been described yet, and demonstrates further possible development alternatives.

6   A Short Outlook

6.1 Buddhist Macroeconomics and Gross National Happiness

Buddhist macroeconomics was examined briefly in this paper. Its development is very similar to the evolution of Buddhist microeconomics. Anyone can uncover unequivocal guidelines from the Pali Canon on this subject, confirmed by many sources (Wee 2001, Pryor 1991). Nonetheless the most fundamental practical achievement of Buddhist macroeconomics was the implementation of Gross National Happiness (GNH) index

---

18   In the book *Leader's Way* Right Action, the fourth part of the Noble Eightfold Path or the Middle Way, is referred to as Right Conduct.

instead of GDP in the kingdom of Bhutan in the early 1970s. Many scholars drew attention to the achievements of Bhutan, and numerous conferences and workshops were held on the subject.[19] As Frank Dixon in his paper 'Gross National Happiness – Improving Unsustainable Western Economic Systems' emphasizes: GNH ensures a system's perspective, eliminates short-term thinking, ensures natural wisdom, and social stability. He describes the development and implementation of GNH goals, which encompass: (i) the articulation of the goals through a wide-range social dialogue; (ii) the development of GNH metrics on every tangible and intangible aspect of social well-being; and (iii) the development of a strategy to achieve the given goals (Dixon 2004: 7–14).

6.2 Buddhist Economics as an Interdisciplinary Scholarship

Buddhist economics is an interconnected discipline unlike mainstream neo-classical economics. Buddhism is a comprehensive spiritual tradition which covers every aspect of people's daily life. Hence Buddhist economics cannot stand apart, without other parts of the Middle Way being considered. It ensures a metaphysical background for the worldly science of economics. Interdisciplinarity is a major characteristic of Buddhist economics. It is related to at least four other disciplines: (i) psychology, especially happiness research, burn-out and depression research, motivation theories; (ii) neurosciences of the self; (iii) business ethics; and (iv) deep-ecology.

7   Conclusions

Some say that Ernst Friedrich Schumacher was the most influential heterodox economist of the twentieth century. The reason may be that he was able to articulate his own imposing intuitive statements with noble severity.

---

19   Read more about GNH conferences and theories at http://www.gnh-movement.org/.

His description of Buddhist economics has flourished through the years, and its conception became popular in the East, where most scholars and Buddhist practitioners try to integrate their tradition in the modern social pattern. It also became popular in the West, because many identified the metaphysical deepness of his statement. Since the 1970s Buddhist economics has evolved to a scholarship. The relevance of Schumacher's intuitive statement is proven by numerous people who deal with Buddhist economics, and approach the subject from various points of view: Schumacher from Right Livelihood, Richard Welford from Right View, Joel Magnuson from Right Mindfulness, and His Holiness the Dalai Lama and Laurens van den Muyzenberg from Right View and Right Action.

Following self-interest and the pursuit of profit-maximising are two axioms which are not be questioned in neo-classical economics. Eventually, the scholarship of Buddhist economics questions exactly these two basic assumptions. It is blunting the science of economics, preventing it from dominating social sciences, and makes sure it fulfils its original purpose: to realize well-being for mankind. Going back to the basic teachings of Buddhism Ernst Friedrich Schumacher could have declared, what the Buddha declared: 'I teach one thing and one only: suffering and the end of suffering':[20] Suffering is the attachment to the detached science of mainstream economics.

References

Alexandrin, G. (1993). 'Elements of Buddhist Economics', *International Journal of Social Economics*, 20 (2), 3–11.

Ash, C. (2000). 'Economics of Sangha. Are Bhikkhus Good for Business?'. In Patricia Sherwood (ed.), *Buddhist Perspective In the Face of the Third Millennium*, pp. 179–83. Singapore: Buddhist Fellowship.

20   It was formulated in The Water-Snake Simile (MN 22).

Ash, C. (2007). 'Happiness and Economics: A Buddhist Perspective', *Society and Economy*, 29 (2), 201–22.

Carson, R. (1962). *Silent Spring*, 2002 edn. New York: First Mariner Books.

Dalai Lama, H.H. and Muyzenberg L. (2009). *The Leader's Way*. London: Nicholas Brealey Publishing.

Daniels, P. (2006). 'Reducing Society's Metabolism'. In L. Zsolnai and K.J. Ims (eds), *Business within Limits. Deep Ecology and Buddhist Economics*, pp. 103–49. Bern: Peter Lang AG, International Academic Publishers.

Dattajeevo, Ven. P. (2010). *Buddhist Economics*, <http://www.urbandharma.org/udharma5/buddhisteco.html> accessed 10 May 2013.

Dixon, F. (2004). 'Gross National Happiness – Improving Unsustainable Western Economic Systems', *GNH Conference*, Bhutan.

Magnuson, J.C. (2007a). 'Pathways to a Mindful Economy', *Society and Economy*, 29 (2), 253–84.

Magnuson, J.C. (2007b). *Mindful Economics*. New York: Seven Stories Press.

Meadows, D.H., Meadows, D.L., Randers, J. and Behrens, W.W. (1972). *Limits to Growth: A Report for the Club of Rome's Project on the Predicament of Mankind*. New York: Universe Books.

Nelson, J. (2006). 'The Relational Firm: A Buddhist and Feminist analysis'. In L. Zsolnai and K.J. Ims (eds), *Business within Limits. Deep Ecology and Buddhist Economics*, pp. 195–219. Bern: Peter Lang AG, International Academic Publishers.

Payutto, Ven P.A. (1994). *Buddhist Economics: A Middle Way for the Market Place*, <http://www.buddhanet.net/cmdsg/econ.htm> accessed 10 May 2013.

Pryor, F.L. (1990). 'A Buddhist Economic System – in Principle: Non-attachment to Worldly Things is Dominant But the Way of the Law is Held Profitable', *American Journal of Economics and Sociology*, 49 (3) (July), 339–49.

Pryor, F.L. (1991). 'A Buddhist Economic System – in Practice: The Rules of State Policy Making of the Ideal Kings Sought a 'Middle Way' Between Right and Left', *American Journal of Economics and Sociology*, 50 (1) (January), 17–33.

Puntasen, A. (2004). *Buddhist Economics: Evolution, Theories and Its Application to Various Economic Subjects*. Bangkok: Amarin Press.

Puntasen, A. (2007). 'Buddhist Economics as a New Paradigm toward Happiness', *Society and Economy*, 29 (2), 181–200.

Schumacher, E.F. (1973). *Small is Beautiful: Economics as if People Mattered*. London: Abacus.

Schumacher, E.F. (1978). *A Guide for the Perplexed*. New York: Harper & Row Publishers.

Schumacher, E.F. (1979). *Good Work*. Great Britain: The Anchor Press Ltd.

Wee, V. (2001). 'Buddhist Approach To Economic Development'. In Patricia Sherwood (ed.), *Buddhist Perspective in the Face of the Third Millennium*, pp. 102–10. Singapore: Buddhist Fellowship.

Welford, R. (2006). 'Tackling Greed and Achieving Sustainable Development'. In L. Zsolnai and K.J. Ims (eds), *Business within Limits. Deep Ecology and Buddhist Economics*, pp. 25–57. Bern: Peter Lang AG, International Academic Publishers.

Zadek, S. (1993). 'The Practice of Buddhist Economics. Another View', *American Journal of Economics and Sociology*, 52 (4) (October), 433–46.

Zadek, S. (1997). 'Towards a Progressive Buddhist Economics'. In J. Watts, A. Senauke and S. Bhikkhu (eds), *Entering the Realm of Reality: Towards Dharmmic Societies*, pp. 241–3. Bangkok: International Network of Engaged Buddhists.

Zsolnai, L. & Ims K.J. (eds) (2006). *Business within Limits. Deep Ecology and Buddhist Economics*. Bern: Peter Lang AG, International Academic Publishers.

Zsolnai, L. (2007). 'Western Economics versus Buddhist Economics', *Society and Economy*, 29 (2), 145–53.

Zsolnai, L. (2008). 'Buddhist Economic Strategy'. In L. Bouckaert, H. Opdebeeck & L. Zsolnai (eds), *Frugality*, pp. 279–304. Bern: Peter Lang.

ROY VARGHESE
K.U. LEUVEN

5 Authentic Development and Responsibility in Economics

1 Introduction

E.F. Schumacher draws on the Gandhian outlook on development as a source of inspiration and motivation to explain economic life in his work *Small is Beautiful*. In this paper I re-read Schumacher from a Gandhian perspective on responsibility in economics and business. These two legacies are mutually complementary and rewarding to re-think on the present economic activities and the developmental paradigms. Gandhian understanding of authentic development consists in four key concepts: truth (*satya*) as the ultimate goal of development, non-violence (*ahimsa*) as the ethos of development, household materials (*swadeshi*) as the resource of development, and individual and social freedom (*swaraj*) as the environment of development. Simplicity, non-violence, regional approach and smallness are the hallmarks of Schumacher's way to development.

2 The Ends of Development

The role of traditional wisdom in the process of development has gained special attention in the present economic and political scenario. Gandhi makes this clear when some of his friends asked him to read great authorities like Mill, Marshall, Smith and others before experimenting economic matters. He was pretty sure that there are few moments in life when about some things 'we need no proof from without'. Gandhi says: 'a little voice within us tells us, "you are on the right track, turn neither to your left nor right, but keep to the straight and narrow way"' (Gandhi 1993a: 93). With such help we march forward, slowly indeed, but surely and steadily'. This does not mean that we do not listen to the academic voices in the economic decision making. Rather it underlines the persistent need to look for a deeper understanding of inner wisdom in human development than the formal studies can do. Schumacher also believes that the exclusion of wisdom from economics, science and technology leads to an unsuccessful human life. 'Wisdom demands a new orientation of science and technology towards the organic, the gentle, the non-violent, the elegant and beautiful' (Schumacher 1973: 33).[1] Wisdom is not just about maximising one's own or someone else's self-interest, but about balancing various self-interests (intrapersonal) with the interests of others (interpersonal) and of other aspects of the context in which one lives (extrapersonal), such as one's city or country or environment or even God (Sternberg 2003: 152). Gandhi pleaded for an ideal economy where there is more truth than gold and greater charity than love of the self. He believes that economics is untrue if it ignores or disregards moral values. A normative economics of Gandhian style, which intertwines economics and ethics into one inseparable whole, reflects a vertical, multidimensional image of man where both material and spiritual forces need to embrace each other in the human quest for unity and wholeness (Diwan and Lutz 1985: 12–13). Gandhi finds that the end of economic activity is sought as 'human happiness combined with full mental and moral growth'. He uses the adjective mental as synonymous with spiritual (Bose 1948: 73).

Development can be authentic only when it promotes the total well-being of the individual – integrating both material and spiritual development. They are not two, but one (*A-dvaita*). Gandhi says that all reality comes from, is sustained by, and finds it fulfilment in the Real, in Truth

---

[1]   The *Oxford English Dictionary* defines wisdom as 'the capacity for judging rightly in matters relating to life and conduct; soundness of judgment in the choice of means and ends'.

(*Satya*) (Gandhi 1948: 230). So our goals are not totally independent. He finds that 'the predominant character of modern civilisation is to dethrone God and enthrone materialism' (Gandhi 1958–94: 28.127). In his critical analysis, Schumacher argues that the purpose of the present-day economics is not merely to satisfy wants but to create wants (Schumacher 1979: 27). Multiplication of artificially generated wants is seen at the modern economic theories. This leads to greed and vulgar consumerism. The modern industrial society everywhere shows the evil characteristic of incessantly stimulating greed, envy and avarice. While believing that this crazy model brings satisfaction and ultimate happiness to the human beings, they call it civilisation. Gandhi rejects this model of civilisation. Many of our wants are not necessarily our need. He says: 'civilisation, in the real sense of the term, consists not in the multiplication, but in the deliberate and voluntary reduction of wants. This alone promotes real happiness and contentment, and increases the capacity for service' (Gandhi 1993a: 399). This helps to realize oneself in the ideals of truth and justice. The Zen way to affluence teaches us that we should limit our desires rather than trying to expand the means to fulfil them. The well-being of the whole person demands integrated development of health of body, peace of mind, and happiness. The life-styles that emerge from being part of a developed society tend to minimize human interactions.

2.1 Purpose and the Spirituality of Wealth

Many economists do not take human conduct into account while estimating prosperity. Accumulated wealth alone does not provide happiness. Human beings have an ethical dimension also (Gandhi 1958–94: 8.371). In everyday life a conversation amongst a couple on the possibility of earning more money is not unusual. But having access to such a conversation in the eighth century BCE is quite revealing. In the *Brihadaranyaka Upanishad* (part 4: 57) we find a conversation between a woman named Maitreyee and her husband, Yajnavalkya. 'How far would wealth help us to get what we want?' is the question. Maitreyee wonders: if 'the whole earth, full of wealth' were to belong just to you, could you achieve immortality through it? 'No', responds Yajnavalkya, 'like the life of rich people, so also will be your life. There is no hope of immortality by getting more wealth'. Maitretyee asks, 'What should I do with that by which I do not become immortal?' Maitreyee's rhetorical question has been cited time and again in Indian religious philosophy to illustrate the human predicament and the limitations of the world. However, we can read it in a different and positive way. This conversation points to the intrinsic and extrinsic motivation of the wealth one obtains. As Schumacher states, proper development engages the fundamental questions of life that includes how to discover and achieve Truth (*Satyam*), Goodness (*Sivam*) and Beauty (*Sundharam*).

Similarly, Aristotle notes in the very beginning of the *Nicomachean Ethics* (echoing the conversation between Maitreyee and Yanjnavalkya about 3000 miles away), 'wealth is evidently not the good we are seeking; for it is merely useful and for the sake of something else' (Aristotle 1980: 7). Indeed, we are not looking for wealth as such, but for something more. Yet we cannot denounce the value of wealth and ignore its mediating function. The usefulness of wealth lies in the important things that it allows us to do. Wealth is a means that helps us to improve the quality of our life and to reach our transcendent ends. Man cannot be trapped in the quest for material means forgetting the ends of his existence. From time immemorial, the great aims of human endeavour (*purusharthas*) have been classified into four in the Indian tradition – wealth (*artha*), aesthetic pleasures (*kama*), righteousness/ethical living/harmony with the global environment (*dharma*), and blissfulness (*moksha*). All human endeavours are interdependent and should be pursued equally. It is indeed argued that material possessions are essential prerequisites in the daily life for the upkeep of a household, raising of a family and the discharge of various social and religious duties and obligations. Implicit in this doctrine of *artha* is a concept of multi-order utility: if a person feeds himself, he derives a certain order of utility; if he feeds his family he derives a higher order of utility; if he feeds the hungry outside the family, he derives an even higher order of utility. This is indeed qualitative ordering of utilities which is to be distinguished from the concept of utility in the ordinary sense that is still quantitative (Huq 1985: 79). *Artha* gets higher meaning when someone reflects over it in a multi-order utility sense. Hence, wealth has individual, social and transcendent purposes.

Money has only an instrumental value. The destructive element of civilisation, as Schumacher identifies, is 'the pretence that everything has a price' (Schumacher 1973: 42). Money is the highest of all values. The nature of money explains exchange. But, the nature of exchange does not explain money. How do we understand the function of money? Adam Smith famously describes money as the 'great wheel of circulation' (Aristotle 1981: 385) 'The great wheel of circulation is altogether different from the goods which are circulated by means of it. The revenue of society consists altogether in those goods, not in the wheel which circulates them'. As a mere vehicle or means of exchange, money contributes nothing to the overall output of the society. As Aristotle reminds, king Midas died from hunger, because everything he touched turned into gold. Money is not wealth or value. It is a mere token of value. Money is good in as far as it functions as a measure of value and as a mere means of circulation. Gandhi tried to explain this by an example: 'The circulation of wealth among a people resembles the circulation of blood in the body. The concentration of blood at one spot is harmful to the body, and similarly, concentration of wealth at one place proves to be a nation's undoing' (1958–94: 8.303). The more evenly social wealth is distributed, the better it serves society.

Aristotle made an important distinction between *'oikonomia'* and 'chrematistics' (Aristotle 2008: 24–5). *Oikonomia* is the use of wealth, while chrematistics is the provision, production or acquisition of wealth. *Oikonomia* is the art of using wealth, not just for mere survival (to *zên*) but also for the Good Life (*eû zên*). It is teleological. It considers costs and benefits to the whole community, not just parties to the transaction. Chrematistics tends to simple money-making. It is short-termish, whereas *oikonomia* looks for the 'management of the household so as to increase its use to all members of the household in the long-run' (Daly and Cobb 1994: 138). Economists have the responsibility to reverse the modern usage of the academic discipline of economics that is closer to chrematistics than *oikonomia*.

2.2 Sustainable Economics

A sustainable economics of peace and permanence involves three factors: first, consideration of meta-economic aspects of life; second, need of divergent thinking; and third, looking for a comprehensive approach. The religion of economics has its own code of ethics that is shrouded by economic, calculative or market-based thinking. Cost-benefit analysis is at the heart of economic thought. This instrumental rationality fails to consider non-economic values like beauty, health, cleanliness, environment etc. Economics as a 'derived' science has to accept the instructions of what Schumacher calls 'meta-economics'. Meta-economics involves two aspects: that which deals with human beings, and that which deals with the natural environment in which they live (Schumacher 1973: 42–7). When modern economics moves up largely in a market-oriented way, it ignores man's dependence on the natural world. It forgets the Mother Earth. The symbiotic relation with nature around us is vital for our total health. 'A human being is made of earth. His body springs from the earth and derives its sustenance from the various forms which earth takes' (Gandhi 1958–94: 28.206). Life may be seen as a continuum: the individual is nurtured by the family constituted by blood relations. This family is a member of a large family, the world of life around us, and this is in turn sustained by the complex network of living and non-living creatures that surround us. The evolution of the universe and of life upon planet earth tells us that we are born not merely from the womb of our mother, but also from the womb of the earth, from the womb of the cosmos. Authentic development should not only avoid distancing us from mother earth, but will also safeguard the integrity of creation and promote a more beautiful environment (Anand 2007). Development is not merely to have more, but to know better, to do better, to live better and to be better. We need to develop a cosmic consciousness in order to live peacefully with other beings. This consciousness is a prerequisite for responsible economic life.

Similarly, economic thinking fails to understand the 'divergent' problems that cannot be solved by logical reasoning alone. Instead of taking into consideration actual human nature and actual circumstances, what really considers in present economics is a fictitious nature in fictitious circumstances. A.N. Whitehead calls this 'the fallacy of misplaced concreteness' (Whitehead 1929: 11).[2] We need art and literature, poetry and yoga, love and beauty etc. to make our life peaceful. The loss of these tastes, Schumacher says, is a 'loss of happiness' and is injurious to the intellect and probably to the moral character (Schumacher 1973: 88–9). These are essential factors of a good leader in a business firm. While evaluating large-scale organisation, Schumacher identifies the potential danger of lack of creative freedom since they strive constantly for 'the orderliness of order' (Schumacher 1973: 227). Man of creative freedom is the real entrepreneur. Sacrificing creativity and imagination at the expense of order and centralisation makes human life static and stagnant.

The judgment of economics is 'extremely fragmentary'. (Schumacher 1973: 38). Economists have the responsibility to see economic activities in the midst of a wide range of various non-economic activities like social, aesthetic, moral or political activities. Lack of comprehensiveness may apparently good economic decision lead to a bad result. Schumacher argues that the economic calculus and judgments are '*methodologically* narrow' due to two reasons: first, 'they give more weight to the short than to the long term'; and second, they exclude all natural 'free goods' or 'non-individualised public goods' including the entire environment (Schumacher 1973: 39). Let me explicate these elements in the language of the great hermeneutical thinker Hans-Georg Gadamer (1996: 6–11). He explains the fragmentary impact of technology in the modern man in two respects: First, in this age, human beings have got a scientific-technical mastery of nature which is qualitatively different from earlier centuries. Science becomes the primary productive factor of the human economy. This is not the pre-modern implication of *techne*, which means 'to fill out the possibilities of further development left open by nature (Aristotle)'. Now, it is moved upward to the level of an artificial counterpart of reality. We tend to think development,

---

2   It is a fallacy involved in abstraction in the process of thought. Generally, economists forget the level of abstraction they have reached and draw unwarranted conclusions about a concrete reality. To 'abstract' means 'to draw away from'. We can draw away from concrete experiences.

not in terms of evolution, but in terms of creation (Schumacher 1973: 155). Today the technical exploitation of natural resources and the artificial transformation of environment become so carefully planned and extensive that its consequences endanger the natural cycle of things and bring about irreversible developments on a large scale. There is a 'superstitious faith in science which strengthens the technocratic unscrupulousness with which technical know-how spreads without restraint'. Second, our progress of knowledge is subject to the law of increasing specialisation and, hence, to increasing obstacles to comprehensiveness. This dogmatism of specialisation within a narrow worldview reduces our vision and makes us forget that we have to preserve peace. Economics eliminates the inherent value of goods. It decides value according to the market price. We do not love the good; we call good what we have or what is useful. Human beings driven by greed or envy fail to see things as they are, in their wholeness (Schumacher 1973: 27). Intrinsic goodness of objects is neglected in the process of objectification of goods. We forget the fact that we are unable to decide the value of many goods exclusively from the point of view of market, where values are decided by bargaining power. This is what the present economics seems to do.

3   The Ethos of Development

Gandhi believes that 'the perfect vision of Truth can only follow a complete realisation of Ahimsa'. Ahimsa (literally translated as 'non-violence') can be positively translated as 'responsible love' (Gandhi 1993: 420). It is the supreme law for all human beings. It can functionally be considered as 'social affection'. This demands our responsibility to do good for oneself and to the other. In a broader sense, it keeps intact the sacredness of every being. Utilising resources without respect is violence. Ahimsa includes the whole creation. While taking the wholeness of beings, we should not fall into atomistic visions. The reduction of wholeness into parts, and taking parts as a whole is idolatry. It is violence also. Today, we suffer from universal idolatry of gigantism against the virtues of smallness (Schumacher 1973: 60). Gandhi maintains that a non-violent social order will have to be constructed on the basis of economic equality, which guarantees a minimum standard of consumption for all. We have at least three-dimensional responsibility in the practice of non-violence: responsibility to oneself, to the other and to the environment.

3.1 Responsibility to Oneself

Involving in economic activities with self-interest itself is not bad. You cannot love the other without loving yourself. Hence, self-love is the starting point of human transcendence. However, it is a bad dogma to argue that every economic action is entirely motivated *only* by self-interest.[3] Here even an apparently altruistic act is the result of calculated maximisation of some kind of a utility index. But this may not be always true. Self-interest does not necessarily exclude altruism. A business man has to decide what kind of the self he wants to serve. Reflexive rationality precedes instrumental rationality. A sensible egoist should try to develop a rich and integrated personality. According to Aristotle, a human being aims not just at mere survival but also at 'a good life' (Aristotle 1980: IX, chapter 8). This demands an inner unity of egoism and self-transcendence. Two factors are important to strengthen this inner unity: self-esteem and recognition. A good manager should always create a climate in which self-esteem and collaborative action for the common good can flourish. This helps employees to deal with their fellow colleagues with respect, dignity and affection.

---

3   For example, economists from Albert Carr to Milton Friedman argue that people responsible for decisions and actions in business should not exercise social responsibility in their capacity as company executives but concentrate on increasing profits for their companies. Eventually they could engage in philanthropic activities in their private life, but not in business life. This view is not acceptable for the defenders of a stakeholder's conception of the firm. Business life can only be sustainable if firms take into account the interests of all those who are affected by the activities of the firm.

Social recognition by peers and colleagues is an almost indispensable pre-condition for self-esteem. According to Adam Smith (1982: 13) the desire for recognition more than love of ease and pleasure is the most powerful psychological motive for business activity. For modern man, recognition is the greatest good, while public humiliation is the greatest evil. Anonymity is more dreadful than disgrace. Hence, a good manager has a responsibility to develop both these qualities.

As Hans Jonas (1974: 91–4) says, economic activity is grounded in the biological fact of metabolism and creaturely need. This need cannot be limited to the present generation alone. That means when we make 'affirma-tion of life', by using goods and materials, we should consider the future as well. In other words, the metabolism of the present and the reproduction of the future generation are two sides of the same economic activity. Here, the inclusion of reproduction within the gamut of economic behaviour makes 'responsibility for future' a constitutive element in ascertaining the proper goals of economic choices. Economic behaviour should be steered by, what Jonas calls, 'the principle of responsible providence' which acts as a principle of restraint in two respects: First, it means that our pursuit of economic goals has to consider the possible externalities in the behaviour of human beings and that of the nature. Second, this principle allows us to see that many of the consequences of economic actions propelled by technology are beyond our foreseeing. Our lack of foreknowledge may indulge us to move after short-term advantages. Hence Jonas suggest this very 'fact of ignorance' of the future consequences itself be incorporated in the imperative of future responsibility. This knowledge of ignorance makes us humble and cautious while using human power in the economic policies. Your responsibility includes the acceptance of your ignorance.

3.2 Responsibility to the Other

To be responsible is to go beyond oneself: one's ego, self-interest, and univo-cal thinking. Transcending oneself amounts to accepting external values and submitting to inter-subjective standards. A good economy is an economy of sharing and commitment. This leads to an inclusive development of a society.

Sharing makes our life meaningful. A good leader should share his money and strength in order to empower his colleagues in the firm. A manager has to participate to the inter-subjective zones of the organisation. Our self-interest involves taking interest in the others. This includes various forms of familial, social and political relationship. Aristotle argues: 'self-sufficiency applies not to a person on his own, living a solitary life, but to a person living alongside his parents, children, wife, friends and fellow-citizens generally, since the human being is by nature a social animal' (Aristotle 1980: 11). The same applies to the corporate world. It is the not the self of an individual alone, but the self of all that counts. Quite often, we can distinguish a 'corporate self' within firms. A strongly individualistic, self-assertive view of the organisation, based on so-called atomistic individualism, could explain the organisation as a temporary nexus of contracts and 'calculative' ties and bonds. However, this is not a very plausible image of a firm. Indeed it is opposed to the corporate values, goals, visions, and to the organisational consciousness of the firm that stresses very clearly its inevitable collective dimension – 'a collective self'. Hence individual identity in contemporary highly differentiated society is multilayered: individuals accept their role in collective entities, yet keeping their personal identity. This points to the multidimensional and equivocal engagement of managers endowed with varied motivations. While using their authority for making judgments and economic evaluation, leaders should see ethics, emotions, aesthetics and ecological considerations. This calls for *ex ante* social responsibility.

We should distinguish organisational excellence from organisational greatness. Organisational excellence is a limited concept as it is preoccupied with organisation-centered goals and concerns. But for greatness it is also necessary that the organisation makes an exalted social contribution which can be in the form of striking positive externalities, an unusual degree of altruism, idealism, contribution to human efflorescence, contribution to positive human transformation, and so on. This can be explained by the story of an Indian corporate idol, N.R. Narayana Murthy, the Founder-Chairman of Infosys Technologies (Murthy 2009: 159). He responds to his friends when they asked him what he wanted to do with his business: 'I want this [Infosys] to be the most respected software service in the world'. He continues, 'If you seek respect, you will not short-change your customers, you will be fair to your colleagues in the company, you will be transparent with your investors, you will treat your vendor partners with care and understanding, you will not violate the laws of the land in whichever country you operate, and you will live in harmony in whichever society you operate in [...]'.[4] Society contributes customers, employees, and investors who frame corporation. It contributes politicians and bureaucrats who frame policies that influence the success and failure of a corporation. Long-term success and sustainable growth of a corporation, Murthy argues, depends on how it demonstrates social responsibility. Society is an important stakeholder for corporations.

A society characterized by an extreme gap between the rich and the poor will not be able to sustain peace in the long-run. A 'dual society' without inner cohesion is subject to political instability and appalling violence (Schumacher 1973: 153). Every business organisation has a responsibility in contributing to social cohesion in order to make a healthy society. Economic destitution may not lead to immediate violence, but it would be wrong to presume that there is no connection between both (Palatty 2009b: 334–50). Gandhi argues that economic equality is the master key to non-violent independence (Gandhi 1981: 20–1). Working for economic equality means abolishing the eternal conflict between capital and labour. A non-violent system of government cannot be realized without abolishing the wide gulf between the rich and the hungry millions. A violent and bloody revolution is a certainty one day unless there is a voluntary abdication of wealth and the power. Gandhi formulates the doctrine of trusteeship to stimulate a non-violent redistribution of wealth. If property and wealth are held as a trust to be used for the public good, there will not arise any conflict. Human beings are basically trustees of the wealth. Our responsibility should be 'neither mere sentimentalism nor the naïve romanticism of being moved by the miserable and marginalised poor. Its affectiveness must turn into effectiveness, its dedication to the other into "works" of care for others' (Levinas 1990: 93).

---

4   *The Economist* ranked Narayana Murthy among the ten most-admired global business leaders in 2005. He is one of the India's most powerful CEOs. Today Infosys operates in thirty-eight countries with 50,000 people from forty-five nationalities.

Dual economy is 'mutually poisoning' and destructive. Schumacher argues that the ruling philosophy of present-day economics is: 'What is best for the rich must be best for the poor' (Schumacher 1973: 156). But it is not. 'A rising tide may not lift up all the boats'. Sometimes, a quickly rising tide, especially when accompanied by a storm, dashes weaker boats against the shore, smashing them to smithereens (Palatty 2009a).[5] What economic man needs is a sense of 'commitment'. Amartya Sen defined commitment in terms of 'a person choosing an act that he believes will yield a lower level of personal welfare to him than the alternative that is also available to him' (Sen 1977: 327). Commitment, however, cannot be easily explained entirely in rational terms. It insists us to break our self-centered thinking. Development can be inclusive only when we serve our interest by considering the interests of others as well.

Today, big MNCs, for instance, either are shifting their factories from the home nations to developing or under developed countries, or are opening new factories in poorer nations to bag comparative advantage. Gandhi argues: 'there is nothing more disgraceful to man than the principle to buy in the cheapest market and sell in the dearest' (Gandhi 1958–94: 8.371). For example, when a country like Ghana or Guatemala decides to do free trade with the USA, they have taken the decision to specialize in particular commodities due to the comparative advantage and comparative demand. Industrialisation has led Ghanaian agricultural workers to mine bauxite (the raw material of aluminum), which is plentiful in West Africa. Consequently, Ghana is now dependent upon the USA for food and other necessities. Because Ghana needs food more than the USA needs bauxite, the dependency has been abused in order to drive labour and bauxite costs well below the free-market price. Taking comparative advantage is usually not a bad thing. But, if it results in complete dependency, it is violence against others' freedom. 'Many things which are legal are not just'. Growing rich by devouring others by way of reducing them to beggary is violence

5   A rising tide in Bangalore city (India), for example, with mushrooming of Big Bazaars and Metros, does not substantially contribute to other parts of the State. The small grocery shops and retailers are dismantled and unemployment problems persist. This leads to a violent society with an extremely high criminal record.

(Gandhi 1958–94: 8.337). Our inter-connectedness means that we cannot think of development just for one's nation. Love has no boundary. Unfair developmental approaches are forms of violence, and violence always begets violence. A good economics or business has to compensate the negative externalities and try to build up an organic development.

3.3 Responsibility to the Environment

The Earth Charter (March 2000) approved at a meeting of the Earth Charter Commission at the UNESCO headquarters in Paris, declared:

> We stand at a critical moment in Earth's history, a time when humanity must choose its future. As the world becomes increasingly interdependent and fragile, the future at once holds great peril and great promise. To move forward we must recognize that in the midst of a magnificent diversity of cultures and life forms we are one human family and one Earth community with a common destiny. We must join together to bring forth a sustainable global society founded on respect for nature, universal human rights, economic justice, and culture of peace. Towards this end, it is imperative that we, the peoples of Earth, declare our responsibility to one another, to the greater community of life, and to future generations.

The main issues of development revolve around what Joseph Schumpeter (1954) calls a 'preanalytic vision'. The pre-analytic vision of economy finds economy as a subsystem to the total system. Here, beyond an optimal scale of production, growth becomes anti-economic. The alternative preanalytic vision is that economy is the total system and is unconstrained in its growth. This vision concedes that nature may be finite, but sees it as just a sector of the economy. This vision rests on a misconception: human beings are creators rather than creatures (Daly 1996: 218–19). These two visions are enormously different: the vision of economy as a subsystem leads to the quest for an optimal scale of the human niche, beyond which growth should cease. The economy as a total system leads to infinite growth, which leads to a total catastrophe for the present and future generations.

I believe that our responsibility towards the environment involves at least three aspects: first, to accept the intrinsic goodness of all beings;

second, to develop a good sense of sacredness; and third, to reflect on the gift-dimension of life. Creatures on the earth cannot be reduced to mere 'factors of production'. Indeed, they are means-to-the ends of human life. They have some intrinsic goodness though that is meta-economic in character. Human being is primarily shepherd of being. We are both guardians and guests on the earth. We have the responsibility 'to cultivate and to conserve' (Genesis 2: 15) the environment. This planet earth is given as a trust. We are guests in the sense that our presence on the earth is not eternal. Someone cannot domesticate what is given in common. We cannot deplete in one generation natural resources that have been built during thousands of years. This Mother Earth has an intrinsic value. All beings on this earth are valuable. A healthy geo-economics is presupposed for a peaceful environment. As Buddhism teaches, we have to work with true love for all beings, in a spirit of benevolence, not only for human beings but also for all kinds of beings on the planet earth. Extreme utilisation of resources is fundamentally problematic. We need to develop an ecological economy (Schumacher 1973: 48–68). It leads us to transform our inner values in the direction of saving planet from crisis. Both at the micro and macro levels, corporations have to transcend their limited short-term goals in order to attain sustainable development. Economic growth has no discernible limit; but, environmental sustainability has limits. Therefore, regulating economic growth is inevitable. As Gandhi rightly says, earth provides enough to satisfy everyone's need, but not for anyone's greed.

To recognize the intrinsic goodness of beings, one has to develop a good sense of sacredness. Human being, as the highest of all creatures, has the duty to take care of other beings (Schumacher 1973: 98–9). The Spirit of the Creator pervades all beings, let they be plants or animals. Hence, they all are sacred. They give us the vital factors that make life possible on earth: food, oxygen, clothing, shelter, medicine, etc. In the Indian tradition, trees and plants are considered as sacred. Sacredness entails reverence. Reverence is more than just respect. It is both respect and love. Indian Scriptures ask us to plant ten trees if, for any reason, we have to cut one. This sense of sacredness urged us to ask apologies to a plant or a tree before it is cut down.[6] They may have a story of feeding thousands of animals, sheltering hundreds of birds and protecting millions of small creatures. A human being devoid of reverence can easily turn into a monster. Some scientific proponents of enlightenment argue that reverence betrays us, for it stops critical thinking, and reverence is submission and consent. Hence, to be scientific, suspend reverence. This kind of enlightenment is itself darkness (Desmond 2000). All our developmental programmes and scientific involvement must employ an ontological reverence. Levinas identifies the 'temptation to murder' – to reduce the other into my subject without recognising the dignity of the 'otherness' of the other – as inherent in every human person (Levinas 1992: 14). Keeping responsibility as a virtue or a mandatory value in the business and contractual relations should not be out of mere respect, but rather out of reverence. This helps economists and businessmen to see life in a comprehensive way. This sense of sacredness and reverence brings them to look for the meta-economic dimension of objects in the world. We realize that many things cannot be priced according to the demand and supply theory since the dignity cannot be cashed. 'The loss of reverence is the source of ontological tyranny of which human beings are the autocrats' (Desmond 2000: 224). We need an expanded notion of dignity. We now need to talk not only about lives in accordance with human dignity but also about lives that are worthy of dignity of a wide range of sentient creatures (Nussbaum 2011: 161). Each being has its own dignity.

It is important to recognize the gift dimension of life. This garden of earth is a gift that is given to everyone. The logic of gift also encompasses reciprocity (Vandevelde 2000). It is difficult to quantify the gift dimension of life. The earth on which we live, the environment we enjoy or the relationships we experience are all saturated with gifts. As it is impossible to return this superabundance of gifts, we can only take our responsibility

---

6   In the Hindu tradition someone who cuts a tree without asking apologies incurs a
     specific sin called *soona*. In Proverbs we read that the just man takes care of his beast,
     but the heart of the wicked is merciless. St Thomas Aquinas wrote: 'It is evident that
     if a man practices a compassionate affection for animals, he is all the more disposed
     to feel compassion for his fellowmen' (Schumacher 1973: 99).

by passing on these gifts to others. We have responsibility for our environment in the same way as a good ruler feels responsible towards his people or as a good steward who takes care of the goods that he has been entrusted with. In an industrial society, human beings are no longer living in a natural environment but live in 'created environment'. A proper use of things involves a sense of ontological gratitude (Palatty and Vandevelde 2011).

4 The Resources of Development

Development, in general, is popularly explained in terms of replacing the traditional labour-intensive activities with capital-intensive technologies. This leads to gradual declining and elimination of the limited exchange systems of traditional village economies. The pull of labour force to the city and the concomitant problems of dislocation, displacement and misery, are the usual outcomes of such process of development. Gandhi's perspective was more on village empowerment. He foresaw the central and ever-worsening problems of stagnation and decay of the traditional sector resulting directly from extensive modernisation and the single-focused growth on urban, capital-intensive development. This is what today we call the 'backwash effect'. Schumacher argues that we should make a regional approach to development to avoid the homogenisation of cultures and social security (Schumacher 1973: 162–3). Human development is about realising one's potential and creativity. But today, development is more market-centered and metro-centric. We hear, for example, a lot about India's emergence as a fast-growing economic power. This is not completely true. Prosperity and progress have not touched millions of villages, where India's soul exists. If the villages perish, India will also perish (Gandhi 1958–94: 63.241). As Sen (2005: 197) rightly says, even a hundred Bangalores and Hyderabads will not solve India's tenacious poverty and deep-seated inequality. The very poor in India get a small share of the cake of information technology and related developments that generate. Unprecedented migration to metros and large unemployment will not make development sustainable. This is mainly due to lack of labour-intensive and village-empowerment programmes. Regional approach considers the possibility to establish workplace nearby villages, labour-intensive business, intermediate technological application and creative utilisation of local resources. This does not mean that all business and manufacturing enterprises should be concentrated in villages. But, rather we take villages also as important as cities. In a highly populated world, we cannot completely underestimate the large-scale production.[7] However, when we go for it we reflect on the possible positive and negative externalities.

Swadeshi invites us to take our immediate neighbourhood seriously, to believe that we have within ourselves and the given surroundings the resources we need for development. It means reliance on our own strength (Gandhi 1993a). Self-reliance however, neither means lack of a net-work of relationship nor a narrow, exclusive or chauvinistic outlook, but the desire to develop a non-violent, non-exploitative society that would provide utilisation of home resources. There are several elements involved in it: (a) Society must be capable of satisfying the basic minimum needs of its people without dependence on external sources. This also means that each society will have to define its minimum standards in terms of economic capacity. They must be attainable within the productive limits of the society. (b) Self-reliance also means the maximum use of indigenous resources and technology. Society will make an effort to obtain needed commodities from within by utilising unemployed resources and by the development of an appropriate skill profile of the labour force and by the growth of appropriate technology. (c) Self-reliance does not mean absence of trade with other societies. However, a self-reliant economy buys goods only if they are essential for the growth of its people, if they are not produced locally, and it is not possible to produce them locally. In an extremely globalized world, we must learn the art of living by striking a balance between our dependence on internal and external sources.

---

7   Even in Gandhi's time, he could not realize a completely *swadeshi* approach to village empowerment. Time has changed; models of economies have changed; people and their preferences have also changed. However, we cannot devalue the importance of villages.

5   The Environment of Development

The Gandhian idea of development is based on individual and social freedom. *Swaraj* means self rule. This has two dimensions: individual *swaraj*
and a village *swaraj*. Every individual should have the freedom to determine his or her destiny. Sen, for instance, argues that expansion of human
freedom is both the primary end and the principal means of development
(Sen 2000: xii). Development consists in the removal of various kinds of
unfreedoms that leave people with little opportunity of exercising their
reasoned agency. Development is not merely about income or wealth, but
about the totality of human-being and human happiness. Anything that
is detrimental to or disregarding of the way towards human fulfilment is
slavery. Empowering individuals to decide their destiny and good of life
is an inevitable element of authentic progress. Government action with its
instruments of technology many a time disregards this element, believing
that 'having' is always more important than 'being'. This is wrong. A state
that undermines the genuine individual freedom and individuality is violence. Hence, Gandhi says, *ahimsa* comes before *swaraj* (Gandhi 1939).
The means must be as pure as the ends. A reckless technology can destroy
a responsible life and thus, man should keep a control over his machines.
According to Schumacher bigger machines entail more concentration of
economic power and that brings greater violence against the environment
and human life in general (Schumacher 1973: 29). It is not progress, but
denial of wisdom.

Gandhi in a consistent and articulate fashion pleaded for village *swaraj*.
This means every village must be an independent unit. Self-rule of a village does not mean that it should separate itself from the neighbouring
villages. Rather, the village as an independent unit is to be taken seriously
for development and progress. A village is not a 'windowless monad'. If a
village is organized in a truly democratic way, it can make decisions by way
of democratic discussions and public debate on issues related to public life
and common good. Gandhi believes that perfect democracy is possible
only when individual freedom is given. The individual is the architect of

his own government, where non-violence rules and leads. This kind of responsible freedom makes each one in a particular locality to define his or her ends of life. Industrial society with mass production and a centralized economic system exploit the poor villages and destroy the rootedness and relatedness of human beings in a particular locality. Man can languish in the midst of affluence without enjoying the warmth of human bonds and the intimacy and reciprocal recognition and response of a community living. Revitalising agriculture and reviving small-scale industries, for instance in the Indian economy, are not only important for economic living but they are essential also for strengthening human well-being in the villages. The social character of human existence may be sacrificed on a radical abstraction of the classical *Homo economicus* model. Our wealth is not the sum of money or possessions, but has much more to do with the quality of our human relations, the values of the society in which we live, and the physical environment which all human beings have to share. To make a workable globalisation, as Joseph Stiglitz rightly says, we need not just markets, governments, and individuals as three pillars of successful development strategy (Stiglitz 2006: 51). But, we want another important fourth pillar, communities, where people work together, live together with government and non-governmental organisations. Collective action at the local level is very important. Development refers to qualitative change, realisation of potentialities, and transition to a fuller or better state (Daly 1996: 167).

6   Conclusion

Authentic development involves search for the ultimate goodness, social affection, utilisation of local resources and responsible freedom. Prudence is the mother of all the virtues. We have to learn to lead a prudent way of economic life (Schumacher 1973: 278). This is antithetic to a calculative way of economic life. 'Politics without principles, science without humanity, commerce without morality, wealth without work, worship without sacrifice, pleasure without conscience, and knowledge without character' will not bring a good society (Gandhi 1958–94: 8.362). Our responsibility lies in establishing a just society which is free from all kinds of deprivations. I may conclude with the words in the *Atharva Veda* (Bloomfield 1897: 12):

> We are the birds of the same nest, We may wear different skins, We may speak different languages, We may believe in different religions, We may belong to different cultures, Yet we share the same home – Our Earth. Born on the same planet; Covered by the same skies; Gazing at the same stars; Breathing the same air. We must learn to happily progress together. Or miserably perish together, for man can live individually, but can survive only collectively.[8]

References

Anand, S. (2007). 'Authentic Development: Some Gandhian Criteria', *Jnanadeepa*, 10 (1), 5–26.

Aristotle (1980). In D. Ross (ed.), *Nicomachean Ethics*. Oxford: Oxford University Press.

Aristotle (2008). In B. Jowett (ed.), *Politics*. New York: Cosmio Inc.

Bloomfield, M. (ed.) (1897). *Hymns of the Atharva Veda*. Baltimore: The John Hopkins University Press.

Bose, N.K. (1948). *Selections from Gandhi*. Ahamadabad: Navajivan Publishing House.

Daly, H.E. (1996). *Beyond Growth: The Economics of Sustainable Development*. Boston: Beacon Press.

Daly, H.E. and Cobb, J.B. (1994). *For the Common Good: Redirecting the Economy toward Community, the Environment and a Sustainable Future*. Boston: Beacon Press.

Desmond, W. (2000). 'On the Betrayals of Reverence', *Irish Theological Quarterly*, 65, 211–30.

Diwan, R. and Lutz, M. (eds) (1985). 'Introduction'. In *Essays in Gandhian Economics*. New Delhi: Gandhi Peace Foundation.

---

8   *Atharva Veda* is one of the Four Vedas – treatises on knowledge of ancient India – believed to have been written eight thousand years ago.

Gadamer, H.G. (1996). *The Enigma of Health: The Art of Healing in a Scientific Age.* Transl. J. Gaiger and N. Walker. UK: Polity Press.

Gandhi, M.K. (1939). *Harijan.* 24 June, 174.

Gandhi, M.K. (1958–94). *The Collected Works of Mahatma Gandhi,* vols. 1–60. New Delhi: Government of India.

Gandhi, M.K. (1981). *Constructive Programme: Its Meaning and Place.* Ahamadabad: Navajivan Publishing House.

Gandhi, M.K. (1993a). Iyer, R. (ed.), *The Essential Writings of Mahatma Gandhi.* New Delhi: Oxford University Press.

Gandhi, M.K. (1993b). *The Story of My Experiments with Truth.* Ahamadabad: Navajivan Publishing House.

Huq, A.M. (1985). 'The Doctrine of Non-Possession: Its Challenge to an Acquisitive Society'. In R. Diwan & M. Lutz (eds), *Essays in Gandhian Economics,* pp. 76–85. New Delhi: Gandhi Peace Foundation.

Jonas, H. (1974). *Philosophical Essays: From Ancient Creed to Technological Man.* New Jersey: Prentice-Hall.

Kautilya (1992). *The Arthashastra.* Transl. L.N. Ranganatha. New Delhi: Penguin Books.

Levinas, E. (1990). *Difficult Freedom: Essays on Judaism.* Trans. S. Hand. Baltimore: The John Hopkins University Press.

Levinas, E. (1992). '*Derrière la couleur, un visage*' (Interview with Catherine David), *Le Nouvel Observateur,* 1429, 14–15.

Murthy, N.R. (2009). *A Better India, A Better World.* New Delhi: Penguin Books.

Nussbaum, M.S. (2011). *Creating Capabilities: The Human Development Approach.* Cambridge: Harvard University Press.

Palatty, R.V. (2009a). *Cathedrals of Development: A Critique on the Developmental Model of Amartya Sen.* Bangalore: Christ University, Centre for Publications.

Palatty, R.V. (2009b). 'Prodigal Freedom and Asymmetric Violence: A Development Audit', *Journal of Dharma,* 34 (3), 334–50.

Palatty, R.V. and Vandevelde, A. (2011). 'Economic Life and Human Transcendence: A Paradigm for Everyday Spirituality', International Conference on *Mysticism without Bounds.* 1–18. Bangalore: Dharmaram Vidya Kshetram and Christ University.

Schumacher, E.F. (1973). *Small is Beautiful: A Study of Economics as if People Mattered.* London: Blond and Briggs.

Schumacher, E.F. (1979). *Good Work.* New York: Harper and Row.

Schumpeter, J. (1954). *History of Economic Analysis.* New York: Oxford University Press.

Sen, A. (1977). 'Rational Fools: A Critique on the Behavioural Foundations of Economic Theory', *Philosophy and Public Affairs,* 6 (4), 317–44.

Sen, A. (2005). *The Argumentative Indian: Writings on Indian Culture, History and Identity*. New Delhi: Penguin Books.

Smith, A. (1981). *An Enquiry into the Nature and Causes of the Wealth of Nations*. Indianapolis: Liberty Fund.

Smith, A. (1982). *The Theory of Moral Sentiments*. Indianapolis: Liberty Fund.

Sternberg, R.J. (2003). *Wisdom, Intelligence, and Creativity Synthesized*. Cambridge: Cambridge University Press.

Stiglitz, J. (2006). *Making Globalization Work*. New Delhi: Penguin Books.

The Earth Charter (2000). <http://www.earthcharter.org> accessed 2 March 2011.

Vandevelde, A. (2000). 'Towards a Conceptual Map of Gift Practices'. In idem (ed.), *Gifts and Interests*, pp. 1–21. Leuven: Peeters.

Whitehead, A.N. (1929). *Process and Reality*. New York: Harper.

ZUBIN MULLA
TATA INSTITUTE OF SOCIAL SCIENCES INDIA

6   Karma-Yoga and Schumacher's Theory of Good Work

1   Introduction

The Indian worldview comprises a belief in a just world, existence of a soul, and rebirth of the soul in various bodies in order to experience rewards and punishments for past actions. The goal of life according to the Indian worldview is to live in this world and perform actions in such a manner that the soul can be liberated from this eternal cycle of birth and death. Arising from this worldview is the belief that individuals find themselves in situations which are an outcome of their past actions and hence are most appropriate for them to discharge past obligations. Hence, Karma-Yoga is a philosophy of work which focuses on doing one's duty to society with full equanimity to pain and pleasure, and without expecting any rewards.

In this paper, I suggest a conceptualization of Karma-Yoga based on several contemporary commentaries on the Bhagawad Gita and show how it constitutes a comprehensive moral philosophy of work. While the Western model of development lays emphasis on the ethics of autonomy, Karma-Yoga is a moral philosophy which lays emphasis on the ethics of community and the ethics of divinity. The philosophy of Karma-Yoga was an inspiration for deriving the fundamental propositions of an economy of permanence as envisioned by Mahatma Gandhi (1960) and J.C. Kumarappa (1945).

The thoughts of Gandhi and Kumarappa were further elaborated in E.F. Schumacher's (1973) collection of essays published under the title, *Small is Beautiful: A Study of Economics as if People Mattered*. Schumacher's ideas had a huge impact not only when they were published but to this day (Bawa

1996; Corrywright 2004). According to Schumacher the most important need of our times is a 'proper philosophy of work' (Schumacher 1973: 23). This philosophy would provide a meaning to work beyond merely earning money and as a fulfilment of life's purpose. Most of the ill effects of our current model of development would be eliminated if only we could understand and follow this new philosophy of work. Schumacher suggests a Buddhist perspective on work (Schumacher 1973: 38–46) as one of the philosophies which can provide meaning to work. In this paper, I argue that Karma-Yoga, the Indian philosophy of work motivation, is a philosophy of work which can meet all the requirements of an ideal work philosophy laid down by Schumacher and if followed can prevent some of the disastrous consequences of materialistic progress. In other words, Schumacher's recommendations are applications of Karma-Yoga suited to modern times. First, I explain the Indian worldview and how Karma-Yoga, the Indian philosophy of work arises out of that worldview, and then I explain how Schumacher's recommendations provide a means of realizing the ideals of Karma-Yoga in today's times.

2   The Indian Worldview

In a series of widely acclaimed ethnographic studies conducted in rural India, Richard Shweder and his colleagues (Shweder, Much, Mahapatra and Park 1997) have tried to understand the worldview of Indians. The studies involved an analysis of why various actions involved moral transgressions according to the inhabitants of Bhubaneswar, a city in the state of Orrisa in eastern India. Finally, after statistical analysis all moral transgressions could be reduced to just three themes, viz. ethics of autonomy, ethics of community, and ethics of divinity. Each of these three themes was built upon a distinct worldview having a different conception of the nature of the individual and the relationship of the individual with the rest of society and the cosmos.

The ethics of autonomy conceptualizes the self as an individual distinct from the rest of the world and aims to promote an individual's freedom and choice in the exercise of his or her preferences. It involves protecting the individual from harm, securing his or her rights and ensuring justice. The ethics of community conceptualizes the self as an integral part of a larger collective and aims to promote the integrity of the collective as a whole through an emphasis on duty, hierarchy and interdependency. The ethics of divinity conceptualizes the self as a spiritual entity which has within itself an unrealized divine potential. This divine potential can be realized by protecting the spirit from degradation and pollution through functioning in harmony with the established natural order of things.

While one or more of these ethical discourses may be used to justify or explain moral transgressions often they are in conflict with each other. In India, the ethics of autonomy is in the background while the ethics of community and the ethics of divinity are emphasized and institutionalized in the form of social institutions and belief systems.

2.1 Indian Belief Systems

The Indian worldview is characterized by three fundamental beliefs, which are common to all the six systems of Indian philosophy (Dasgupta 1922/1991: 71; Prabhavananda 1960: 201). First, the belief in the karma theory, i.e., that all actions that are done have the power to ordain for their doers joy or sorrow in the future depending on whether the action is good or bad. Often, individuals may be required to take birth in another body to experience fully the joy or suffering that is due to them because of their past actions.

The second belief is in the existence of a permanent entity, the soul (*atma*), which is our true unknown nature, pure and untouched by the impurities of our ordinary life. In the Rig Veda, the soul or self is denoted by the word *atma* (Ghanananda 1958). The soul is the eternal subject which is free from all impurities like sin, old age, death, grief, hunger, and thirst. The soul is complete and hence, it is free from all forms of desires (Radhakrishnan 1940).

The third belief is about the doctrine of salvation (*moksha*). Since actions lead us through this endless cycle of birth and death, if we could be free of all such emotions or desires that lead us to action, there would be no fuel (in the form of joys or sorrows to be experienced) to propel us into another birth and we would be free of this eternal cycle.

The doctrine of karma is equivalent to the belief in a just world (Connors and Heaven 1990; Hafer and Begue 2005) which states that individuals get what they deserve (Connors and Heaven 1990). Karma extends the concept of justice to other worlds and other births, thereby implying that all good and bad deeds of all previous lives are accounted for cumulatively. Accordingly, in every life one reaps what one has sown in one's previous lives (Radhakrishnan 1926). Similar to the belief in a just world, belief in karma reaffirms one's faith in natural justice and makes every person responsible for his or her own well-being and suffering. Thus, positive deeds are believed to lead to good outcomes, while tragic happenings are explained as an outcome of negative deeds done in the past (Agrawal and Dalal 1993; Dalal and Pande 1988).

2.2 Indian Metaphysics

The metaphysical explanation of the law of karma is derived from the concept of spiritual law (*satya*) and law in its working process in the cosmos (*rita*). Conformity to this law leads to material and spiritual progress, while its violation is punished with a series of transmigrations. Actions which are motivated by a sense of personal individuality or which are incongruous with the universal order create disequilibrium in the cosmos, which is then set right by inflicting the effect of an action upon the doer of it. This metaphysical, ethical, and psychological regulative force is called karma (Krishnananda 1994). The law of karma serves as a moral causal ontology which suggests that the cause of one's suffering is the non-fulfilment of some obligation (Shweder, Much, Mahapatra and Park 1997).

The law of karma is not a blind mechanical framework in which man is trapped for eternity. Freedom from the cycle of karma is possible and is the ultimate goal and destiny of every being (Mahadevan 1958). This freedom from the cycle of birth and death is termed *moksha* or liberation. It results when the bonds of ignorance have been broken and is a state which is free from all imperfections and limitations (Prabhavananda 1960).

3   Karma-Yoga: The Indian Philosophy of Work Motivation

The philosophy of Karma-Yoga is built around the ethics of community and divinity. The self is conceptualized as a divine entity which the human form and intelligence cannot easily comprehend. Hence, the goal of human life is to realize that divinity. However, the barrier to realization of the divinity is the multitude of births that we are forced to endure in order to repay for our past misdeeds. The only way to break this cycle of birth and death is to ensure two things: first, to exhaust one's quota of suffering based on past misdeeds, and second, not to accumulate any more balance of good and bad deeds for which one may need to be repaid in future.

Exhausting your quota of suffering based on past misdeeds is possible by dispassionately executing the duties expected of you in your immediate environment. This is especially useful since those individuals who are in your immediate environment are most likely those who are your karmic creditors from the past. Hence, the only way one can be free of these karmic debts is by selflessly serving those who are nearest.

The second way of breaking the cycle of birth and death is to stop accumulating new karma (rewards and punishments for actions). This is done by cultivating an attitude of complete disinterestedness in rewards or any form of returns from one's actions. In other words, if we can work selflessly without expecting any rewards for our actions we will not accumulate further karma and will be eligible for liberation.

The beliefs in karma, *atma*, and *moksha* serve as a logical basis to explain the necessity of Karma-Yoga. When one is convinced of the law of universal cause and effect, the existence of an eternal soul, and the objective of life as liberation of the soul from the eternal cycle of birth and death, one seeks opportunities for eternal salvation. Indian philosophy suggests that the path to be selected for liberation must be suited to the temperament and disposition of the seeker. Karma-Yoga provides one such path for freedom from the cycle of birth and death, which is suited for people with an active temperament who have chosen to remain in the world and aspire for liberation.

The word karma comes from the Sanskrit root *kri*, which means doing, affairs, or activity and includes all actions that a person performs whether they are of body, speech, or mind. The word yoga comes from the Sanskrit root *yuj*, which means, to join. However, in the Mahabharata it is used in three ways: as a special skill, device, intelligent method, or graceful way of performing actions (Gita Chapter 2, Verse 50); as equability of mind towards success or failure (Gita Chapter 2, Verse 48); and as the device for eliminating the natural tendency of karma to create bondage (Gita Chapter 2, Verse 50). Since the latter two definitions of yoga speak of the relationship of yoga with action, the terms 'yoga' and 'Karma-Yoga' are used interchangeably at various instances in the Gita (Tilak 1915/2000). For the purpose of this study, we will use the word 'yoga' to mean 'device' or 'intelligent method' and hence the term 'Karma-Yoga' would mean 'a technique for intelligently performing actions'.

Since the ultimate goal of all beings is to free the soul from the cycle of birth and death, any method that enables release from this perpetual cycle is preferable to any other method that is likely to bind the human soul to the cycle. Hence, whether we define Karma-Yoga as 'a technique for intelligently performing actions' or 'a technique for performing actions in a manner that the soul is not bound by the effects of the action', we mean the same thing (Tilak 1915/2000).

The essence of Karma-Yoga is given in the Bhagwad Gita (Radhakrishnan 1948/1993) Chapter 2, Verse 47, which says, 'To action alone hast thou a right and never at all to its fruits; let not the fruits of action be thy motive; neither let there be in thee any attachment to inaction'. This verse of the Gita is also mentioned by Tilak (1915/2000: 895) as giving the entire import of Karma-Yoga in a short and beautiful form. Later in the Gita (Radhakrishnan, 1948/1993: Chapter 3, Verses 12, 13, and 16), Arjuna is told that persons who survive on this earth and use its resources without working are living in sin, and hence man is obliged to work selflessly in order to fulfil his duty towards the world. A content analysis of the text of the Bhagwad Gita conceptualized Karma-Yoga as made up of three dimensions: duty-orientation, indifference to rewards, and equanimity (Mulla and Krishnan 2006). Subsequently, other studies (Mulla and Krishnan 2007; 2008) have validated the relationship between these three dimensions.

3.1 The Eternal Cycle of Birth and Death

The metaphysical explanation of Karma-Yoga is explained as follows. The eternal cycle of birth and death driven by reincarnation and the karmic law is defined in the form of a three-step procedure (Tilak 1915/2000). The first step is the interaction of the five senses with external objects; this in turn leads to a perception of pain or happiness in the mind of the agent of the action (Gita Chapter 2, Verse 14). Perceiving pleasure or pain further leads to a desire to experience again what has been experienced (in the case of happiness) or a desire to avoid what has been experienced (in the case of pain). The presence of an unfulfilled desire to experience or avoid a certain experience is the essential fuel, which drives a soul to being reborn again in a body most suited to its experiencing its latent unfulfilled desires. In this manner, the cycle of birth and death is repeated to eternity. The cycle can be broken in three ways. First, an individual may choose to avoid all interaction of his or her senses with external objects. However, in the case of an active person, this path is not suitable. Hence, the only two ways of breaking the cycle of birth and death are to endure pleasure and pain with equanimity and to be indifferent to the rewards (and punishments) of one's actions (Tilak 1915/2000).

3.2 Breaking the Cycle of Birth and Death through Equanimity and Indifference to Rewards

One way out of this perpetual cycle of desire is to be able to control in one's mind the experience of pain and happiness i.e., being neutral to the experiences of our senses (Tilak 1915/2000). According to the Gita, when one does what one has to do, with perfect mental control and after giving up the desire for the result and with a frame of mind that is equal towards pain and happiness, there remains no fear or possibility of experiencing the unhappiness of actions. If one can perform actions with such a spirit, it does not become necessary to give up actions. Hence, the Gita recommends that we keep our organs under control and allow them to perform the various activities, not for a selfish purpose, but without desire, and for the welfare of others (Tilak 1915/2000).

In addition, since the outcomes of one's actions are dependent on an elaborate chain of cause and effect, all that is in the individual's control is performance of that action. Hence, one ceases to have a feeling of ownership towards one's actions and believes that the actions happen naturally and the bodily organs are just an instrument for their execution. This lack of ownership for actions coupled with the sense of obligation to others creates a complete disinterest in the mind of the seeker for any form of material or social rewards (Tilak 1915/2000).

3.3 Duty-Orientation as a Precursor to Developing Equanimity and Indifference to Rewards

A question that is often asked is: how is it possible for an individual to maintain equanimity to pleasure/pain and be indifferent to rewards? By integrating elements of the Indian worldview and developing duty-orientation, it is possible to develop equanimity and indifference to rewards.

The belief in the law of cause and effect makes us realize that we are placed in a particular situation because of unfulfilled past obligations on our part and we develop a sense of connectedness with all beings. In other words, irrespective of the situation that we are placed in, we can look upon those around us as our creditors in our past lives to whom we are obliged to discharge certain obligations (which were unfulfilled earlier). The belief in the law of cause and effect coupled with the belief in the doctrine of salvation makes us strive to discharge our obligations to those around us. In this manner, all actions become a repayment of a debt and the actor is free of any motive for the actions.

For example if A borrows money from B, then A feels a sense of obligation (duty-orientation). Later when A is making efforts to return the borrowed amount back to B, A will not be affected by any pain or pleasure that is encountered in the process of repayment (equanimity). Finally, when A has repaid B, then A will not expect to be praised or rewarded by B (indifference to rewards) since whatever was done by A was out of a sense of duty or obligation towards B.

4 Schumacher's Call for a Proper 'Philosophy of Work'

Schumacher (1973: 11) identifies a strange paradox in our current way of thinking i.e., striving for prosperity will bring us peace. In other words, we assume that the Western industrialized nations have discovered the secret of production and hence all that is now needed for world peace is for the developing nations to copy the Western economic model. The roots of this paradox lie in two faulty assumptions. First, blinded by our scientific and technological achievements, humans have come to believe that we have unlimited power over nature. Second, we feel that resources that we have not created ourselves (but have come to us from nature) are completely without value. Because of this, instead of treating our natural resources as capital (which they truly are), we erroneously treat them as income which can be freely spent without any attempt at conservation. According to Schumacher (1973: 11), the faulty belief that Western nations have discovered the secret of production coupled with the faulty assumption that single-minded pursuit of production will bring about all other desirable values such as freedom, equality and peace is likely to lead to disastrous economic, social and moral problems as explained in the paragraphs that follow.

4.1 Economic Consequences

Believing that natural resources are unlimited and available for free, the mindless pursuit of growth in consumption without any regard for nature is likely to lead to complete depletion of natural resources of the planet. In addition, development of alternative resources (such as nuclear power) in a hurry to fuel humankind's increasing hunger for goods is likely to lead to more serious problems of safety and health.

4.2 Social Consequences

In order to meet the huge demand for material consumption at low costs, there is a drive towards attaining economics of scale. This leads to large factories being concentrated in a few locations. Because of these concentrated labour opportunities, there is often an exodus from rural areas to a few commercial hubs, which develop into unmanageable metropolises. Finally, since the large cities become unmanageable and rural areas remain underdeveloped and impoverished, neither the rural nor the urban people benefit.

4.3 Moral Consequences

In the quest for material prosperity, our educational, legal, and social institutions have systematically sought to cultivate baser aspects of human nature such as greed and envy. Over a period of time, this single-minded pursuit of material progress fuelled by greed and envy is likely to destroy all traces of 'intelligence, happiness, serenity, and thereby the peacefulness of man' (Schumacher 1973: 19) and finally lead to a complete breakdown of human intelligence and wisdom.

4.4 The Way Out of the Problem

To avoid the harmful economic, social, and moral consequences of the current developmental trajectory, Schumacher suggests that we create a new lifestyle with new methods of production and consumption, which are designed for permanence. In order to do this, we will need to encourage small-scale technology with a human face and enable people to work for not just money but spiritual fulfilment. The first step in doing this is to cultivate an attitude of 'wisdom' (Schumacher 1973: 19). An attitude of wisdom suggests insight or an ability to discern inner qualities beyond what is apparent and an ability to see interrelationships between objects and events which appear independent (Merriam-Webster online dictionary 2012). One of the methods suggested by Schumacher to cultivate this wisdom is to design work processes which encourage and sustain human creativity. This can be done only if we subscribe to a philosophy of work which is able to appreciate work as a means to human perfection and not just as a tool for meeting one's material needs.

Schumacher further suggests that the Buddhist approach to work in terms of 'right livelihood' recognizes the role of work as being not just a means of production but a vehicle to develop one's character and overcome one's selfishness by working for others. This is quite different from the conventional economic view which considers the objective of work to be merely the satisfaction of an individual's material needs (Schumacher 1973: 38–40).

In this essay I will further show how the Indian worldview and specifically the doctrine of Karma-Yoga as described in Gita is clearly expressed in Schumacher's philosophy of work. In this way, Schumacher's ideals are a contemporary manifestation of the Karma-Yoga philosophy.

5 The Role of Karma-Yoga in Enabling an 'Economy of Permanence'

The doctrine of Karma-Yoga has been an essential part of Indian philosophy and culture since earliest times. It was first articulated in the battlefield by Lord Krishna to the warrior prince Arjuna as part of the Gita in the epic Mahabharata. Later during the Indian nationalistic movement in the nineteenth and early twentieth centuries, two thinkers used the doctrine of Karma-Yoga to inspire and motivate the Indian people to participate in the struggle for freedom from British rule.

The first of these was the politician-scholar, Lokmanya Bal Gangadhar Tilak. Prior to Tilak, many scholars including the highly influential scholar-saint Adi Shakara had advocated renunciation of action as the message of the Gita and the best way to liberation. While he was in a British jail, Tilak (1915/2000) wrote a treatise on the Gita called the *Gita Rahasya* (the secret of the Gita) which rejected renunciation and advocated an active life as the most conducive to liberation. In addition, Tilak suggested that according to the Gita, it is the duty of all citizens to work for their country (Mackenzie Brown 1958). The other great thinker who popularized the doctrine of Karma-Yoga was Swami Vivekananda. According to Vivekananda there were four means to liberation – viz. Raja-Yoga for the mystic, Gyan-Yoga for the intellectual, Bhakti-Yoga for the devotional, and Karma-Yoga for the active. Thus, each individual could select the path that was most conducive to his or her temperament. For those just entering spiritual life, Karma-Yoga was the safest and the best path. In fact, Vivekananda famously said, 'You will be nearer to Heaven through football than through the study of the Gita' (Vivekananda, 1897/1989: Vol. 3, 242).

In more recent times, the philosophy of Karma-Yoga was emphasized by Gandhi in his translation of the Gita entitled *Anasakti Yoga* (the Yoga of Selflessness). Gandhi went further to develop his philosophy into a complete way of life encompassing an individual's lifestyle, dress, food, and occupation. Gandhi's ideas were further elaborated by an economist, J.C. Kumarappa (1945), in his classic work, *Economy of Permanence*.

Kumarappa (1945) categorizes various types of relationships amongst forms of life into five types. The most violent kind of economy is the parasitic economy where one life form thrives at the expense of the life of the host life form e.g., a tiger killing a sheep for food. The next is the predatory economy where one life form benefits from another without any return contribution e.g., a monkey eating a mango from a mango tree. The third form of economy is the economy of enterprise where one individual takes from another and renders a service in return e.g., honey bees taking honey from a flower and fertilizing the flower in return. The fourth form of economy is the economy of gregation where an individual does not work for himself or herself but for the benefit of a larger group or community e.g., a bee collecting nectar for the entire hive. The last and most mature form of economy is the economy of service or the economy of permanence. An example of this kind of economy is seen in the love of parents for their children. Parents of all species of living beings selflessly endure pain and suffering in order to provide for their offspring. Bringing about an economy of permanence requires one to recognize the essential interconnectedness and harmony amongst various natural phenomena.

6   Schumacher's Theory of Good Work and the Tradition of Karma-Yoga

The Karma-Yoga doctrine provides a comprehensive religious and moral philosophy of life based on Indian cultural beliefs. Over the years, this philosophy has been used by leaders to guide religious and social life of Indians. For meeting the challenges of today it can complement Schumacher's ideas by being a 'proper philosophy of work' (Schumacher 1973: 23). There are three arguments which suggest that Karma-Yoga is a good candidate for being an adequate philosophy of work in line with Schumacher's ideals.

6.1 Belief in Karma Eliminates Envy and Greed

Belief in the law of karma suggests an essential interconnectedness of all beings. If individuals have to pass through an infinite number of births prior to being liberated and if the main objective of one's being born in a particular circumstance is the fulfilment of past rewards and punishments, then it is obvious that every being we meet is likely to have been intimately related to us in some life or the other. And all our acquaintances are our debtors or creditors. Since it is not clear who our debtor is and who our creditor, and our objective is to get rid of our past karma, it is safer to assume that all those we meet are our creditors and our duty is to serve them to the best of our ability.

Envy is a 'painful or resentful awareness of an advantage enjoyed by another joined with a desire to possess the same advantage' (Merriam-Webster online dictionary 2012). Envy is the start of numerous other negative emotions such as hate and greed. It is said that envy can occur only amongst equals or individuals who are perceived as similar. Underlying the emotion of envy is a feeling of injustice. In other words, we believe that equal inputs should beget equal outcomes and when we find that those whom we perceive to be equal to us get outcomes which are superior to us we feel a sense of injustice and resent the superior outcomes of others in the form of envy (Smith and Kim 2007).

Individuals who strongly believe in the law of karma are likely to believe that the outcomes of others are justly deserved (based on actions done in this life or earlier lives) and hence are less likely to be victims of envy. In addition, if we can recognize our essential relatedness to all beings, then our envy is likely to be converted into pride (since the person who enjoys the superior benefit is perceived as intimately related to us) and is hence less likely to lead us towards greed and hate.

In this manner, karma and Karma-Yoga strike at the very raw material which is fuelling the current mindless pursuit of production so characteristic of the current developmental paradigm. Schumacher (1973: 18–20) also discusses the limitations of the modern economic paradigm built on envy and greed. According to him, by encouraging an individual's envy and greed through a system of economic incentives, we are losing the ability to think rationally and holistically, which further leads to a breakdown of peace and civilization. On the other hand, individuals who are free of envy and greed are unlikely to succumb to the thoughtless growth for its own sake. If at all they choose to expand their enterprise, they are likely to do so as a response to some genuine need of communities around them.

6.2 Ethics of Divinity Eliminates Exploitation of Natural Resources

The Indian worldview is built upon an ethics of divinity (Shweder, Much, Mahapatra and Park 1997) that emphasizes the essential interconnectedness of all beings and the entire cosmos. This interconnectedness is described in the form of a universal spirit, life force, or Brahman: aspects of which are manifested in the form of an individual soul or atman. The concept of *rita* in the Rig Veda suggests that the universe functions according a subtle yet powerful cosmic order. As an integral part of the cosmos, humankind is expected to recognize this cosmic order and subordinate its will to it. Individuals who fail to recognize this divine order and forcibly impose their will are punished through the law of karma. In this manner, the ethics of divinity in the Indian worldview cultivates in individuals an attitude of wisdom, which can recognize the interdependence of humans on nature.

According to Schumacher one of the errors of the subject of economics is to *'ignore man's dependence on the natural world'* (Schumacher 1973: 29; emphasis in original) which had led individuals to be 'relieved of all responsibility to except oneself' (1973: 30). Individuals who recognize the interdependence of various elements of nature (including man) are less likely to exploit natural resources and instead are likely to nurture and sustain nature.

6.3 Doing One's Swadharma Prevents Needless Expansion and Labour Migration

A concept closely related to Karma-Yoga is *swadharma*. Swadharma implies that task which comes to us naturally or the code of conduct which ought to govern our actions based on our temperament and our station in life (Sinha 2008). In other words, swadharma consists of duties that arise out of one's being part of a community or duties appropriate for a given time (Bhave 1940/2005). According to Vinoba Bhave (1940/2005), in order for us to fully relinquish the fruits of our actions (i.e., become completely selfless), we must only take up those actions which are obligatory. In other words we must not go out of our way and seek out opportunities and actions which may appear attractive to us nor give up those actions which are naturally ours by virtue of being born in a particular family at a particular point in time. Vinoba argues that only by doing those actions which are obligatory can we easily give up the fruits of our actions and strive towards the ideal of Karma-Yoga.

Schumacher too criticizes needless expansion of organizations and cities. Related to expansion is the extensive development of means of transport and communication which 'makes people *footloose*' (Schumacher 1973: 51, emphasis in original) thereby increasing migration to large cities, which in turn creates severe problems of their assimilation and integration into meaningful occupations (Schumacher 1973: 53).

6.4 Karma-Yogis Seek Meaning and Purpose in Their Work

A Karma-Yogi serves those around him or her with an attitude of selflessness. This spirit of service comes naturally to the Karma-Yogi since it is driven by recognition of the essential oneness or relatedness of all beings and hence the Karma-Yogi expects no reward in return for the service. In contrast to others, the Karma-Yogi sees a deeper purpose and meaning in his work. At one level this meaning is to be of service to those around him or her. At a deeper level, the Karma-Yogi realizes that through work one can liberate oneself from the cycle of birth and death.

In addition to creating meaning for themselves in their work; Karma-Yogis have been found to be more inspirational as leaders. In a study of 205 Indian leader-follower pairs it was found that individuals who were rated high on Karma-Yoga were found to be charismatic role models for their followers, providing meaning and challenge to the follower's work (Mulla and Krishnan 2009).

Schumacher also emphasizes the role of work in creating meaning and purpose in an individual's life through his essay on 'Buddhist Economics' where he says: '[...] the Buddhist sees the essence of civilization not in a multiplication of wants but in the purification of human character. Character, at the same time, is formed primarily by a man's work. And work, properly conducted in conditions of human dignity and freedom, blesses those who do it and equally their products' (Schumacher 1973: 40).

7   Conclusion

Schumacher (1973) expressed his concern with humankind's single-minded obsession with material progress since he believed that this would lead to economic, social, and moral ruin for the human race. In fact if humankind continues on its trajectory of exploiting natural resources, making large institutions bigger, and dehumanizing work, its very existence could be at stake. In order to overcome this lethal momentum, Schumacher suggests that we create a new lifestyle based on an economy of permanence, which can be developed by cultivating in ourselves an attitude of wisdom. In this chapter, I described the philosophical foundations of Karma-Yoga and I defined Karma-Yoga in operational terms. In addition, I showed how Karma-Yoga and its antecedent beliefs are manifest in Schumacher's philosophy of work.

There are four common threads in Karma-Yoga and Schumacher's thoughts. First, belief in the law of karma helps us to eliminate envy and greed which according to Schumacher are the drivers of our faulty growth trajectory. Second, Karma-Yoga is based on an understanding of the essential interconnectedness of all beings and Schumacher too urges us to recognize man's interdependence on nature in order to save the world from ruin. Third, Karma-Yoga recommends that we focus on achieving perfection in the task allotted to us based on our role in society rather than hankering after growth and material progress for its own sake. Schumacher too criticizes needless expansion of organizations and mindless migration from small towns to large cities. Finally, Karma-Yoga enables us to find meaning and purpose in work and Schumacher too emphasizes that the role of work is to help build character and enable us to progress spiritually rather than just materially. In this manner, Schumacher's philosophy provides a modern interpretation to the age-old Indian philosophy of work, i.e., Karma-Yoga.

Economics and business education have recently been at the receiving end of society's ire due to the large number of scandals and increasing wage disparities between top executives and frontline workers. Organizations and leaders are being subjected to increasing scrutiny about their ethics and moral obligations to society. Echoing Schumacher's (1973) criticisms of economics, Sumantra Ghoshal (2005) argued that by propagating ideologically inspired amoral theories, business schools have actively freed their students from any sense of moral responsibility. Social science theories, while attempting to describe human behaviour in precise 'scientific' terms, invariably contain powerful behavioural norms for students who are exposed to these theories. In this way instead of merely being a description of human behaviour, they become self-fulfilling. One such theory that is said to be self-fulfilling is the theory of the self-interested behaviour of human beings in organizations (Ghoshal and Moran 1996; Ghoshal 2005; Miller 1999). The fact that business education leads to behaviour that is more self-interested was validated in a longitudinal study of business school students over a period of five years (Krishnan 2003). In order to reverse the damage caused by these theories and to reinstitute ethical or moral concerns in the practice of management, Ghoshal (2005) called for teaching theories which would help build moral/ethical organizations. Goshal's (2005) concerns are evidence of the fact that economics and business educators have not yet heeded Schumacher's call for a new philosophy of work nor embraced the theory of Karma-Yoga. Karma-Yoga is a precious jewel of Indian philosophy which has been successfully harnessed by Indian scholars, saints, and freedom fighters to awaken a dormant India and inspire the Indian people. Similarly, E.F. Schumacher's ideals have been immensely popular across the world (Bawa 1996; Corrywright 2004). However, despite being well known both these philosophies have not been extensively applied to transform social institutions. Perhaps it is now time to let the rest of the world know about Karma-Yoga and the legacy of E.F. Schumacher. This time the very survival of the human race may be at stake.

References

Agrawal, M., and Dalal, A.K. (1993). 'Beliefs about the World and Recovery from Myocardial Infarction', *The Journal of Social Psychology*, 133 (3), 385–94.

Bawa, V.S. (1996). 'Gandhi in the Twenty-first Century: Search for an Alternative Development Model', *Economic and Political Weekly*, 31 (47), 3048–9.

Bhave, V. (1940/2005). *Talks on the Gita* (translated by Parag Cholkar). Wardha: Paramdham Prakashan.

Connors, J., and Heaven, P.C.L. (1990). 'Belief in a Just World and Attitudes toward AIDS Sufferers', *The Journal of Social Psychology*, 130 (4), 559–60.

Corrywright, D. (2004). 'Network Spirituality: The Schumacher-Resurgence-Kumar Nexus', *Journal of Contemporary Religion*, 19 (3), 311–27.

Dalal, A.K., and Pande, N. (1988). 'Psychological Recovery of Accident Victims with Temporary and Permanent Disability', *International Journal of Psychology*, 23, 25–40.

Dasgupta, S. (1922/1991). *A History of Indian Philosophy*. Vol. 1. New Delhi: Motilal Banarasidas.

'Envy' (2012). In *Merriam-Webster.com* <http://www.merriam-webster.com/diction-ary/envy> accessed 24 March 2012.

Gandhi, M.K. (1960). *Trusteeship*. Ahmadabad: Navajivan.

Ghanananda, S. (1958). 'The Dawn of Indian Philosophy'. In S. Radhakrishnan, H. Bhattacharyya, R.C. Majumdar, S.K. Chatterji, H. Kabir, S.K. De et al. (Series Eds) and S.K. Chatterji, N. Dutt, A.D. Pusalker, and N.K. Bose (Vol. Eds), *The Cultural Heritage of India: Vol. 1. The Early Phases*, 2nd edn, pp. 333–44. Kolkata: The Ramakrishna Mission Institute of Culture.

Ghoshal, S. (2005). 'Bad Management Theories are Destroying Good Management Practices', *Academy of Management Learning and Education*, 4 (1), 75–91.

Ghoshal, S., and Moran, P. (1996). 'Bad for Practice: A Critique of the Transaction Cost Theory', *Academy of Management Review*, 21 (1), 13–47.

Hafer, C.L., and Begue, L. (2005). 'Experimental Research on Just-World Theory: Problems, Developments, and Future Challenges', *Psychological Bulletin*, 131 (1), 128–67.

Krishnan, V.R. (2008). 'Impact of MBA Education on Students' Values: Two Longitudinal Studies', *Journal of Business Ethics*, 83 (2), 233–46.

Krishnananda, S. (1994). *A Short History of Religious and Philosophic Thought in India*. India: The Divine Life Society.

Kumarappa, J.C. (1945). *Economy of Permanence*. Varanasi: Sarva-Seva-Sangh-Prakashan.

Mackenzie Brown, D. (1958). 'The Philosophy of Bal Gangadhar Tilak: Karma vs. Jnana in the Gita Rahasya', *The Journal of Asian Studies*, 17 (2), 197–206.

Mahadevan, T.M.P. (1958). 'The Religio-Philosophic Culture of India'. In S. Radhakrishnan, H. Bhattacharyya, R.C. Majumdar, S.K. Chatterji, H. Kabir, S.K. De et al. (Series Eds.) and S.K. Chatterji, N. Dutt, A.D. Pusalker, and N.K. Bose (Vol. Eds.), *The Cultural Heritage of India: Vol. 1. The Early Phases*, 2nd edn, pp. 163–81. Kolkata: The Ramakrishna Mission Institute of Culture.

Miller, D.T. (1999). 'The Norm of Self-Interest', *American Psychologist*, 54, 1053–60.

Mulla, Z.R., and Krishnan, V.R. (2006). 'Karma Yoga: A Conceptualization and Validation of the Indian Philosophy of Work', *Journal of Indian Psychology*, 24 (1/2), 26–43.

Mulla, Z.R., and Krishnan, V.R. (2007). 'Karma-Yoga: Construct Validation Using Value Systems and Emotional Intelligence', *South Asian Journal of Management*, 14 (4), 116–36.

Mulla, Z.R., and Krishnan, V.R. (2008). 'Karma-Yoga, the Indian Work Ideal, and its Relationship with Empathy', *Psychology and Developing Societies*, 20 (1), 27–49.

Mulla, Z.R., and Krishnan, V.R. (2009). 'Do Karma-Yogis Make Better Leaders?: Exploring the Relationships between the Leader's Karma-Yoga and Transformational Leadership', *Journal of Human Values*, 15 (2), 167–83.

Prabhavananda, S. (1960). *The Spiritual Heritage of India*. Hollywood, CA: Vedanta Society of Southern California.

Radhakrishnan, S. (1926). *The Hindu View of Life*. India: Harper Collins Publishers.

Radhakrishnan, S. (1940). *Indian Philosophy: Vol. 1*. London: George Allen & Unwin.

Radhakrishnan, S. (1948/1993). *The Bhagvadgita*. India: Harper Collins Publishers.

Schumacher, E.F. (1973). *Small is Beautiful: A Study of Economics as if People Mattered*. London: Vintage.

Shweder, R.A., N. Much, L. Park and M.M. Mahapatra (2003). 'The "Big Three" of Morality (Autonomy, Community, Divinity) and the "Big Three" Explanations of Suffering'. Originally from Allan Brandt and Paul Rozin (eds), *Morality and Health*. New York: Routledge, 1997. Reprinted in R.A. Shweder, *Why Do Men Barbecue? Recipes for Cultural Psychology*. Cambridge, MA: Harvard University Press.

Sinha, J.B.P. (2008). *Culture and Organizational Behaviour*. New Delhi: Sage.

Smith, R.H., and Kim, S.H. (2007). 'Comprehending Envy', *Psychological Bulletin*, 133 (1), 46–64.

Tilak, B.G. (1915/2000). *Srimad Bhagavadgita-Rahasya*. (B.S. Sukhantar, Trans.). Pune: Kesari Press.

Vivekananda, S. (1897/1989). *The Complete Works of Swami Vivekananda*. Calcutta: Advaita Ashrama.

'Wisdom' (2012). In *Merriam-Webster.com* <http://www.merriam-webster.com/dictionary/wisdom> accessed 24 March 2012.

GERRIT DE VYLDER
LESSIUS UNIVERSITY COLLEGE ANTWERP/LEUVEN UNIVERSITY/
THOMAS MORE

7 The East as a Practical and Spiritual Basis for Economics

1 Introduction

What is needed, according to E.F. Schumacher, is 'technology with a human face'. While he found his inspiration in 'Eastern' traditions (Gandhi and Burmese Buddhism), his message was directly addressed to the so-called 'Western' world. He was a Christian economist taking the Buddhist point of view that the function of work was to give a man a chance to utilize and develop his faculties, to enable him to overcome his ego-centeredness by joining with other people in a common task, and to bring forth the goods and services needed for a becoming existence. That his message was derived from Eastern sources but aimed at a 'Western' public puts Schumacher in a long line of nineteenth- and twentieth-century Orientalists.

In this contribution we put Schumacher in the broader perspective of West-European Orientalism by referring to two different Sanskrit concepts of justice in ancient Indian jurisprudence: *niti* and *nyaya*. Amartya Sen introduces both concepts in his *The Idea of Justice* (Sen 2009: xvi and 20–1). *Niti*, on the one hand, relates to organizational propriety as well as behavioural correctness. *Nyaya*, on the other hand, is concerned with what emerges and how, and in particular the lives that people are actually able to lead. Early Indian legal theorists talked about the need to avoid *matsyanyaya* or 'justice in the world of fish', where the big fish can freely devour a small fish. A clear distinction was made between judging the institutions and rules on the one hand, and judging the societies themselves.

Sen refers to Ferdinand I, the Holy Roman emperor, who in the sixteenth century claimed 'Let justice be done, though the world perishes', reflecting an extreme type of *niti*-thinking. Many West-European Enlightenment authors actually confirmed this way of thinking. They concentrated on identifying perfectly just arrangements, taking the form of perfectly just institutions. Thomas Hobbes in the seventeenth century and later John Locke, Jean-Jacques Rousseau and Immanuel Kant gave their interpretation of a hypothetical 'social contract' which reflected a shift from *niti* to *nyaya*. This culminated into John Rawls's pioneering paper ('Justice as Fairness') in 1958 which preceded his classic book, *A Theory of Justice*. One interpretation is that while the predominant Western thinking increasingly became *niti*-oriented and accordingly emphasized perfect ideologies, almost like utopias, Eastern thinking remained more practical and *niti*-oriented.

However, the Enlightenment philosophers did not speak in one voice. There were philosophers who were interested in how institutions, no matter how perfect they were, failed to directly influence people's life. Other factors like people's actual behaviour, emotions and social interactions were studied by Adam Smith, Condorcet, Wollstonecraft, Bentham, Marx, J.S. Mill, even though their ideas were afterwards interpreted as alternative 'social contracts' leading to *niti*-oriented utopias. In the mid-twentieth century the pioneering contributions of Kenneth Arrow would result in the 'social choice theory' which consolidated an alternative *nyaya*-approach in the West and on an international level.

In this contribution we argue that most West-European philosophers who were influenced by Eastern philosophies were explicitly *nyaya*-oriented. More specifically we argue that E.F. Schumacher was the ultimate translation of this tendency into socio-economic terms. In a way Schumacher's *Small is Beautiful* was the final answer to the *nyaya*-influence from the East. In order to assess this we should identify the socio-economic characteristics of the Orientalist tradition and the Orientalist orientation of economists during the nineteenth and twentieth centuries in Western Europe.

2   Paternalist Utilitarian Approaches versus
      Eastern Spiritual Solutions

While since the sixteenth century, starting with Thomas More himself, West-European utopias had considered the 'East' to be a more advanced culture, with the advent of nineteenth-century romantic Orientalism the notion of the 'East' would radically change. The industrialization of England was too fast and too radical and all of a sudden it seemed that 'East and West would never meet again'. Around the turn of the century, however, Europe still felt inferior towards the East and chances for a peaceful co-existence were still high. This was also reflected in economic thinking. The Indologist William Jones (1746–94), who founded the Asiatic Society in Calcutta in 1784, was aware of economic liberal ideas like those of David Hume (1711–76) and Adam Smith (1723–90), who referred to India as the ultimate example of comparative advantages in textiles throughout world history in his famous *Wealth of Nations* (1776; 2003: 563–5). Gradually economists would radicalize Smith's ideas into utilitarian philosophies, like those of Jeremy Bentham (1748–1832) and David Ricardo (1772–1823). Up to the end of the eighteenth century the notion of racial superiority would remain largely unknown but the new concept of 'public utility' would gradually allow paternalistic thoughts to emerge.

At first also the Romanticists did not oppose the tradition of admiration for the East. Orientalist Romanticists were looking for 'Divine Remembrance' originating from the East. In Germany, the philosopher G.W.F. Hegel (1770–1831) described India as the 'richest country in the world', both in terms of physical and metaphysical richness. But it was Germany's *uomo universale*, Johann Wolfgang Goethe (1749–1832), who gave Eastern religion and philosophy also socio-economic relevance. Human beings are caught in *das Trübe*. According to Goethe a scientific approach to nature, including artificial instruments and mathematical considerations, is useless as it is about rediscovering and reconfirming 'what is unconsciously already known'. Goethe's interpreting of nature is a philosophical and religious experience. It somehow illustrates why Vedanta (the dominant school of Indian philosophy) did not result in science as an independent activity. It also illustrates that as 'man' is trapped in an unbalanced situation, economics also is to be considered as unbalanced (Friedenthal 1993).

Significantly, Thomas Raffles (1781–1826), the East India Company clerk who founded Singapore, investigated the Javanese temple ruins of Prambanan and Borobudur, and assumed the existence of an advanced Indian civilization in Java's history. For Raffles civilization obviously had no skin colour (Grabsky 2000). Likewise, Warren Hastings (1732–1818), the first governor-general of British India, spoke fluent Urdu, Bengali and Persian. He even suggested that Persian (the language of the Mogul Court and as such still the official language of India) should be included in the curriculum of Oxford University and be made a part of a British 'gentleman's' education.

One of the last great European admirers of Indian culture was Sir William Jones. In 1783 he took up his position as a judge in the High Court of the British East India Company. Throughout his life, Jones's greatest passion had been the study of Oriental languages, including Arabic and Persian, and on his arrival in India he turned to the ancient and then almost forgotten language of Sanskrit. He discovered that Sanskrit shared many characteristics with Greek, Latin, German and other European languages. This led him to the conclusion that all these different tongues were branches of the same Indo-European family. An interesting conclusion followed: India and Europe had common roots. From that point of view Jones introduced an Orient which is no longer utopian but actually very much like the 'West'. But Jones' conclusions came at the wrong time because for the next century the psychological distance between India and Europe would only become larger (Hobson 2004).

Gradually, a new Eurocentric and Victorian world was born in which most Orientalists were considered eccentric. It was the classical economist James Mill, with his famous *History of India* (1817), who marked a turning point in the way West-Europeans considered Asia. At the end of a comprehensive attack on supposed Indian achievements particularly in mathematics and science, Mill came to the conclusion that the Indian civilization was similar to other inferior ones like the Chinese, Persian and Arab civilizations. Unfortunately Mill's book became a 'bible for the British Indian officer', without Mill having set one foot in India during his lifetime...

Most nineteenth-century Orientalists essentially supported the classical school of economics in the utilitarian interpretation of the term. However, this manifested itself in two completely different ways. The first, predominant way was to assume that all blessings came from Western Europe. These Orientalists assumed that India had to adopt West-European concepts and technologies in order to promote economic growth. They are the so-called 'Said' types.[1] It should be pointed out that many of them were socialists. Karl Marx (1818–83) saw Hinduism, like all religion, as the reflection of social and economic realities of despotism and inertia. And Max Weber (1864–1920) saw the poor social and economic condition of India as the result of Hinduism. Both their views were based on inadequate sources and a deeply rooted Euro-centrism. They were also essentially a reaction against the utopian interpretation of the 'East'. The *nyaya*-message was completely ignored and the static interpretation of Eastern civilizations was taken for an extreme fatalistic *niti*-orientation.

The second way was to assume that all blessings came from Asia itself and that therefore an ancient and genuine Asia had to be rediscovered. Theosophical speculation placed an emphasis on mystical experience:[2] a deeper spiritual reality exists, and direct contact may be established with that reality through intuition, meditation, revelation, or some other state transcending normal human consciousness. Theosophists claimed that all world religions, including Christianity, contain such an inner teaching, and that the richest and most profound source of theosophical views is Hindu or Vedantic thought. Through theosophy the tradition of Orientalism continued.

---

1   After Edward Said, a strong opponent of Orientalism, emphasizing its collusion with imperialism (Macfie 2000: 87–114).

2   Theosophy is a doctrine of religious philosophy and mysticism. It holds that all religions are attempts to help humanity evolve to greater perfection, and that each religion therefore has a portion of the truth.

In reality, most commentators were somewhere in between. Levallois and Moussa (2006) support this view by referring to the Saint Simonians (the 'saint-simoniens'), followers of the French utopian economist, the Count of Saint Simon (1760–1825). Many of them were involved in the imperialist designs of France on the Maghreb and Egypt. Following in the footsteps of Napoleon they sojourned in Egypt, and from the 1830s increasingly in Algeria. Most of them genuinely tried to open up to the Muslim society and culture, and to find common ground for their utopian socialism. This attitude of 'ouverture à l'autre' left its impact on Orientalist literature and was not completely irrelevant to the French colonial policies in the Maghreb.

The 'East' also received mixed comments from Victor Hugo (1802–85) who dominated French literature during the mid-nineteenth century. The depiction of Turks in his Les Orientales (1829) mixed condemnation, idealization, and crude envy. It is often cited as being representative of the 'Orientalist' attitudes in much of French literature. In his essay on Shakespeare (1864) Hugo was more positive about the East. The Roman poet and philosopher Lucretius, one of the characters, studies Greece and its philosophers and finally, just like Shakespeare, realizes the importance of India, described as l'infini impersonnel (Laurent 2006: 72). India cannot attain the level of individuality but at the same time transcends it, again indirectly referring to the problem of classical economics that its sole reference point is the individual.

Germany's and France's appreciation for Vedanta (Michelet, Burnouf, Lévy, Rolland, Müller, Schopenhauer, Hegel, Kant, Von Schlegel) generally combined admiration, fascination and paternalism. In the same way the relationship between utopian and scientific socialism on the one hand and the early ancient Indian-Buddhist concept of sanghas or democratically organized monastic communities on the other should be considered (Tathagatananda 2002 and 2005).

However, for Irish theosophist Annie Besant (1847–1933) India was no longer an abstract concept but a very close reality. With her the Said type gradually lost terrain. She was a foreigner who 'genuinely' sought to restore a 'genuine' India which supplied a 'genuine' socio-economic alternative to the Victorian world. Since the late nineteenth century theosophy was represented by the Theosophical Society whose headquarters moved from New York to Chennai in South India. The leadership of the charismatic Besant gave Indians a sense of pride that they were exporting ideas of importance to the West (Ramaswami, 1992). In 1911 she proclaimed Jiddu Krishnamurti (1895–1986), an obscure South Indian youth, as the vehicle of a coming World Teacher, an act that led to much controversy. Krishnamurti subsequently renounced any claims to being a World Teacher and began a career of writing and teaching. Beginning in the 1920s he spent much time in the United States and Europe, where his books enjoyed considerable popularity. The relevance of Krishnamurti's thought for economics and other social sciences became obvious when Europe was confronted with the absurdities of the inter-War period and the Second World War. Krishnamurti argued that the ultimate pitfall of the human sciences in general, and of man's approach to life in general, is the continuous intellectual effort to identify schools of thought and ideas. He considered thinking the ultimate problem of humankind: 'There is only one freedom-religious freedom; there is no other freedom. The freedom that the so-called welfare state brings, the economic, national, political, and various other forms of freedom that one is given surely are not freedom at all, but only lead to further chaos and further misery-which is obvious to anyone who observes' (Krishnamurti 2005: 2–5).

Concrete influence from Vedanta reached European socio-economic thinking through the visits and the writings of the Bengali monk and philosopher Swami Vivekananda, who became the subject of the French novelist and pacifist Romain Rolland's (1866–1944) essays 'La vie de Vivekananda' (1930) and 'l'Evangile universel' (1930). The writings of Swami Vivekananda mixed both socialist and classical-utilitarian solutions for socio-economic problems but were essentially about overcoming duality in a genuine Vedanta-sense. Economists should acknowledge that the main issue of today's socio-economic problems is not primarily of an economic nature, but rather of a psychological or behavioural nature (whereby spiritual capital is the key to the solution). Essentially that is what Swami Vivekananda meant when he stated: 'What will save Europe is the religion of the Upanishads [i.e. Vedanta]' (Dasgupta 2005: 474).

Another famous Bengali, the 1913 Nobel Prize Winner for Literature, Rabindranath Tagore (1861–1941), also influenced Romain Rolland and introduced a spiritual, literary but also broad-minded India to Europe and the world (cf. Rolland's 'Conversations with Rabindranath Tagore'). Tagore may have formulated the most explicit attacks on a *niti*-approach to life (Basu 2000). Lacking any economic training, he nevertheless contributed, especially in his speeches on nationalism, to Indian thinking on politics and economics. Tagore argued that all positive social relations which are not mechanical nor impersonal are contrary to the notion of a 'nation'. One of the major crimes of the nationalistic cults was the surrender by individuals of their own free will, replacing it by an abstract, strictly organized national will. Tagore explained: 'I am not against one nation in particular, but against the general idea of all nations. What is the nation?' (1917; 2002: 53–104). When applying nationalism, economic means are being redrawn from the higher nature of man where he is creative and in solidarity. Nationalism, in the eyes of Tagore, is immoral, mechanical, self-destructive and counterproductive. As early as 1908 he had written: 'Patriotism cannot be our final spiritual shelter; my refuge is humanity. I will not buy glass for the price of diamonds, and I will never allow patriotism to triumph over humanity as long as I live' (Sen 2005: 108). His words would linger on during the First World War and when fascism took over in Italy, and Nazism in Germany. Not surprisingly he became a hero to the European anti-war movement.

The popularity of characters like Krishnamurti, Vivekananda and Tagore in Europe can only be explained by reference to a continuing utopian tradition within European orientalism. From a European perspective Asian philosophies still reflected non-existent and mystical realities which were identifiably better than the existing ones. However, it should also be emphasized that gradually, because of the nature of the writings of the Indian philosophers themselves, the divide between East and West was gradually disappearing. The East was no longer an alternative but another dimension of one self. In that sense the East became a 'practical' alternative offering *nyaya*-solutions. As already mentioned, it was especially the famous French Nobel Prize winner for Literature in 1915, Romain Rolland (1866–1944), who embraced the work of the philosophers of India ('Conversations with

Rabindranath Tagore' and 'Mohandas Gandhi'). Rolland was strongly influenced by the Vedanta philosophy of India, primarily through the works of Swami Vivekananda. However, in his later years he turned more towards Christianity and became interested in Christian mysticism. Rolland successfully combined this with continued sympathies for communism and Indian philosophies and religions (Berdyaev 1945). In this way he transcended the East-West divide and saw no contradiction between both. It also allowed a consequentialist approach to the ideologies which had originated from the West and had almost destroyed the world (e.g. nationalism, state capitalism, etc.). It strongly advocated a *nyaya*-approach against a deontological approach which had created false utopias.

Interestingly, it was in Germany that Oswald Spengler's *Der Untergang des Abendlandes* (*The Decline of the West*, 1918; 1991) made explicit room for heterogeneities within each culture and for the cross-cultural similarities that can be clearly observed. In fact Spengler argued that there was nothing special about Socrates, Epicurus or Diogenes, who all have their more ancient Indian and Chinese counterparts. For Spengler Asia was not a utopia but a mirror, reflecting one's own reality. Unfortunately, as Germany got trapped in economic crises and subsequently the Nazi regime, both the time and the location were wrong for introducing such ideas.

Other West-European scholars like the Protestant theologian, Dr Albert Schweitzer (1875–1965), writing his *Indian Thought and Its Development* in 1935 (English edition: 1936), were influenced by Vivekananda and Tagore. Schweitzer searched for the meaning of activity and work within Hinduism and challenged the Weberian view that religions like Hinduism and Buddhism were by nature fatalistic and counterproductive. He argued that Hindu thinking, instead of merely tolerating activity, prizes activity as a valuable thing. He agreed with Sen that the *Mahabharata* illustrates that 'An appropriate understanding of social realization – central to justice as nyaya – has to take the comprehensive form of a process-inclusive broad account' (Sen 2009: 22–4).[3] The philosophically oriented treatise of the *Bhagavad-Gita*, contained in the *Mahabharata*, explicitly linked activities to an ethical awareness: Krishna defines it as the totality of the obligations

3   One of the two major Sanskrit epics of Ancient India, the other being the Ramayana.

which naturally belong to a man's stations in life. This is how Schweitzer expressed his preoccupation with affirming life. His view was that 'Western' civilization was in decay because it was gradually abandoning its ethical foundations, those of affirmation of life. He looked forward to a renewed and more profound Renaissance and Enlightenment of humanity through the philosophies of the European Middle Ages, and the essence of Indian Hindu thought. In this way Schweitzer was the first West-European to derive a direct economic-ethical message from ancient Hindu thinking related to West-European reality.

During the 1920s a Russian painter and philosopher, Nicholas Roerich (1874–1947), started expeditions to Buddhist, Hindu and Islamic regions in Central Asia, China and India. In his philosophic and artistic essays, Roerich created an absolutely new concept of culture based on the idea of 'Living Ethics'. Culture and ethics are based on beauty and knowledge. Economics should focus on artistic expression and beauty, as these are basic needs for a successful and harmonious humanity. Roerich's paintings themselves are an expression of utopian concepts: somewhere deep in the Himalayas or the Gobi desert lies 'shambala', presented as a Buddhist utopia. His emphasis on beauty also resulted in an international pact for protection of cultural treasures, signed in 1935 in the presence of US President F. Roosevelt, and supported by Rolland, Tagore and Albert Einstein. Roerich's son, Svetoslav Roerich (1904–93), while living in India, basically continued his father's work (Roerich 2004a and 2004b).

Finally, also two traditions with roots in Islam reached Europe. First, 'Perennial' Sufism was introduced to Europe through the foundation of the Sufi Order in the West in 1910 by Pir Hazrat Inayat Khan (1882–1927), who initially came to Europe as a representative of classical Indian music, but soon turned to the introduction and transmission of Sufi thought and practice. His universal message of divine unity (*Tawhid*) focused on the themes of love, harmony and beauty. He taught that blind adherence to any book rendered any religion void of spirit. Doctrinally it held views which go against Sunni, Shi'ite and even mainstream Sufi Islam: the nature of Allah/God is changeable, Allah/God and human beings are essentially one and the human being is divine. It also accepted the belief in reincarnation, and promoted the idea of a feminine dimension of the sacred (Hazrat Inayat Khan 2004).

Second, the Bahá'í faith was a monotheistic religion founded by Bahá'u'lláh (1817–92) in nineteenth-century Persia, emphasizing the spiritual unity of all humankind. Under the leadership of his son, 'Abdu'l-Bahá (1844–1921), the religion gained a footing in Europe and America. As Bahá'i did not consider man innately sinful (like many of the Christian churches or conventional Islam), a free market system is considered a perfect way to distribute resources in a fair way. Not surprisingly the movement reacted against the extreme forms of protectionism implemented during the Inter-War period. British IMF economist and member of Bahá'i, John Huddleston, describes this point of view: 'A spiritual society will have more rational methods of protecting its members from economic hardship than restrictions on movement of trade and peoples which cause gross inequalities and inefficiencies in the economic system' (Huddleston 2008: 140–1).

A natural evolution of mankind implies the growth of the higher, spiritual nature of man in a free market environment. However, an emphasis on marriage and family life resulted in a certain degree of exclusiveness.

It is clear from this summary that Orientalist thinking identified itself increasingly with a way of protesting against nationalistic ways of thinking which reflected the ideal of *niti*-justice. Orientalism contributed to paving the way for the *nyaya*-approach to socio-economic justice (and in particular E.F. Schumacher) in the new world that would emerge after the Second World War.

3   Schumacher and Post-War Europe: From Environmentalism to Business Ethics

Post-War Europe saw the emergence of two new religious fashions: Buddhism and Hinduism. The Second World War had once again demonstrated how Europe was self-destructive and once again 'Eastern' ideas were considered as possible alternatives.

Consequently, E.F. Schumacher's interest in Buddhism fits into the spirit of the time. From the 1960s the public showed specific interest in

Zen Buddhism which stressed the importance of applying meditation to work and art. Mahayana (Greater Vehicle or Great Way) Buddhism, emphasizing complete Buddhahood, the perfection of wisdom and compassion, was introduced by Japanese movements in the 1960s. Together with an increasing sympathy for the Tibetan cause also Tibetan communities became very popular, attracting not only Tibetan refugees but also native French and other European nationalities. Native French *lamas* and monks 'Europeanized' the movement. Later, in the 1980s and 1990s, a widespread interest developed in Vajrayana Buddhism, which involves the use of rituals to achieve both Buddhahood itself and this-worldly benefits. One of the principal agents in the advancement of 'engaged Buddhism' was the Vietnamese monk Thich Nhat Hanh. Through his publications and the foundation of the *Eglise Bouddhique Unifiée* he advocated a non-violent engagement through Buddhism with all aspects of life, including economic activities (Clark 2006: 87–92).

However, Schumacher's interest was strongly influenced by his research in Burma in 1955. The Burmese constitution and the law code included prefaces that explicitly connected the modern legal system with a Buddhist utopia that was believed to have existed in the past. Sargent concludes: 'Thus, in Burma the utopian past remained a touchstone of life until the late twentieth century' (Sargent 2010: 68). It was a concept that could be used and abused. By the time the army took over power in Myanmar (the new name for Burma) and the concept started to be abused Schumacher's interaction with the country had stopped. Schumacher came to believe that 'a Buddhist economy would make the distinction between renewable and non-renewable resources' (Lindley 2007: 131).

Schumacher's other exposure to the East was through research in the development problems of the newly created republic of India, which he visited for the first time in 1961 at the urging of the Marxist scholar, Jayaprakash Narayan. Schumacher's writings and that of many of his colleagues derived a lot from Mahatma (Mohandas Karamchand) Gandhi (1869–1948), the so-called 'Father of the Indian Nation', who was inspired by both *Vedanta* and Buddhism. While industrialist J.N. Tata and to some extent Swami Vivekananda had been industrial pragmatists, the Mahatma represented a complete economic alternative, emphasizing a 'voluntary limitation of needs', leading to a better equilibrium between man and nature. He suggested to set up self-sufficient village communities in order to reach these goals. After studying the *Bhagavad-Gita* and other (including Christian and Muslim) religious and philosophical sources, he had concluded that a peaceful basic needs approach should replace the modern demand oriented economy. 'True economics' coincided with 'just economics'. Regardless of the objective utility of their production, 'Western' economies only focused on profit and return maximization. As long as industries alienate themselves from local and appropriate technologies the economy will continue to lose touch with the objective needs of people. Man is being made subordinate to technological progress, economic policy and the game of power this implies. He is delivered to invisible and unpredictable economic laws which in one stroke can make thousands of people lose their jobs. A citizen living in an industrialized environment is no longer self-sufficient, becoming increasingly vulnerable, and is not satisfied with what he or she produces him or herself.

Being an economist Schumacher was even more directly influenced by J.C. Kumarappa, the first Gandhian economist and collaborator of the Mahatma. Schumacher's arguments are in many ways like those set out by Kumarappa. Gandhians in India consider Schumacher's article 'The Economics of Permanence' to have been derived from Kumarappa's 'Economy of Permanence'. Lindley (Lindley 2007: 128–36) argues, however, that whereas Kumarappa had avoided promoting this or that religion Schumacher celebrates Buddhism. Considering that Schumacher never abandoned his Christian roots this conclusion may only be applicable to the chapter on 'Buddhist Economics' in *Small is Beautiful*.

Actually, these 'ecological' points of view *avant la lettre* contradicted the 'spirit of the time' in India. Gandhi and his disciples were described as moralizing old men who lacked any theoretical basis. In Europe, however, his timing couldn't have been better. He inspired generations of green and small-scale socio-economic philosophers like Schumacher and Michael Lipton (1937-). Basically, the Mahatma paved the way for the success of the green movement in Europe from the 1960s onwards.

Against this background Schumacher published *Buddhist Economics* (1966), which was widely understood as a call for an economics of peace. In the essay Schumacher imagines a multitude of vibrant, self-sufficient villages which, from their secure sense of community and place, work together in peace and cooperation. This idea was repeated in his 'utopian' *Small is Beautiful* (1973).

However, the Hindu and Buddhist messengers would gradually adapt to a more globalized, capitalist and competitive world. From the 1980s onwards, the emphasis gradually moved from alternative 'green' messages to a more practical code for businesses. A new generation of holistic thinkers explored Asian philosophical and religious traditions and applied them to modern socio-economic leadership wisdom (Chakraborty 2006). All these traditions refer to a basic oneness of existence whereby the inner and outer worlds merge into one reality. The success of new religious movements (NRMs) and the New Age Movement (NAM), both frequently inspired by Asian traditions, in Europe and elsewhere reflected the need for the 'un-churched but spiritual'. However, the 'integration of the whole person' has been interpreted either as 'intensified concentration' and eventually as 'greater job efficiency', or as a way for extreme alienation from society. Now, the study of the origins of concepts, principles, and rituals, and thereby uncovering their spiritual meanings, became relevant for mainstream socio-economic ethics. Similarities with mainstream West-European Christian-inspired humanism were noted. Norwegian economist Oyvind Jaer (Oyvind Jaer 1998) referred to a common reference point shared by capitalism and Hinduism in the concepts of action (Karma) and structure (Dharma). He argued that the duality of action-structure is a particularly fertile 'bridgehead' for cultural translation and comparison. Lindsay Falvey (2005) identified agricultural sustainability in both Christianity and Buddhism. Polish film director M. Skiba focused on the ecological awareness of the Rajasthani community of Bishnois in her documentary film 'Eco Dharma' (2006). The Sant Nirankari Mission, an open-minded movement among Sikhs which had its formal beginning as early as 1929, attracted attention in the UK and elsewhere because of its views against ritualism, emphasizing that God is formless and the need to maintain a balance between spiritual and material life. From an economic point of view the Mission emphasized the importance of economic activities within the context of responsibilities for family life and service to the society (Gulati 2003). These are only a few examples of how a new economic ethical awareness grew from a new approach to Eastern traditions.

More specifically, the new business ethical approach also involved the Sufi concept of 'self-help through remembering God' (constant remembrance and respect for origin and historical perspective), the concept of *Darshan* (seeing the divine image in everything, resulting in the sacredness of nature and its implications for ecological awareness), the concept of *Prasad* (blessed offering to the God as a reflection of the right product, salary and price), the tradition of gurus and pilgrimages (e.g. the *Maha Kumbha Mela*, allowing both gurus and followers to cleanse themselves, reflecting the need for mutually beneficial interactions, e.g. fair play relations), the principle of *Ahimsa* (reflecting non-violent interactions), connected to the law of *Karma* (of cause and effect, e.g. violent interactions invite more violent interactions), and the concept of *Dharma* (emphasizing the 'path', e.g. the way of doing business, rather than the outcome, e.g. the profits). Simultaneously Eurocentric views of the world received exhilarating critique by thinkers such as the development economist Andre Gunder Frank (1929–2005), who forcefully argued that Asia had played the leading role in the world economy up to the eighteenth century (Frank 1998).

Schumacher's perspective seemed all of a sudden out of fashion. However, despite the fact that the perspective moved from the public sphere to the business sphere, the messages remained the same. Both Schumacher's and a business ethics' approaches are *nyaya*-oriented. They are dealing with the reality of consequences. Corbett (Corbett 2009) sums it up from a personal point of view: '[...] when the financial crisis of 2008 hit, I began to reflect back that many of the troubles we currently see were the sort of things that Schumacher anticipated back in 1973 and earlier, and that it might be good for me to return to his book, reread the essays and reassess them in light of today's economic situation'.

Corbett (2009) argues that Schumacher's *Buddhist Economics* differs metaphysically from classical Western economics – which since the Second World War has increasingly dominated the whole world and devalues labour. The Buddhist view of the role of a well-organized economy is to develop the character of individuals. Work is a part of that. Buddhism's respect for life – all living things – leads economically to very different attitudes toward the human use of nature.

However, it is clear that Schumacher only challenged neo-classical Western economics. He did not challenge the physiocrats or the economic liberals before and after Adam Smith who were inspired by Christian ideas. In *A Guide for the Perplexed* Schumacher expressed his own Christianity and as such I would argue that he did not see a great division between East and West. About the chapter on 'Buddhist Economics' in *Small is Beautiful* he even confessed 'if I had called the chapter 'Christian Economics', nobody would have paid any attention!' (Fager 1977: 325).

On the contrary, he pragmatically used Eastern ideas for the West to find again its own original Christian ways of dealing with economics and society. From this point of view the East and West are identical. Unlike some Orientalists and New Agers who consciously rejected Christianity, Schumacher saw no reason to prefer Buddhism in favour of his own Christianity, following in the footsteps of Albert Schweitzer, Nicholas Roerich, Romain Rolland, and many others. This resulted in a clear-cut *nyaya*-approach to economics and society. What mattered most to Schumacher were the actual consequences for people.

4   Conclusion: A Message Transcending Cultures

This contribution focused on how Europe perceived Asian traditions and how it used them for advancing a *nyaya*-approach in economics. Though nineteenth-century utilitarianism initially invited paternalistic behaviour, it nonetheless paved the way for a genuine intellectual interaction between Europe and Asia and a strong *nyana*-oriented alternative to the excesses of imperialism, nationalism and state-capitalism. During and after the World Wars, the spread of totalitarian regimes, and the economic crises of the 1920s and 1930s, some intellectuals reacted against economic chaos, violence and fascism by referring to 'Asian (especially Indian) wisdom'. E.F. Schumacher was no exception, as a German who took up his exposure to Asia as an opportunity to criticize mainstream economics from a practical and consequentialist point of view (a *nyana*-approach). In the 1960s many religious movements came over from the East, and while yoga seemed to offer a solution to many physical problems, Buddhism and

Vedanta fascinated environmentalist and alternative economists. Of late post-modernism provided the framework for yet another renaissance of Asian thinking in Europe. This time 'Asian wisdom' was introduced to business ethics. As Indian wisdom adapted so did Schumacher's perspectives which were now translated from a business point of view. Only the perspectives changed, not the *nyaya*-approach.

References

Basu, S.P. (2000). *Economic and Political Ideas: Vivekananda, Gandhi, Subhas Bose.* New Delhi: Sterling Publishers.

Berdyaev, N.A. (1945). *In Memory of Romain Rolland,* <*http://www.berdyaev.com/ berdiaev/berd_lib/1945_454.html*> accessed 17 April 2011.

Chakraborty, S.K. (2006). *Ethics in Management. Vedantic Perspectives.* Oxford-New Delhi-etc.: Oxford University Press.

Chakravarthi, U. (2004). *The Social Philosophy of Buddhism and the Problem of Inequality.* New Delhi: Critical Quest.

Chanda, Nayan (2007). *Bound Together. How Traders, Preachers, Adventurers and Warriors Shaped Globalization.* London-etc.: Penguin Viking.

Chang, Ha-Joon (2007). *Bad Samaritans. Rich Nations, Poor Policies & The Threat To the Developing World.* London: Random House Business Books.

Clark, P. (2006). *New Religions in Global Perspectives.* London-New York: Routledge.

Corbett, B. (January 2009).<http://www.webster.edu/~corbetre/personal/reading/ schumacher-small.html> accessed 17 April 2011.

Dasgupta, A. (1993). *A History of Indian Economic Thought.* London-New York: Routledge.

Dasgupta, S. (2005). *Social Philosophy of Swami Vivekananda.* Kolkata: The Ramakrishna Mission Institute of Culture.

De Vylder, G. (1987). 'India in Belgian Literature, Plastic Arts and Scholarship'. In *Sevartham. Indian Culture in a Christian Context,* Vol. 12, pp. 65–74. Ranchi: St Albert's College.

De Vylder, G. (2009). 'Light From India. Europe's Search for Indian Economic Wisdom'. In L. Bouckaert and J. Eynikel (eds), *Imagine Europe. The Search for European Identity and Spirituality.* European SPES Cahiers 3, pp. 113–28. Antwerp-Apeldoorn: Garant.

De Vylder, G. (2010). 'Identical Pitfalls for East and West: Different Socio-Economic Interpretations of Hindu-Buddhist Philosophy'. In H.-Cl. de Bettignies and M.J. Thompson (eds), *Leadership, Spirituality and the Common Good. East and West Approaches*. European SPES Cahiers 4, pp. 97–114. Antwerp-Apeldoorn: Garant.

Drury, N. (2004). *The New Age. The History of a Movement*. London: Thames & Hudson.

Fager, Ch. 1977. 'Small Is Beautiful, and So Is Rome: Surprising Faith of E.F. Schumacher', *Christian Century*, April 6, 1977, 325, <www. Religion-online.org> accessed 17 May 2011.

Falvey, L. (2005). *Religion and Agriculture. Sustainability in Christianity and Buddhism*. Adelaide: Institute for International Development.

Frank, A.G. (1998). *Reorient: Global Economy in the Asian Age*. Berkeley-Los Angeles-London: University of California Press.

Friedenthal, R. (1993). *Goethe. His Life and Times by Richard Friedenthal*. London: Weidenfeld.

Fuwei, Shen. (1997). *Cultural Flow Between China and Outside World Throughout History*. Beijing: Foreign Languages Press.

Ghosh, S.P. (2006). *Swami Vivekananda's Economic Thought in Modern International Perspective: India as a Case Study*. Kolkata: The Ramakrishna Mission Institute of Culture.

Grabsky, Ph. (2000). *The Lost Temple of Java*. London: Seven Dials.

Gulati, C.L. (2003). *A Mission for All*. Delhi: Sant Nirankari Mandal.

Gunn, G.C. (2003). *First Globalization. The Eurasian Exchange, 1500–1800*. Lanham-Boulder-New York-Toronto-Oxford: Rowman and Littlefield Publishers.

Hazrat Inayat Khan (2004). *The Sufi Message*, XIII vol. Delhi: Motilal Banarsidass Publishers.

Hobson, J.M. (2004). *The Eastern Origins of Western Civilization*. Cambridge: Cambridge University Press.

Huddleston, J. (2008). *The Earth Is But One Country*. New Delhi: Bahá'i Publishing Trust.

Inden, R. (2000). 'Orientalist Constructions of India'. In A.L. Macfie (ed.), *Orientalism. A Reader*, pp. 277–84. Cairo: The American University in Cairo Press.

Jaer, Oyvind. (1998). *Capital and Karma. Hinduism and Capitalism Compared*. Bangkok-Oslo: Orchid Press-The Institute for Comparative Research in Human Culture.

Jhingan, M.L., Girija, M., Manimekalai, A., and Sasikala L. (2006). *History of Economic Thought*. Delhi: Vrinda Publications.

Krishnamurti, J. (2005). *What Is a Problem?* Chennai: Krishnamurti Foundation India.

Krishnamurti, J. (2004). *Why Are You Being Educated? Talks at Indian Universities.* Chennai: Krishnamurti Foundation India.

Laurent, F. (2006). 'L'Orient de Victor Hugo: un nom de Génie'. In M. Levallois, and S. Moussa (eds), *L'orientalisme des saint-simoniens*, pp. 65–74. Paris: Maisonneuve & Larose.

Levallois, M. and Moussa, S. (eds) (2006). *L'orientalisme des saint-simoniens.* Paris: Maisonneuve & Larose.

Lindley, M. (2007). *J.C. Kumarappa. Mahatma Gandhi's Economist.* Mumbai: Popular Prakashan.

Macfie, A.L. (ed.) (2000). *Orientalism. A Reader.* Cairo: The American University in Cairo Press.

Madan, G.R. (1981). *Economic Thinking in India.* New Delhi: S. Chand.

Mill, J. (1975/1817). *The History of British India.* Chicago: University of Chicago Press.

Parameswaram, P. (1987). *Marx and Vivekananda. A Comparative Study.* Madras: Vivekananda Kendra Prakashan Trust.

Ramaswami Aiyar, C.P. (1992). *Annie Besant.* New Delhi: Ministry of Education and Broadcasting.

Roerich, S. (2004a). *Art and Life.* Moscow: International Centre of the Roerichs.

Roerich, S. (2004b). *Creative Thought.* Moscow: International Centre of the Roerichs.

Rushby, K. (2007). *Paradise. A History of the Idea that Rules the World.* London: Robinson.

Rutten, M. (2004). 'Rethinking Assumptions on Asia and Europe: The Study of Entrepreneurship'. In S. Ravi, M. Rutten and B.-L. Goh (eds), *Asia In Europe. Europe in Asia*, pp. 102–30. Leiden-Singapore: International Institute for Asian Studies-Institute of Southeast Asian Studies.

Saberwal, S. (2004). 'Civilizational Encounters: Europe in Asia'. In S. Ravi, M. Rutten and B.-L. Goh (eds), *Asia In Europe. Europe in Asia*, pp. 15–35. Leiden-Singapore: International Institute for Asian Studies-Institute of Southeast Asian Studies.

Said, E.W. (1995). *Orientalism. Western Conceptions of the Orient.* London-New York-Ringwood-Toronto-Auckland: Penguin Books.

Sargent, L.T. (2010). *Utopianism. A Very Short Introduction.* Oxford: Oxford University Press.

Schumacher, E.F. (1993). *Small is Beautiful. A Study of Economics as if People Mattered.* London: Vintage.

Schweitzer, A. (2006/1936). *Indian Thought and Its Development.* Mumbai: Wilco Publishing House.

Sen, A. (2000). *On Ethics and Economics.* New Delhi: Oxford University Press.

Sen, A. (2005). *The Argumentative Indian. Writings on Indian History, Culture and Identity.* London-etc.: Penguin Books.

Sen, A. (2006). *Identity and Violence. The Illusion of Violence.* London: Allen Lane-Penguin Books.

Sen, A. (2009). *The Idea of Justice.* Cambridge, Mass.: The Belknap Press of Harvard University Press.

Skiba, M. (2006). *Ecodharma.* PSBT & Prasar Bharati (documentary film).

Smith, A. (2003/1776). *The Wealth of Nations.* New York: Bantam Dell. A Division of Random House.

Smith, D. (2003). *Hinduism and Modernity.* Malden-Oxford-Carlton South-Berlin: Blackwell.

Sprengler, O. (1991/1918). *The Decline of the West.* New York-Oxford: Oxford University Press.

Tagore, R. (2002/1917). *Nationalism.* New Delhi: Rupa.

Tathagatananda, S. (2002). *Journey of the Upanishads to the West.* New York: The Vedanta Society of New York.

Tathagatananda, S. (2005). *Light from the Orient. Essays on the Impact of India's Sacred Literature in the West.* Kolkata: Advaita Ashrama.

Thakur, V.K. (2006). *Social Background of Buddhism.* Patna-New Delhi: Janaki Prakashan.

Uppal, J.S. (1986). 'Hinduism and Economic Development in South Asia', *International Review of Economics & Ethics*, 1 (1), 20–33.

Vivekananda, S. (2003). *The Complete Works of Swami Vivekananda.* 8 volumes. Kolkata: Advaita Ashrama.

Zsolnai, L. (ed.) (2008). *Europe-Asia Dialogue on Business Spirituality.* Antwerp-Apeldoorn: Garant.

PHILIP BRUCE
SCOTT BADER

8   The Legacy of Schumacher in the Scott Bader Company Today

1   Introduction

Not everyone may be aware of Schumacher's involvement with the Scott Bader company. Life President, Godric Bader, the son of the founder Ernest Bader, told me that he was surprised but delighted, not only in the interest that Schumacher had in Scott Bader, but more importantly that a man of such importance was prepared to be personally involved with us. The Scott Bader Commonwealth was founded in April 1951, and uniquely registered as a charity to take over the original Scott Bader Company, which was founded in 1921. This neutralized all the shares and safeguarded us from being taken over by anyone else. It was given into the hands of those in the workforce that, having a normal contract with the operating company – signed up and committed themselves to a deeper undertaking – a covenant with The Commonwealth, undertaking not only responsibility for the company assets, but also for the fundamental purposes of The Commonwealth. In essence to develop their own livelihood but also to serve the wider community – the world, and bring about an altogether better way of living for themselves and for coming generations!

So far the development and establishment of our truly international Common Trusteeship company, with its organisation of offices and manufacturing companies around the world, is certainly a unique achievement – most assuredly as it is now, with our democratic Members' Assembly at the centre – learning to be the strong beating heart of our organisation. Those sixty years required a lot of hard, reliable work... many different lives came and went during all those years for there was good work, good innovation which was a key theme propagated by Schumacher... work to keep up Scott Bader's standards and reputation, especially to please and supply our customers and always in competition with some of the largest chemical companies in the world (some of them no longer exist but we do)!

2   Schumacher's Involvement with Scott Bader

Schumacher had got to know Ernest Bader at a Conference in Geneva. He saw the decision that Ernest took in 1951, to give up the ownership of the company that he had created and developed into a charitable holding company, the Scott Bader Commonwealth Limited, as practical action par excellence. Schumacher wanted to see it encouraged, developed and lived out. When writing his world renowned book *Small is Beautiful* he included a whole part of a chapter about Scott Bader. He described the ethos of the company as 'the development of the power over the responsibility for a bundle of assets – not ownership'.

Schumacher was personally involved with Scott Bader as a Non Executive Director and Trustee at a time when he was in great demand as an advisory by many world governments. We are told that it was a concern to his supporters that he should travel to the sticks of Northamptonshire during the 1960s to give his time free of charge to support us. It was during his involvement with Scott Bader that Godric was eager to listen to and learn from Schumacher. In fact Godric had hoped that Schumacher would take over as Chairman of Scott Bader after him, but sadly he died before this was approved.

3   The Legacy of Schumacher in Scott Bader Today

Firstly, Scott Bader has manufacturing operations around the world. The challenge for us going forward is not only how to survive alongside our huge competitors but how to be better than them. Our legacy and our structure gives us the framework from which to do this. Scott Bader is not immune from the challenges of the global economy where we compete with capitalist behemoths in a difficult market and have had to expand geographically to be competitive. Over the last fifty years, the company has successfully expanded, and now has manufacturing companies in France, South Africa, Dubai and Croatia, along with distribution outlets in the Czech Republic, Sweden, Spain, USA, China and Eire. Around 600 people are employed worldwide, producing polyester resin, adhesives and water-based emulsions for the transport and construction markets. Turnover is £200m and we are investing strongly in new innovation technologies.

Schumacher was a strong advocate of investing in research and development as the way forward – to develop new products. Today innovation is still seen as the key to our continued success and indeed our survival. We are working to reduce dependence on oil products, increasing our water based products, reducing VOC emissions and e.g. developing resins for the production of light weight parts to be used in trains, trucks and cars to improve fuel efficiency. Sustainability is critical to reducing dependence on oil products, which Schumacher, possessing great prescience, saw their availability coming to an end!

Secondly, the development of an international democracy. When Scott Bader became a Common Trusteeship Company, it only operated in the UK. The global expansion has seen us move from more of a participative to a representative democracy. Scott Bader certainly is very different to the Scott Bader Schumacher would have known but, what remains at the core, is what Ernest Bader passed on and the desire to continue to do so from generation to generation. Indeed Scott Bader (in the tradition of R.H. Tawney) remains on its way to finding a principle of justice upon which association for the production and distribution of wealth could be found. A number of separate bodies are involved in the governance process: the Commonwealth Board, the Group Board that runs the Business and the local site Community Councils. The people within these bodies are all part of Scott Bader, but, at times, they have different responsibilities and play different roles to help realize the Principles.

I specifically want to comment on the newest body – the Members' Assembly – which we have established as a global voice and involvement to the future direction of our Company. It has elected representatives, approximately one per fifty people, from around the company and the Members' Assembly meets three times per year. As the MD I have to provide input to the Members' Assembly and more importantly we use the forum to share and help strategy development, consult on policies, share ideas for investments etc. The Assembly is very valuable and supports the two way flow of information, encouraging questioning from around the company on how we are and need to operate.

I will explain how we are organized and show that we remain true to the concept of *Small is Beautiful*. I see the model of a spider plant depicting the way Scott Bader operates. The UK and Commonwealth remain the 'mother plant' with other operations emulating the Scott Bader Founder's philosophy, genetics and ideals. The largest Site is 250 people and I see future growth focussed in small and local operations as we move into new regions.

From the spider plant diagram and the structure you will see that Group companies are integral in The Commonwealth. Interdependent bodies are working in an atmosphere of collaboration and co-operation within a set of formal checks and balances to ensure the continuing development of The Commonwealth.

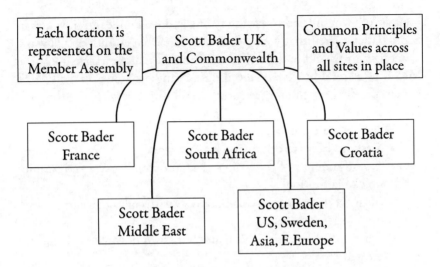

Spider Plant Model in Scott Bader

4 Principles and Values

Ernest Bader wanted to ensure not only the financial security of the company but also that we thought of others less fortunate than ourselves. Over the last sixty years we have donated in excess of £3m to charitable activities. Other large organisations may give larger amounts of money to charity but given that our profitability is not huge the percentage of our profits that go to charity is approximately 5 per cent. We have been doing this for sixty years and will continue to do so. The more profits we make then the more we can contribute to the wider world.

Schumacher explained in *Small is Beautiful* that the essence of education is the transmission of values. When The Commonwealth was formed, Ernest and the company provided a set of Principles that were ahead of the time in terms of Corporate Social Responsibility for Scott Bader. We remain fully committed to having strong and well understood values in Scott Bader. Given that we operate now in eleven countries this was a challenge for us and in 2010 the international representative body, the Members' Assembly, were involved in restating our values in words that are acceptable throughout the Scott Bader Group, but without losing any of the originals outlined by Ernest Bader.

Four values are central:

- Responsibility to others and how we work
- Commitment to Scott Bader as a Common Trustee and sustainable organisation
- Team working to work collaboratively with colleagues and customers and across functions
- Fairness – to be fair, ethical and honest in how we work and are treated

We are currently working to embed these values throughout Scott Bader and to explain what they mean so that people know what is expected of them and what they can expect in return. If everyone works to these values we are confident that in business terms Scott Bader will be a Partner for Excellence.

5   Conclusion

Ernest Bader's highly generous and imaginative act established a common trusteeship business. I am sure Schumacher would have been pleased that we now describe ourselves in this way. As all the shares are held in trust, we are totally independent. This means we are self governing and allows us to improve our lives as individuals, and show that there is a better way of doing things. So, by our example, we can help improve society at large – albeit in a small way. We must relentlessly strive to refresh the vision and excitement of 1951 and we feel it is appropriate to read the conclusion of

Godric Bader's speech at our sixtieth anniversary celebration: 'So, moving forward with these sixty years behind us, our company surely has the experience now, the strength, the desire, and much deeper drive and confidence behind it to brave this, our 21st century. Thank goodness we are now more broadly based in the world than most of us in the last century ever expected. Our worldwide companies have given us wider horizons to excite us, and stimulate our outlook, and to make more imaginative progress across the world... our current goal!'

PART II

Responsibility

CHRISTIAN ARNSPERGER

UCLOUVAIN

9 Small is Beautiful: But is it Responsible? A Critical Reappraisal of E.F. Schumacher's Contribution to Ecological Economics and Political Ecology

1 Introduction

In this chapter, I investigate the meaning and content of responsibility in economics as it emerges from Ernest F. ('Fritz') Schumacher's writings on small-scale economics and on metaphysics. My endeavour is not intended to be a promotion of Schumacher's ideas; rather, I offer an attempt at laying bare some of the more hidden – and radical – presuppositions that underlie the now all too common and overused slogan 'Small Is Beautiful' that has come to virtually identify Schumacher as a 'new age' thinker. I hope to show that he was more than that, and that – regardless of whether or not one ends up agreeing with his ideas – he built a coherent, albeit demanding, set of philosophical and economic ideas.

In section 2, I argue briefly that although Schumacher's thought has been identified as the linchpin of decentralized bioregionalism, there is actually a paradox at the heart of his approach: decentralism and centralism may be more complementary than opposed. (This will come back as the main point of the paper as it ends on concrete proposals for institutional reform in section 5.)

Section 3 then argues in more detail that Schumacher was a liberal and that, in terms of form and procedure though not in terms of political options, his approach shares common features with the more conservative liberalism of Hayek. Comparing the two men actually offers enlightening insights. Basically, I submit, Schumacher shares with Hayek the puzzle of how individuals can become responsible agents in a world about which they possess massively incomplete knowledge.

Section 4 then introduces a crucial distinction between conscious responsibility – which is what Schumacher calls for – and reactive responsiveness – which is what Hayek reduces responsibility to. In that context, I discuss the reasons why today's trend towards conveying agents' responsibility through the economic evaluation and pricing of 'ecosystem services' may be problematic from Schumacher's perspective. He is calling for a shift in rationality that will lead an individual to *aim consciously and deliberately for* the very things an economic incentive mechanism would only make her *participate in unconsciously and grudgingly*. This, in essence, differentiates Hayek's reactive responsiveness from Schumacher's proactive responsibility.

Which leads me, in section 5, to ask how 'smallness' – which obviously plays such a central role in Schumacher's approach – links up with responsibility. My idea is this: Given the huge and irreducible uncertainty characterizing our ecological future, *Schumacher conceives of small economic units as a specific precautionary principle* – advocating smallness is an attempt to guarantee that decentralized actions will not generate ecological catastrophe. In that sense, operational smallness is intimately linked with his idea of a responsible economic agent. However, as I also show, his arguments as to the *sufficiency* of smallness are... insufficient, mainly due to the existence of the 'tragedy of the commons' and, more generally, congestion externalities.

This allows me, in the final section 6, to argue that if small scale is to be generalized on a large scale – as Schumacher no doubt thought it had to be – we need new social and economic institutions. Some of them will, of necessity, be highly centralized, but this is no problem unless one dogmatically sticks to 'decentralism' as the key doctrine supposedly underlying Schumacher's economic philosophy. Therefore, making responsibility concrete from a Schumacherian perspective entails creating institutions – some of them centralized, some of them decentralized – so that a global federation of bioregions, populated by economically and ecologically responsible agents, can form the backbone of the world economy.

2   The Paradox of Decentralism

Fritz Schumacher's thought, just like Ivan Illich's, emerged at a time when the affluent West started to struggle with limits, more and more citizens feeling that certain developments towards 'gigantism' – especially in the area of political and economic decision making – were threatening the very collective prosperity in whose name they had been tolerated. To put it in a nutshell, by the late 1960s and early 1970s political and economic bureaucracy, seemingly called forth by the demands of technological and productive efficiency, was showing clear signs of becoming 'counterproductive' – one of the major themes of Illich's critique of the industrial model at the time. Political ecology grew out of the twin realization that industrial growth was straining the limits of nature and society, and that the postwar 'politics of affluence' was powerless to address the mounting problems of social congestion and resource depletion.

There seems to me to be a frequently overlooked paradox in the reflections of Schumacher and Illich. Both of them were clearly rooted within what one might call a left-wing – or progressive – anarchical tradition of thought. This tradition, in the words of Kirkpatrick Sale, one of Schumacher's most ardent disciples, 'drew from, and built upon, what [...] is best described as the *decentralist* tradition of Western society, that of institutions built to the human scale within harmonious self-regarding communities run by participatory democracy and fueled by self-sufficient regional economies deeply conscious of the limits of natural resources and the need for ecological harmony' (Sale 1989).

The paradox is that the problems thrown up nowadays by runaway economic growth are, in fact, due precisely to inputs, throughput and output *not being the subject of any regional or international coordination*, so that actually it is the very decentralization Sale is putting forward that is causing the ecological problem today. How can 'self-sufficient regional economies' become 'deeply conscious of the limits of natural resources and the need for ecological harmony' unless there are *centralized institutions* that transmit to them the right signals about scarcity and disruption?

Should not the current predicament of humanity as a whole lead us, in the very spirit of Schumacher, to also re-think the *centralist* tradition of Western society and, perhaps, to question the validity of the centralization/ decentralization divide?

This question has a crucial bearing upon the whole issue of responsibility in economics.

3 Centralism versus Decentralism: Hayek and Schumacher as Bedfellows?

The subsidiarity-based bioregionalism which Schumacher and his followers are espousing (Sale 2000) is the left-wing, progressive pendant to the incomplete-knowledge-based free market championed by Hayek and his right-libertarian, conservative disciples. In fact, it is striking that in both cases, a decentralized setup is being proposed – small-scale localism in Schumacher's case, adaptive evolutionism in Hayek's case – on the basis of the inherent patchiness of human knowledge.

As a staunch liberal individualist writing in the 1930s and 40s, Hayek was blissfully ignorant of ecological limits. He also considered so-called 'social limits to growth' (which he never really addressed explicitly) as irrelevant, contrary to Illich three decades later. Schumacher was no less of an individualist than Hayek, and in a sense no less of a liberal, either – but he did not espouse at all the same views on *what constitutes fully-fledged knowledge for an individual*.

As evidenced by works such as *The Sensory Order* (Hayek 1952), Hayek's decentralism was rooted in empiricist naturalism, which led him to epitomize complexity and brain science – knowledge as used in society being of the purely situated, contextual, self-centred kind that a 'boundedly rational' adaptive creature (whom he calls free) uses in its everyday economic dealings. As made clear in works such as *Guide for the Perplexed* (Schumacher 1977), Schumacher's decentralism started out from the metaphysics of the 'levels of being' and the individual's destiny (which he calls freedom) is to become both self-aware and aware of her own belonging to the Great Chain of Being – an operation of gradual broadening and deepening whereby the individual moves away from self-centeredness and towards a 'cosmo-centric' form of reason, so that she can make decisions from a holistic viewpoint. *Hayek's and Schumacher's views of the individual are two variants of liberal individualism based on widely differing assumptions as to what constitutes individual freedom and individual knowledge.*

However, let us be very careful here. Hayekian self-centeredness and Schumacherian 'cosmo-centricity' are actually not mutually exclusive. At first glance, it might look as if, in Hayek's brand of liberalism, individual knowledge is patchy while, in Schumacher's, it is all-encompassing. In fact, this is not at all the case. Schumacher is just as adamant as Hayek in insisting that no human being can actually know everything that would need to be known in order to make perfectly informed decisions. Social responsibility, both from Hayek's vantage point and from Schumacher's, rests in recognizing one's structural ignorance and in creating institutions and decision algorithms that realistically take this constitutive limitation into account.

This, I would say, is the very essence of liberalism – that a genuinely free, and therefore socially responsible, human agent is someone who lucidly acknowledges her ignorance and her inability to gain full knowledge of the Whole, *but who at the same time* recognizes the need for a form of collective, social organization that will somehow act as an impersonal, 'collective brain' that blindly processes knowledge gathered from decentralized sources and redistributes it to the relevant people. *In genuine liberalism the very function of individual freedom is to enable the individual to relinquish her illusions of omniscience and to delegate the processing and systematizing of holistic knowledge to social institutions.* This is a very liberating insight: it means that with the advent of liberalism, individualism is inextricably institutional and institutions are inherently individualistic.

More to the point perhaps, Hayek's decade-long attempt to spell out a truly liberal social order has shown that the distinction between centralization and decentralization is basically nonsensical, as is the divide between bottom-up and top-down approaches to regulation. Decentralization requires elements of centralization if it is to avoid disintegration – and the pure anarchical idea of atomized spontaneous order is a utopian pipe dream. Conversely, centralized governance will avoid brittleness and sclerosis only if substantial decentralization is introduced. In a truly free society, there are only ever *enabling institutional frameworks* and *self-centred, knowledge-seeking individuals*. The real and burning issue is how the two are *combined*: Do institutions keep self-centred individuals narrow and ignorant or do they allow a gradual broadening of mind and reason so that their 'sense of self' changes over time? What is it, actually, that institutions such as civil law, the constitution, democracy, money, technology, and the market enable individuals to do? In any free society, or at least in any society on its way towards liberation, decentralization and centralization are dual manifestations of one another – and the manner in which they are shapes the society's trajectory in very crucial ways.

4   Responsibility in Economics: Beyond Reactive Responsiveness?

It is a truism to say that the word 'responsibility' is intimately connected with the notion of responsiveness. A socially respons*ive* individual or organization is one who perceives, and responds to, the calls and demands coming from its social environment to which it considers it legitimate or inevitable to respond. An individual or organization is then socially repons*ible* when its general intention is to be socially responsive whenever needed. Thus, according to my definition here, social responsiveness is a punctual action, while social responsibility is an ongoing, processual attitude or inclination. This also implies that one can be responsive without being responsible: a reflex reaction betrays responsiveness (to a given stimulus) but signals no deliberate responsibility. We might say that responsiveness is refle*x*ive or reactive while responsibility is refle*ct*ive or proactive.

Using these categories, we can easily see that depending on the type of rationality we postulate, economic agents will or will not turn out to be socially responsible. In fact, in Hayek's brand of liberalism, agents are constantly adapting to their contextual situation by reacting to economic stimuli, be they prices or profits. These agents have not only bounded rationality based on cognitive limitations and incomplete knowledge – they have adaptive rationality based on an absence of search for a 'broader picture'. In Schumacher's view, economic rationality is also bounded by cognitive limitations and incomplete knowledge, but agents know one thing: they are a part of a much broader whole – the Great Chain of Being – which they can never fully comprehend or embrace, but in which they have a moral or sacred duty to participate by remaining in their rightful place as human beings within the Cosmos. In his *Guide for the Perplexed*, he calls this specific faculty 'wisdom' and links it to the main spiritual traditions of humanity.

Despite the *prima facie* religious undertones, there is in fact nothing in Schumacher's categories that goes against liberalism – any more than liberalism's own insistence on the categorical validity of human rights and on the unconditional promotion of 'freedom' or 'justice'. Schumacher is simply saying here that responsibility entails a reflective adhesion to something that is routinely invisible and hard to perceive with one's own senses – namely, *the overall finiteness of nature and of the ecosystems in which we live*.

An economically conservative liberal such as Hayek – or, more recently, Wilfred Beckerman (2002) – would claim that no specific form of wisdom is needed here, since firms and consumers will end up reacting to the scarcity and depletion of non-renewable resources when market price signals warn them that they should gradually adapt away from them towards (say) renewables. Although no one knows the overall state of non-renewable resources, the conservative liberals claim, the markets will, through prices, summarize whatever parts of the Big Picture are needed so as to guide agents towards efficient resource use. As the overall finiteness of nature and ecosystems starts to 'bite', market prices will inform us, no matter how ignorant or even unwise we started out. From that perspective, competitive markets are indeed, in and of themselves, a 'guide for the perplexed'. All that is needed, in this economic worldview, is market liberalization: it will make all agents reactively responsive and it will allow prices to transmit to them the 'correct' information to which to react despite the drastically limited scope of their knowledge.

Of course, this requires well-defined private property rights in resources, and such rights do not always exist. Most natural resources are public goods. Surrogate markets must therefore be organized in order to supplement agents' constitutive lack of wisdom and prevent the blind depletion of unpriced – and therefore effectively free – resources. The whole movement towards the economic evaluation and pricing of 'ecosystem services' has been a response to this challenge.[1] It requires no ecological consciousness whatsoever on the part of economic agents. The finiteness of nature and ecosystems is (supposedly) conveyed to resource users through a usage fee that is a function of how few natural substitutes the resource has, how limited its replacement through technological capital is, and how heavily – albeit invisibly – it currently contributes to throughput and output. This, so is the claim, will prompt adaptation by reactively responsive users through either a reduction in exploitation and a search for substitutes, or the adoption of more resource-efficient technologies.

What is problematic about this stance from Schumacher's 'cosmocentric' vantage point? Essentially, it seems, that it replaces responsibility with reactive responsiveness, which reduces most economic agents to being manipulated externally by economic incentive mechanisms. This, according to Schumacher, goes against the *qualitative, internal evolutionary drive towards self-enhancement* inscribed into the human condition:

> [...] everything in the world around us must be matched, as it were, with some sense, faculty or power within us; otherwise we remain unaware of its existence. There is, therefore, a hierarchic structure of gifts inside us; and, not surprisingly, the higher the gift the more rarely is it to be found in a highly developed form, and the greater are the efforts required for its development. To enhance our Level of Being we have to adopt a life-style conducive to such enhancement, which means one that grants our lower nature just the attention and care it requires and leaves us with plenty of time and free attention for the pursuit of our higher development. (Schumacher 1977: 147)

---

1   See, e.g., De Groot, Wilson and Boumans (2002), Spangenberg and Settele (2010) and Salles (2011).

But – so environmental economists might argue – do adequate economic valuations for ecosystem services (and for nature in general) not simply force agents, whether they like it or not, to 'adopt a life-style' that will make them more conscious of the finiteness of nature and of ecosystems? The whole issue is whether an attitude of responsibility – which is necessarily open-ended and consists of a general readiness to respond to calls to action one has internalized as legitimate if not desirable – can ever be generated through a sequence of reactively responsive adaptations to incentives one perceives as coercive but often illegitimate or, at the very least, cumbersome. For most economists as well as lawyers, this issue does not really matter – what counts, at the end of the day, is the result in terms of consequences.

Schumacher has a less consequentialist view of human rationality. He believes that 'some sense, faculty or power within us' has to be unlocked and mobilized if we are going to be genuinely responsible, as opposed to merely reactively responsive. A *deontological evolutionary dimension* is at stake, which behavioural approaches in terms of economic incentives routinely neglect: Reactive stimulation has to give way to proactive openness, and that openness has to be directed toward 'the pursuit of our higher development', by which Schumacher means the gradual shift from self-centeredness to cosmo-centricity:

> [A human being's] first task is to learn from society and 'tradition' and to find his temporary happiness in receiving directions from outside. His second task is to interiorise the knowledge he has gained, sift it, sort it out, keep the good and jettison the bad; this process may be called 'individuation', becoming self-directed. His third task is [...] 'dying' to oneself, to one's likes and dislikes, to all one's egocentric preoccupations. To the extent that he succeeds in this, he ceases to be directed from outside, and he also ceases to be self-directed. He has gained freedom, or, one might say, he is then God-directed. (Schumacher 1977: 149)

Only such a shift in rationality can actually allow an individual to *aim consciously and deliberately for* the things an economic incentive mechanism would only make her *participate in unconsciously and grudgingly*.

This, to my mind, is the essence of responsibility in Schumacher's thought. While rather demanding spiritually, it is certainly humanistic – but, needless to say, it is not without problems, not the least of which is whether it makes any sense at all to base a liberal social ethic on a traditional, perhaps even theistic, metaphysics of freedom. What might being 'God-directed' mean that might be of any relevance at all to the issues of social ecology that so urgently beset us today?

5   Is Small Responsible?
On 'Smallness' as a Precautionary Principle[2]

Let us note that Schumacher equates being 'God-directed' with being *neither directed from outside nor self-directed*. This would, at first brush, seem to make little sense from a logical point of view. Until, that is, one realizes that Schumacher's use of the word 'God' can be taken as a pointer towards some *telos*, some goal or horizon that is neither purely sociological – 'society' and 'tradition'– nor purely psychological – 'one's likes and dislikes, one's egocentric preoccupations'. To understand what might be meant here, we must remember that, although Schumacher became Catholic towards the end of his life, he had for quite some time before that been deeply interested in Buddhism. While not even remotely theistic, Buddhism is not merely consequentialist either – and this twin property may hold the key to understanding what Schumacher means by a responsible economic agent.

Central to the Buddhist view of the world is that all of reality – both our minds 'inside' and the world 'outside' – is ruled by so-called *dependent co-origination*. This means that both mental and natural phenomena can be witnessed as a vast network of mutually interdependent causes and effects. Actually, all effects can also be seen as causes, and all causes also as effects, so that no entity within reality (however conventionally delineated) possesses any intrinsic autonomy. As Joanna Macy writes,

2   For a different take on related ideas – but not involving Schumacher or the notion of 'smallness' – see chapter 5 of Thiry (2012).

The self, if causality is mutual, is not the knower and actor we conventionally posit, so much as a series of events, occurrences of knowing and. [...] If there is in my internal organization no separable and acting continuous agent that decides, can I be accountable for my acts? Does it matter what I do? The basic issue, then, is the connection between what we do and what we are. Or, if we understand our being as our conscious participation in reality, the question is whether our acts affect that participation – that is, our capacity to know, choose, and enjoy. If not, then notions of responsibility are tangential to one's life, noble but inconsequential. If they do [i.e., if our acts do affect our participation], then distinctions between the pragmatic and the moral dissolve. In the perspective of mutual causality, this is the case. (Macy 1991: 161)

So I would venture that the capacity to be 'God-directed' in Schumacher's theistic vocabulary corresponds, in Buddhism, to the capacity to act not from a self-enclosed perspective, nor from a pure obedience to social conventions, but *from a rational recognition that what one does has effects which reverberate through the whole fabric of reality, one's 'self' included*: 'The effect is inescapable, not because God watches and tallies, or an angel marks our acts in a ledger, but because in dependent co-origination, our acts co-determine what we become' (Macy 1991: 165). This is not a moral idea but a purely pragmatic one – although it does entail a moral or ethical decision to participate in reality in ways that are more or less harmless or hurtful, including for oneself.

From the non-theistic viewpoint of Buddhism, 'God-directed' rationality is, in essence, *ecological rationality*: the agent recognizes that she is herself of a composite nature, as a psycho-physical entity generated by multiple causes and effects,[3] and she also recognizes in the same stroke her capacity to 'co-shape' herself and reality through deliberate choices that take as their starting point the systemic, ecological, dependently co-originating nature of reality. I would express this as a principle of *individual attunement to an eco-systemic Whole about which one's knowledge can never be exhaustive and definitive*. 'Attunement' is of a different order from knowledge. It is a readiness to act on incomplete knowledge *as if* one had complete knowledge – as if,

---

3   See Varela, Thompson and Rosch (1992).

in Schumacher's words, one were perceiving a 'message from the universe'[4] – along with a readiness to revise one's criteria for action as new knowledge arises. This attunement is not a substitute for rationality – it *is* ecological rationality.

This is where we encounter the relevance of what, earlier, was presented as the divide between, on the one hand, incentive mechanisms based on the economic evaluation of ecosystem services and, on the other hand, fundamental changes in lifestyle or civilization. The former can work with standard economic rationality intact, whereas the latter requires a shift in the content of rationality itself. Environmental economics seeks to embed standard economic rationality within a system of legal and financial norms designed to reflect ecological constraints. Ecological economics, in keeping with the impulse given by Schumacher, instead seeks to *conceptualize a different form of rationality – ecological rationality – which it embeds in a thermodynamic and ecosystemic view of the economy itself.*[5]

As Joan Martínez-Alier has written:

> Because in ecological economics we see the market economy as embedded in a physical-chemical-biological system, the question arises of the value of natural resources and environmental services for the economy. Is it possible to translate environmental values into monetary values? Ecological economists are very sceptical about the possibility of translating or transmuting future, uncertain, irreversible externalities into monetary values. [...] In the ecological economy, future human generations, and the values attributed to other species, play a role precisely because the time horizon of the ecological economy is much longer, as we take into account slow biogeochemical cycles and irreversible thermodynamics. (Martínez-Alier 1997: 22–3)

Because of the huge uncertainties connected to the non-linear nature of dependent co-origination in complex systems, economic evaluation as a guide to policy is very problematic. Alternatives are, so Martínez-Alier argues, *economically incommensurable* but they can still be compared: 'Incommensurability means that there is no common unit of measurement,

---

4   See Schumacher (1974).
5   For both historical and conceptual elements to distinguish environmental from ecological economics, see e.g. Martínez-Alier (1990) and Daly and Farley (2011).

but it does *not* mean that we cannot compare alternative decisions on a rational basis, on *different* scales of value, as in multi-criteria evaluation' (Martínez-Alier 1997: 29).

In fact, the perception of externalities is socially embedded, and so a major force shaping the way policies can be designed is the existence of *social movements* which represent different 'positionally objective' takes on the environmental impact of economic decisions.[6] 'The economy is embedded in the social perception of externalities, which sometimes give rise to social movements. Therefore, from an ecological viewpoint, the economy lacks a common standard of measurement, because values would depend [...] on the strength of environmental movements and the distribution of power' (Martínez-Alier 1997: 27).[7] *Due to radical uncertainty as to future large-scale externalities (because of the irreversibility and non-linearity inherent in complex, dependent co-origination), economic commensurability breaks down and evaluation becomes a fundamentally political process in which social movements play a central role.* Genuine human responsibility therefore consists in taking this fact seriously – so as to participate in qualitative evaluation whenever possible if one is an individual citizen, and so as to allow citizens' movements to participate in qualitative evaluation if one is a firm, a non-governmental organization or a governing body.

Not all social movements that seek to embody this notion of responsibility will champion the same overall social project. Some will be more technophile than others. Some will question the current economic system and some will not. Some will champion deep lifestyle changes, others will not. Schumacher's contribution is this area, which many of us might find rather disturbing, is to insist that such process-oriented ecumenism is not sufficient. According to him, to actually embody a responsible attitude means that one has to face up to certain – in his eyes – inescapable truths that are not a matter of mere preference or accentuation. He does not share

6   To use the concept of socially embedded objectivity propounded by Sen (1993). For a multi-perspective methodology for analysing environmental and ecological issues, see Esbjörn-Hargens and Zimmerman (2009).

7   For the role of citizens' movements in the ecological economy, see also Healy et al. (2012).

the ecological economist's conviction that the basis for value comparison is either multi-criteria analysis or the politics of social movements. From a Schumacherian perspective, *there are right and wrong ways for an individual to relate to the basic fact of dependent co-origination and to pursue her ultimate goal of becoming 'God-directed'. There are right and wrong ways to claim to be a responsible economic agent.* In that sense, there is definitely a perfectionistic trait in his thought.

In the late 1960s, Schumacher wrote:

> The spirit of violence and impatience has invaded wide ranges of scientific work, producing a flood of innovations of an increasingly dangerous character. The pressures of rivalry, competition and ambition are such that only the minimum of time is allowed for an examination of consequences. The God-given environment is subjected to unlimited degradation until the legislator steps in, normally at a very late stage, to stop the grossest abuses. (Schumacher 2004: 93)

This means that coercive laws and regulations, apart from not being necessarily conducive to a propensity to responsibility, also usually are too little, too late – in particular because the *realpolitik* of irresponsible agents consists in lobbying and influencing the legislator, so that restrictions are often minimal and only stop 'the grossest abuses', leaving the mechanisms and attitudes that created these abuses largely intact until the next time. Making use of specialist scientific knowledge to manipulate natural mechanisms, without heeding the deep inherent uncertainty associated with entropy, generates anxiety:

> This ruthless application of partial knowledge, stimulated by impatient demands for faster growth, quicker returns, and greater speed, now constitutes such a direct threat to human health and happiness that even quite ordinary people, without knowledge of the scientific details, are looking into the future with a deep, often sub-conscious dread. (Schumacher 2004: 93)

Such anxiety and dread cannot be assuaged by policies based on the economic evaluation of nature, since the latter is made questionable and often even impossible by radical uncertainty. Schumacher would argue – and the ecological economists for whom Martínez-Alier speaks would surely concur – that whatever else citizens' groups militate for, the *unquantifiable but realistic danger of technology-driven catastrophe* should impel them to set some minimal benchmark on the changes they call for. In other words, if the science that has been one of the main causes of growth-driven environmental degradation cannot suddenly become a remedy to such degradation (an assumption to which Schumacher clearly subscribes), the politics of ecological responsibility needs to posit an alternative 'founding principle' – and it has to be *a radical precautionary principle that takes into account the anxiety-generating, destructive potential of advanced technology.*[8]

This is, of course, where Schumacher's most popular and most widely cited contribution lies – except that, to the best of my knowledge, it has rarely if ever been derived and presented in this particular light. What founding principle does he suggest for all further reflection on ecological sustainability or, as he calls it, 'permanence'?[9] In a nutshell: For Schumacher, the only plausible basis for a responsible attitude towards the ecological hazards thrown up by industrial-age technology is *smallness as a precautionary principle.* Here is how he expresses it in an often-quoted passage:

> Small-scale operations, no matter how numerous, are always less likely to be harmful to the natural environment than large-scale ones, simply because their individual force is small in relation to the recuperative forces of nature. There is wisdom in smallness if only on account of the smallness and patchiness of human knowledge, which relies on experiment far more than on understanding. The greatest danger invariably arises from the ruthless application, on a vast scale, of partial knowledge

8   For a detailed discussion of what a 'catastrophistic' attitude towards radical uncertainty in the ecological arena entails, see Dupuy (2002). Dupuy argues strongly against those who would limit the precautionary principle to probabilizable situations and disqualify it in situations of radical uncertainty where probabilities cannot be computed.

9   Two decades before the Brundtland Report, Schumacher wrote this, which I personally take to be a deeply apt definition of so-called sustainable development: 'We must study the economics of permanence. Nothing makes economic sense unless its continuance for a long time can be projected without running into absurdities. There can be "growth" towards a limited objective, but there cannot be unlimited, generalised growth. [...] The economics of permanence implies a profound reorientation of science and technology, which have to open their doors to wisdom and, in fact, have to incorporate wisdom into their very structure' (Schumacher 1973: 34).

such as we are currently witnessing in the application of nuclear energy, of the new chemistry in agriculture, of transportation technology, and countless other things. (Schumacher 1973: 37)

Now, strictly and logically speaking, Schumacher's statement is clearly incorrect. It is simply not the case empirically – nor can it be defended as a theorem unless one introduces additional assumptions – that small-scale operations, *no matter how numerous*, are *always* less harmful than large-scale ones. The well-known 'tragedy of the commons' where a multitude of small Kerala fishers ends up depleting a lake of its fish resources, or where a very large number of very small Haitian farmers end up deforesting half the country, shows that, in fact, and especially in highly populated areas with a non-renewable or slowly renewing resource base, sufficiently numerous small-scale operations can be as harmful as a handful of large-scale ones.[10] In fact, all congestion externalities of the traffic-jam type, such as discussed by Ivan Illich in his *Energy and Equity* (Illich 1974), are of the same type: a sufficiently large number of small-scale decisions (in this case, the micro-decision to take out one's car) can lead to highly counterproductive situations and even catastrophic results.

In the light of the literature on collective action and on the difficulties of decentralized management of common resources such as fisheries, open forests or road space, Schumacher's arguments in favour of smallness seem feeble *as principled answers to the problem of how to prevent environmental catastrophes*:

> Although even small communities are sometimes guilty of causing serious erosion, generally as a result of ignorance, this is trifling in comparison with the devastations caused by gigantic groups motivated by greed, envy, and the lust for power. It is, moreover, obvious that men organized in small units will take better care of *their* bit of land or other natural resources than anonymous companies or megalomanic governments which pretend to themselves that the whole universe is their legitimate quarry. (Schumacher 1973: 37)

10   See, e.g., Ostrom (1990).

Massively distributed ignorance, especially if accompanied by corruption and lust for power at the level of individuals in town, local or regional government, can generate as much devastation as greed end envy in large economic units – not necessarily more, but not necessarily less. And while the misdeeds of large, rapacious companies or governments clearly need to be countered, it is not clear from Schumacher's discussion how ensuring technology's 'suitability for small-scale application' (Schumacher 1973: 37) will solve the issue of uncoordinated small-scale destructivity. *The bottom line is that, when interacting blindly within an uncoordinated, complex system from which aggregate results emerge through anonymous composition – whether it is a large number of small market participants or a large number of small fishers around a lake or farmers near a wood – small-scale agents can wreak havoc.* What matters is not so much their smallness as (*a*) what common enterprise, if any, they perceive themselves to be part of and (*b*) what individual preferences or values – that is, what 'level of consciousness or evolution' – they bring to that enterprise in order to make it succeed. These consciousness aspects, as we saw earlier, form part and parcel of genuine responsibility.

Unless these issues are addressed, Schumacher's idea that smallness can, in and of itself, serve as a precautionary bulwark against the dangers of ecological depletion and destruction is simply not plausible.

6 Instituting Small Scale on a Large Scale: Why Responsible Decentralism Might Need (Some) Centralism

What flows from the Schumacherian perspective is a view of the economy – whether at the national or international level – as a *federation of relatively self-contained bioregions*. We saw at the outset of section 1 that Kirkpatrick Sale, one of Schumacher's most ardent followers, envisioned a bioregionalist economic system rooted in 'the *decentralist* tradition of

Western society, that of institutions built to the human scale within har-monious self-regarding communities run by participatory democracy and fuelled by self-sufficient regional economies deeply conscious of the limits of natural resources and the need for ecological harmony'.

We also saw, in our discussion of Hayekian liberalism in section 2, that socially and ecologically responsible economic agents are individuals – and collectives – who relinquish their illusion of omniscience and lucidly delegate the task of gathering relevant higher-level knowledge to social institutions. That such institutions cannot be reduced to price-transmitting markets should by now be clear. In fact, as evidenced by chapter 3 of *Small Is Beautiful*, Schumacher had no strong faith in the ability of markets to either self-regulate or ensure a judicious allocation of resources. Nor did he think a market economy is, in and of itself, particularly conducive to the enhancement of human creativity – outside, that is, the rather narrow spectrum of 'innovation' called for by the very dynamics of competition and power concentration that characterizes industrial capitalism. At the same time, the qualities of free-minded emergence and creative experimentation which thinkers such as Hayek wrongly ascribe to markets should, indeed, be promoted by social institutions: The free emergence of initiatives and the widest possible opportunities to experiment are part and parcel of a genuinely free society, and hence should be protected and advanced by any liberal.[11]

What is needed, in other words, is a set of social institutions that pro-mote decentralized interaction between socially and ecologically responsi-ble economic agents – and Hayek and Schumacher agree on this principle, although they agree neither on the content of 'responsibility' nor on how to translate the principle into actual institutions.

For people to become 'deeply conscious of the limits of natural resources' (in Sale's words), the economic evaluation and pricing of eco-system services we discussed earlier might be a very first and insufficient, though necessary, step. It would impel the least conscious citizens to join the already aware ones in demanding more fundamental change. This would

11   I have discussed this point in detail in Arnsperger (2005).

then, if one follows Schumacher, go along the lines of *a gradual and selective re-localization of economic activities:*

> From the point of view of Buddhist economics, [...] production from local resources for local needs is the most rational way of economic life, while dependence on imports from afar and the consequent need to produce for export to unknown and distant peoples is highly uneconomic and justifiable only in exceptional cases and on a small scale. Just as the modern economist would admit that a higher rate of consumption of transport services between a man's home and his place of work signifies a misfortune and not a high standard of life, so the Buddhist economist would hold that to satisfy human wants from faraway resources rather than from sources nearby signifies failure rather than success. (Schumacher 1973: 62)

Large-scale, globalized industrial production and consumption have carried positive implications (among which, lower consumer prices for many goods) but have also had negative collateral effects: The amenities we purchase on the world market – supposing we have the means to do so – are increasingly abstract, the people and processes that produce and transport them having become more and more remote in the majority of cases. This abstraction and remoteness have been rendered possible by the availability of relatively cheap energy sources, especially fossil fuels, which constitute the backbone of today's globalization of production, transport, and consumption. As the era of globalized trade gradually ends – under the twin pressure of peak oil and of climate change – more local economic units will have to spring up again. Bioregionalism will inevitably shape the global marketplace of the future, and smallness (compared to today's still ongoing drive towards consolidation, multi-nationalization, and merging) will inevitably ensue.

This notion of a world made up of bioregional localities is likely to send shivers down the spine of globalists. How is an economy to work properly without the forces of competition? This important issue is, however, partly independent of whether the market remains globalized or not. Clearly, some trade will always exist – as it virtually always has throughout human history. Long-distance transportation will not disappear altogether, although it is likely to become substantially more expensive. This will mean a strong, cost-driven prioritization of the use of fossil fuels, with the need to coordinate and deliberate about issues (namely, what and how much to import and export) we have been used to leaving to impersonal market forces. Much more of the volume of consumed goods will have to be produced closer to the consumers – and this necessarily will mean smaller units. A combination of localized activity and (limited) globalized trade will ensue, which I call *bioregionally constrained globalization*. The theory of what constitutes an optimal allocation of production tasks from the local to the global will not be offered here. No 'protectionism' is involved at all in this new form of division of labour; simply, it will be a world of reduced cross-border trade flows and increased intra-border production and consumption.

This is not necessarily reassuring. 'Small is beautiful' is a catchy slogan, but it cannot hide all the deleterious aspects of smallness and locality – namely, the pettiness and corruption that can easily follow upon the realization that customers are trapped within borders they cannot, for cost reasons, easily transcend. However, the fact that economic units are small does not imply that they are few in numbers. Indeed, the pure economic theory of perfect competition rests on the assumption of 'atomistic', hence *small and numerous*, sellers for its claim that market outcomes produce efficient allocation.[12] Small might be beautiful if there also is (near-) perfect competition between small units – that is, if these units can be 'arbitraged away from' by consumers even within a restricted geographical area. Economic units should be numerous enough such that any of them should stand to lose a large fraction of its stakeholder constituency if it did not offer acceptable production and selling conditions (prices, working conditions, pollution, etc.). This may be compatible with a duopoly if competition is of the Bertrand type, but we know that in such situations collusion – at least tacit collusion – is more than likely. Therefore, bioregionally constrained globalization will only work if regulatory authorities *increase, rather than mitigate*, the degree of market competition within the bioregion – an idea which, surely, will not be immediately popular within those who have interpreted Schumacher in the direction of 'flower power'.

12   See Aumann (1964). In a perfectly competitive market, the theory says, agents are both infinitely numerous and infinitesimally small (they are of 'Lebesgue measure zero'). In fact, both properties are equivalent to one another since the infinity of points on a segment comes from the fact that they have no dimension.

For each bioregion to know – in keeping with Sale's call to be 'deeply conscious of the limits of natural resources and the need for ecological harmony' – how much it can draw on the planet's (including its own local) resources, there would have to be a global protocol of resource consumption, depletion, and restoration, linked to a global agreement on how to distribute growth and de-growth across bioregions. This cannot possibly be a decentralized endeavour – on the contrary, to be at all effective it has to be highly centralized at world level (possibly within a 'World Sustainability Organization' to be created).

Within each bioregion, local trade could be massively enhanced through the introduction of regional complementary currencies alongside the dollar, the euro and other national currencies used for cross-border trade.[13] Moreover, the right of socially and ecologically responsible citizens to experiment with new, more 'permanence-driven' forms of competitive activities will only be truly effective if some form of unconditional income support is offered them – so that they can gather the nerve to pursue alternatives without risking losing their livelihood and their rights to social security.[14]

These are only some of the most salient institutional reforms that would be called for if we were to seek to create a large-scale dynamic toward small scale. Clearly, as I emphasized earlier, the divide between decentralism and centralism becomes meaningless. And actually, if the economic agents we are dealing with are socially and economically responsible in the sense of Schumacher, this blurring of the border between decentralism and centralism is not only not a problem – it is desirable.

---

13   The literature on complementary currencies is currently burgeoning. For an in-depth synthetic discussion, see Arnsperger, Brunnhuber, Goerner and Lietaer (2012).

14   This idea of an 'economic transition income' (ETI) has been explored in Arnsperger and Johnson (2011).

References

Arnsperger, C. (2005). 'Probing the "Moralization of Capitalism" Problem: Democratic Experimentalism and the Co-Evolution of Norms', *International Social Science Journal*, 185, 433–44.

Arnsperger, C. and Johnson, W.A. (2011). 'The Guaranteed Income as an Equal-Opportunity Tool in the Transition Toward Sustainability'. In A. Gosseries and Y. Vanderborght (eds), *Arguing About Justice: Essays for Philippe Van Parijs*, pp. 61–9. Louvain-la-Neuve: Presses Universitaires de Louvain.

Arnsperger, C., Brunnhuber, S., Goerner, S., and Lietaer, B. (2012). *Money and Sustainability: The Missing Link*. Axminster: Triarchy Press.

Aumann, R.J. (1964). 'Markets with a Continuum of Traders', *Econometrica*, 32, 39–50.

Beckerman, W. (2002). *A Poverty of Reason: Sustainable Development and Economic Growth*. Oakland: The Independent Institute.

Boumans, R.M.J., De Groot, R.S., and Wilson, M.A. (2002). 'A Typology for the Classification, Description and Valuation of Ecosystem Functions, Goods and Services', *Ecological Economics*, 41, 393–408.

Daly, H. and Farley, J. (2011). *Ecological Economics: Principles and Applications*. 2nd edn. Washington D.C.: Island Press.

Dupuy, J.-P. (2002). *Pour un catastrophisme éclairé: Quand l'impossible est certain*. Paris: Seuil.

Esbjörn-Hargens, S., and Zimmerman, D. (2009). *Integral Ecology: Uniting Multiple Perspectives on the Natural World*. Boston: Integral Books.

Gerber, J-F., Healy, H., Martínez-Alier, J., Temper, L., and Walter, M. (eds) (2012). *Ecological Economics from the Ground Up*, London: Routledge/Earthscan.

Hayek, F.A. (1952). *The Sensory Order: An Inquiry Into the Foundations of Theoretical Psychology*. Chicago: University of Chicago Press.

Healy, H., Martínez-Alier, J., Temper, L., Walter, M. and Gerber, J.-F. (eds) (2012). *Ecological Economics from the Ground Up*. London: Routledge/Earthscan.

Illich, I. (1974). *Energy and Equity*. London: Boyars.

Macy, J. (1991). *Mutual Causality in Buddhism and General Systems Theory: The Dharma of Natural Systems*. Albany: SUNY Press.

Martínez-Alier, J. (1990). *Ecological Economics: Energy, Environment and Society*. Oxford: Basil Blackwell.

Martínez-Alier, J. (1997). 'From Political Economy to Political Ecology'. In R. Guha and J. Martínez-Alier (eds), *Varieties of Environmentalism: Essays North and South*, pp. 22–45. London: Routledge/Earthscan.

Ostrom, E. (1990). *Governing the Commons: The Evolution of Institutions for Collective Action.* Cambridge: Cambridge University Press.

Sale, K. (1989). 'Preface to the 1989 Edition'. In Schumacher (1973), pp. xvii–xxiii.

Sale, K. (2000). *Dwellers in the Land: The Bioregional Vision.* New edn. Athens: University of Georgia Press.

Salles, J.-M. (2011). 'Valuing Biodiversity and Ecosystem Services: Why Put Economic Values on Nature?', *Comptes-Rendus Biologies*, 334, 469–82.

Schumacher, E.F. (1969). 'Industry and Morals'. Reprinted in Schumacher (2004), pp. 87–96.

Schumacher, E.F. (1973). *Small Is Beautiful: Economics as if People Mattered*, new edition. New York: Harper and Row.

Schumacher, E.F. (1974). 'A Message From the Universe'. Reprinted in Schumacher (2004), pp. 205–14.

Schumacher, E.F. (1977). *A Guide for the Perplexed.* New York: Harper and Row.

Schumacher, E.F. (2004). *This I Believe and Other Essays.* Totnes: Green Books.

Sen, A. (1993). 'Positional Objectivity', *Philosophy and Public Affairs*, 22, 126–45.

Settele, J., and Spangenberg, J. (2010). 'Precisely Incorrect? Monetising the Value of Ecosystem Services', *Ecological Complexity*, 7, 327–37.

Thiry, G. (2012). *Au-delà du PIB: Un tournant historique – Enjeux méthodologiques, théoriques et épistémologiques de la quantification*, unpublished PhD thesis. Louvain-la-Neuve: Université catholique de Louvain, Economics School of Louvain (ESL).

Thompson, E.T., Varela, F.J., and Rosch, E. (1992). *The Embodied Mind: Cognitive Science and Human Experience.* Cambridge: MIT Press.

CARLOS HOEVEL

PONTIFICAL CATHOLIC UNIVERSITY OF ARGENTINA

10 The Call for Responsibility and the Crisis

1 Introduction

During the last decades many mainstream economists have considered the relative success of globalization to be a general refutation of almost each of Schumacher's warnings and forecasts about the evil consequences of a lack of adequateness of the economy to the qualitative natural, ethical and spiritual limits of man and society. In the first place, these authors argued that the last three decades of accelerated economic growth had not been the product of qualitative and 'adequate' policies but of standardized deregulation policies based on neoclassical 'value free' models that had permitted an indefinite expansion of financial markets and technological innovations. In the second place, these same authors generally also argued that the economic success had been the result of the generalized introduction of monetary incentives and increasing flexibility in the labour market without needing to take into account any other factors, based on the neoclassical assumption that in order to behave rationally people need only extrinsic motivations. In the third place, the same authors believed that consumerism and a massive use of credit was no longer as serious a risk as it had been in the past because the new forms of global financing permitted a sufficient access to money and therefore to consumption in an almost limitless amount. Finally, most of the supporters of this position were very optimistic about the future, based mainly on the assumption that the available economic indicators and indexes were on the whole satisfactory and correct.

In opposition to these four statements I will argue in this paper that, especially after the financial crisis, there are very concrete reasons to believe that these arguments were false and that, as a consequence, and from now on, we should go exactly in the opposite direction. In that sense, I will try to present briefly, on the one hand, some arguments proposed by contemporary economists and business theorists who differ with the opinions of orthodox mainstream representatives about the nature and meaning of these four crucial issues of the last crisis: the use of economic knowledge, the role of monetary incentives, the expansion of credit and the reliability of standard economic indicators and indexes. On the other hand, I will try to connect these arguments with some of E.F. Schumacher's insights into the concept of 'adequateness' – explained by him in his *A Guide for the Perplexed* and applied to many issues in his *Small is Beautiful* and *Good Work* – but adapted to the new context of our post-crisis economy. Finally, I will attempt to propose an ethical agenda of new responsibilities that flow from the four above-mentioned issues, taking into account Schumacher's call to adequate our extremely powerful and risky economic tools to the natural limits of the human being and the planet.

2 Responsibility towards Knowledge

According to analysts as famous as Joseph Stiglitz (2010) and Francis Fukuyama, one of the structural causes of the last financial crisis has been the paradigm of liberalization and deregulation of financial activities, understood not as a prudential measure adequate for certain situations and times, but as an absolute dogma valid in all circumstances and places. 'The authorities should not interfere with the pollinating bees of Wall Street' Alan Greenspan argued in his biography (Greenspan 2008). A crucial role in the promotion of these extremely imprudent policies was played by the dominant neoclassical economic thought, from which were drawn a series of refined theorems, models, econometric techniques and financial instruments of 'firepower' that had never been seen before.

Think only [says the Italian economist Stefano Zamagni] of mechanisms such as the computerized trading program, which is somewhat analogous to a particle accelerator, which amplifies, in a pro-cyclical trend, upward and downward market stock values. It is clear that a speculative bubble in the proportions that we know today would never have been possible without this 'mental bubble' that has made many believe it would be possible to reduce risk to zero, from the time that it had been scattered among a sufficiently large number of operators. But the risk, if it is any, can be moved or reduced but not canceled. This sense of omnipotence, fueled by years of financial euphoria, has mastered the habits of mind, not just of the traders and financial institutions but also of political authorities, the media, and not a few academic and research centers. (Zamagni 2008: 2)

Zamagni also quotes Paul Samuelson' s article in the *Corriere della Sera* of 20 October 2008 where the latter writes: 'I and some colleagues at MIT and at the University of Chicago, Wharton, Pennsylvania, and many others, risk suffering a very rude treatment when we meet St Peter at the gates of Paradise' (Zamagni 2008: 9). Another similar statement was that of Edmund Phelps, also a Nobel Prize winner, in the article of 11 November 2008 in the same newspaper when he wrote: 'The banks have talked about the fall in house prices as if it were the result of any shock [...] However, there have not been really earthquakes, droughts or other external factors that caused the fall in prices. The main cause was a prediction based on totally erroneous theoretical models'.

Thus, this crisis demonstrates the futility of what the Argentine philosopher of the economy Ricardo Crespo calls the 'idolatry of instruments'. According to Crespo, the excessive use of 'a set of techniques such as financial evaluation, accounting norms, incentive systems and interest rates foster the evolution of the crisis and make difficult its detection. Agents, like horses with blinkers, go on directly and inexorably towards the precipice, without real responsibility from any one of them. They produced growing vicious circles that nobody creates individually and intentionally' (Crespo 2009: 28). In the same vein, according to Luk Bouckaert, the use of these models led many people in the financial system to 'ignore the risks and promote irresponsible, and short-time oriented and speculative behavior. It produced a high degree of moral myopia and selective blindness'. Moreover, in Bouckaert's opinion, the apparent safety of the techniques and models 'dazzles people to realize the consequences and to anticipate the catastrophe. In classical tragedies the hero's fall is always preceded by an inability to grasp the ambiguities and the fragility of what is happening. A process of moral myopia and hubris always comes before the catastrophe' (Bouckaert 2009: 14).

For those of us who are teachers in economics and business departments it is easy to see how students are taught to seek means by which they can supposedly find precise answers to complex social and human problems. This claim is favoured and encouraged by the economic disciplines themselves. In fact, according to Michael Naughton, a specialist in business ethics at the University of Saint Thomas, United States,

> the first principles of these disciplines are largely methodological and amoral, abandoning any professional moral responsibility. Warren Bennis and James O'Toole, in a highly critical article on business education in the *Harvard Business Review* ('How Business Schools Lost Their Way'), explained that business schools have adopted a model of academic excellence that reflects a scientific model 'predicated on the faulty assumption that business is an academic discipline like chemistry or geology when, in fact, business is a profession and business schools are professional schools'. This scientific model in business has been highly influenced by the quantification of economics and finance. (Naughton 2009: 38)

This scientific-technical model of teaching induces students to think in compartments and does not allow them to grasp the whole, especially when it has to do with social and moral problems. This is an education, adds Naughton,

> that ignores what is at the heart of a professional understanding of business: practical wisdom, which entails technical competence, a rich moral end, and practical experience. When business education adopts a scientific model over a professional model, it reduces itself to technical training and fails to engage the student in a deeper understanding of the practice of business. It should not surprise us that those trained within our universities with this type of formation would act in such a way that would produce our current financial crisis. (Naughton 2009: 38)

This conception has its roots in what E.F. Schumacher calls the modern Cartesian and empiricist image of man and in the different forms of positivism and neo-positivism derived from it. According to this view, human knowledge can be considered just as any other raw material and can be ruled by the same procedures by which we treat (not very amiably) the natural world. 'Knowledge itself is power' said Francis Bacon (1561–1626), and Descartes promised men they would become 'masters and possessors of nature'. In its further development, 'science for manipulation' almost inevitably tends to advance from the manipulation of nature to that of people (Schumacher 1978: 83).

Therefore, this kind of education impoverishes the subjective dimension of knowledge, precisely the place where intellectual and ethical orientation of actions could be obtained: science and engineering produce 'know-how'; but 'know-how' is nothing in itself; it is a means without an end, a mere potentiality, an unfinished sentence. 'Know-how' is no more a culture than a piano is music. Can education help us to finish the sentence, to turn the potentiality into a reality for the benefit of man? To do so, the task of education would be, first and foremost, the transmission of ideas of value, of what to do with our lives (Schumacher 1983: 83–4).

In that sense, it is urgent to restore gradually at the departments of economics and business, a kind of education that can put in its proper place the exaggerated importance given until now to mathematical models, and to induce students to open their minds to new currents of economic thought, social and cultural realities and problems presented by other disciplines. As argued by Ricardo Crespo,

> before learning about tools (models, etc.), economists should learn Political Philosophy, History, Sociology, Psychology, Anthropology, Moral Philosophy and even Literature. Lionel Robbins had realized about this and proposed it, although a little late. Only in this way we will shape true political economists that will not make such big mistakes. Furthermore, great economists were great because they were also humanists: let us think about Adam Smith, John Stuart Mill, Carl Menger, Ludwig von Mises, John Maynard Keynes, Friedrich von Hayek, Joseph Schumpeter, Herbert Simon or Albert Hirschman. (Crespo 2009: 30)

3   Responsibility towards Work and Property

A second cause of the crisis was the system of incentives and salaries of
financial managers oriented to short-term gains that led to a deliberate
neglect of the long-term and augmented the risks assumed by banks. This
system was the product of the widespread corporate culture of recent decades which was also characterized by short-term financial performance,
a management style with rapid rotation of jobs, highly individual bonus
systems applied to remunerations, a lack of long-term investment in people
and an excessive focus on earnings and benefits. In fact, the main problem of
the work-for-performance incentive system was to undermine the intrinsic
motivation to do the right thing, replacing it with an extrinsic motivation,
which is always weaker than the intrinsic. As was pointed out by the Swiss
experimental economist Bruno Frey, a system can lead to wrong incentives
such as the perverse effects of 'crowding out' by which the incentives end
up weakening the motivation of the conduct that they are supposed to
encourage (Frey 1997).

Taking these arguments into account, it is clear that what we need now
is a different kind of incentive system applied to work that can lead us to
a more responsible behaviour. According to Helen Alford, a specialist in
business ethics at the Angelicum University in Rome, 'a financial incentive doesn't have to be entirely absent, but it is handled in such a way that
it reinforces intrinsic motivation to do the good thing [...] rather than by
"crowding out" that motivation and replacing it with the purely extrinsic
motivation of earning money. It is the difference, as the economists say,
between "price" and "prize" – a prize reinforces intrinsic motivation, while
a price can tend to drive it out' (Alford 2009: 25).

The problem with incentive systems – especially with the ones applied
to the work of financial agents and CEOs – is, in my opinion, in very close
connection with what E.F. Schumacher tries to teach us especially in his
book *The Good Work*. As many experimental economists and business theorists are arguing now, Schumacher considers that there is no way to promote
a more ethical and economically efficient behaviour of managers and workers unless we recognize and promote the intrinsic value of their work as a

crucial factor: 'If we see work as nothing but an unpleasant necessity, it is no use talking about good work, unless we mean less work. Why put any goodness into our work beyond the absolute minimum? Who could afford to do good work? What would be the point of making something perfect when something imperfect would do as well?' (Schumacher 1980: 153).

However, besides the need for 'good work', the problems with incentive systems lead us also to another very important Schumacherian insight: the need for a change in some property structures in order to 're-connect' managers with morally and socially responsible conducts. Indeed, according to Michael Naughton, the lack of responsibility and overall commitment to clients that we have seen during the crisis was due to the phenomenon of what Naughton calls the 'disconnected capital'. According to Naughton,

> the beginning of the financial crisis started in the 1990s when John Gutfreund, then CEO of Salomon Brothers (who was once called the King of Wall Street) turned Salomon Brothers from a private partnership into Wall Street's first public corporation. Besides benefitting immensely from this ownership change, Gutfreund set in motion a transferring of financial risk from connected partners/employees to disconnected shareholders. This ownership system incentivized CEOs and others to take high stake risks, which they probably would not have made with their own capital. The shareholders who financed the risks had no real understanding of what the risk takers were doing, and as the risk-taking grew ever more complex, their understanding of the instruments decreased. (Naughton 2009: 38–9)

This 'disconnection' then spread to a vast area of the financial system. According to Naughton again,

> the faith in the market that so many expressed has had one major problem: it had no ownership of those who were operating in the market. The people whose faith in the market perpetuated this crisis were largely immune from any serious ownership in what they were doing. Homeowners bought with little ownership and bad debt and with little accountability to what homeownership meant. Bankers sold these loans with significant fees and passed them on to investors. Investment banks and others incentivized banks and mortgage brokers to issue problematic loans which they could securitize and pass on to other speculators. Global demand for these securities was high, based on unrealistic returns, pressuring lenders to lower their standards and produce more loans. And so an incentive system developed that passed on to others what many believed were problematic products. (Naughton 2009: 38)

In fact, in Naughton's opinion, 'no bank of employee-owned investment could have leveraged in proportions of 35 to 1 or buy and hold $ 50 billion in collateralized debt obligations (CDOs). In this high-risk operation where only the bonus itself was at stake, failure was usually someone else's problem, as there was no property in the system of those agents operating. No system can prevent structural defect, but some structures are more prone to sin than others' (Naughton 2009: 39). Hence the need to overcome the model of the 'commodity-company', created to be subdivided, merged and resold, and to think about new property models based on the partnership of stakeholders and on a responsible attitude towards society as it was taught by E.F. Schumacher.

4   Responsibility towards Credit and Consumption

A third root of the financial crisis was the replacement of the saving and work culture by the culture of excessive credit and debt. In fact, as stated by Stefano Zamagni (2008), it is true that what has turned the financial free market into a 'greed market' ('Greed is good, greed is right' claimed the famous film star of 1987 *Wall Street*), far beyond mere economic rationality, was the narcissistic desire of many financial agents to have more money, more things, more prestige and more power (Lasch 1999). However, this was for sure not only a Wall Street problem. Indeed, behind an economy based on financial speculation that allows both the reduction of the price of labour and of the price for consumption, we can discover the postmodern culture of 'wanting everything now', the consumption culture described by the sociologist Zygmunt Bauman (2006) that we can see in the queues in front of the malls before the launch of a new technological toy, at the beginning of a new promotion or during Christmas shopping. As Samuel Gregg puts it,

> a little discussed fact is that the financial crisis has also been driven by widespread moral lapses that have manifested themselves just as much on what American politicians like to call 'Main Street' as on Wall Street. A prominent example is the subprime-mortgage fiasco. We now know that thousands of Main St borrowers *lied* about their

income, assets, and liabilities when applying for subprime loans. Likewise, many lenders failed to do even the most rudimentary checks on borrowers' credit history. Recklessness also features among the sins underlying our present financial turmoil. On Main St, thousands of investors mortgaged themselves to the hilt on the highly imprudent assumption that house-prices could only continue to soar. Meanwhile on Wall St, investment banks overleveraged themselves, sometimes at ratios of 30-to-1. Then there is the rampant materialism that has apparently permeated Main Street and Wall Street to equal degrees. The virtue of temperance was also largely forgotten. The thrifty, even parsimonious Adam Smith would have been appalled by the 'I-want-it-all-now' mentality that has helped the personal savings-rate in America to hover around 0 per cent since 2005 – the lowest rate since the Depression years of 1932 and 1933. (Gregg 2009: 51)

Furthermore, this irresponsible behaviour in relation to one's own economic and personal limits was strengthened by technological means which replaced face to face relationships – and their concomitant moral virtues of trust, reciprocity and integrity – by anonymous relations based on purely financial liquidity, moral neutrality and the tendency to imitate others. This excessive artificiality and loss of contact with the local reality of real estate credit systems favored the disconnection of many people from their own limits and real possibilities. In this sense the credit and financial system has become what some analysts called a 'no place' in which thousands of people connected through the Internet lacked a direct contact with the daily reality of the debtors. All this probably contributed no little to the loss of the sense of reality that many people experienced before the crisis, having the false impression that the world was now ruled by different laws from the ones that had governed the life of all generations in the past. The extreme delocalization of relationships was fatal to the moral and realistic fabric that credit and financial markets require to function in a proper and safe way.

Responsibility towards credit would thus imply: first, to leave aside the philosophy of the *homo consumens* that justifies excessive borrowing and speculation on the basis of an unrealistic philosophy of man. The latter should be replaced by a philosophy of the integral human person open to others through the gift of creativity and effort through work and through market relations and exchanges occurring not only as mere exchange of equivalents but as modes of human interaction that include utility but also obligations and responsibilities towards others; Schumacher argues:

Let us try to utilize this opportunity to recall to our minds what a human person really is. I am saying nothing original, I just remind myself of it. First of all, in some way or another, whatever way you try to express it, he comes from the divine level onto this earth. He is a son or daughter of the divine. Second, he is a social being; he doesn't come alone. He is put into this social context. And third, he or she is an incomplete being. He has been sent here to complete himself. From this insight have been formulated all the ethics and all the instructions to the human race. As a divinely arrived being he is called upon to love God in traditional language. As a social being he is called upon to love his neighbor. And as an incomplete individual being he is called upon to love himself. The social organization ought to reflect these three absolute needs. If these needs are not fulfilled, if he can't do it, he becomes unhappy, destructive, a vandal, a suicidal maniac. The social, political, and economic organizations ought to reflect these needs. (Schumacher 1980: 178)[1]

However, this would not be enough. A crucial factor would be the reintroduction of at least a part of the credit and financial system – and of the consumption economy – in the concrete network of social relations. That is why, following Schumacher's perspective, it is so important that, in addition to the actual tendencies to globalized, delocalized and flexible market relationships, we can also return in banking, credit and consumption – at least partially – to localized relations not so excessively dependent on global forces:

The optimal pattern of consumption, producing a high degree of human satisfaction by means of a relatively low rate of consumption, allows people to live without great pressure and strain and to fulfill the primary injunction of Buddhist teaching: 'Cease to do evil; try to do good'. As physical resources are everywhere limited, people satisfying their needs by means of a modest use of resources are obviously less likely to be at each other's throats than people depending upon a high rate of use. Equally, people who live in highly self-sufficient local communities are less likely to get involved in large-scale violence than people whose existence depends on worldwide systems of trade. From the point of view of Buddhist economics, therefore, production from local resources for local needs is the most rational way of economic life, while dependence on imports from afar and the consequent need to produce for export to unknown and distant peoples is highly uneconomic and justifiable only in

---

1   The Schumacher quotations in this article are based on the Spanish editions of his
     works.

exceptional cases and on a small scale. Just as the modern economist would admit that a high rate of consumption of transport services between a man's home and his place of work signifies a misfortune and not a high standard of life, so the Buddhist economist would hold that to satisfy human wants from faraway sources rather than from sources nearby signifies failure rather than success. (Schumacher 1983: 60–1)

5 Responsibility towards Figures

Finally, another aspect of our need for adequateness is in relation to the use and interpretation of economic figures and the building of indexes. It is true that during the last decades economic figures about GDP growth, consumption and reduction of poverty – the latter especially in emergent economies – were impressive. However, as we now know, many acute problems were concealed under these seemingly so good figures. Therefore, there is now a strong debate in economics about the limits of conventional indexes, measuring instruments and the theoretical foundations on which the latter are based. Indeed, many economists and policy makers wonder whether traditional indexes are able to provide relevant information about important issues in such a complex economy and society as the globalized one. In fact, most of the good figures of the overoptimistic views of financial globalization were built on conventional economic quantitative measurements based on relatively simple statistical and mathematical models.

Indeed, how much can we trust in the quality or the value of the information obtained on such a basis? Can conventional macro measurements of production, consumption or even wealth distribution give us the qualitative knowledge that we need in order to understand the general direction of our society? Do they give us the relevant information we need about the cultural and ethical trends in order to detect problems and eventually prevent the crises?

Most of the 'conspicuous developments of economics in the last quarter of a century are in the direction of quantification, at the expense of the understanding of qualitative differences. Indeed, one might say that economics has become increasingly intolerant of the latter, be cause they do not fit into its method and make demands on the practical understanding and the power of insight of economists, which they are unwilling or unable to fulfil. For example, having established by his purely quantitative methods that the gross National Product of a country has risen by, say, five per cent, the economist-turned econometrician is unwilling, and generally unable, to face the question of whether this is to be taken as a good thing or a bad thing. He would lose all his certainties if he even entertained such a question: growth of GNP must be a good thing, irrespective of what has grown and who, if anyone, has benefited. The idea that there could be pathological growth, unhealthy growth, disruptive or destructive growth is to him a perverse idea which must not be allowed to surface. (Schumacher 1983: 49).

Statistics don't have to be accurate; they have to be significant. My theory has always been that figures don't mean anything if you can't make them sing. How can anybody assert that 'growth' is a good thing? If my children grow, this is a very good thing; if I should suddenly start growing, it would be a disaster. Therefore, the qualitative discrimination is the main thing; it's far more important than some mysterious adding-up of everything. We've all learned at school that you must add together only things of essentially the same quality. So you can't add together apples and the number of evenings spent watching television; this is meaningless. Let's look at the qualitative aspect of the whole matter. Surely our job is always to make up our minds what is good and do our best to let the good grow; and to make up our minds what is evil or not so good and try to diminish it. Whether the two processes, put together, mean a new growth or a net diminution shouldn't interest anyone. The quality of life – not the quantity – yes, that's what matters. GNP, being a purely quantitative concept, bypasses the real question: how to enhance the quality of life. (Schumacher 1980: 160–1)

In this regard, it is now crucial to take responsibility in the way we build economic indicators and indexes in order to evaluate the performance of the economy and society and set up the right policies. In fact, against the conventional trend, some economists are becoming increasingly aware of the need for new and more responsible indexes. According to the former, indexes and statistical information should not be based on purely rationalistic and mechanistic models of neoclassical market equilibrium, but should take into account the complex and dense network of links, rules, habits and natural, ethical and cultural particularities of each people, region and country as it was always recommended by Schumacher. As it was noted by Joseph Stiglitz, Jean-Paul Fitoussi and Amartya Sen in their *Report of the Commission on the Measurement of Economic Performance and Social Progress* of 2010 presented to President Sarkozy: 'what we measure affects what we do; and if our measurements are flawed, decisions may be distorted' (Stiglitz, Fitoussi and Sen 2010) The fact that some of today's most important economists, politicians and statisticians are thinking seriously about new ways to measure the complexity of social and economic reality gives us hope to start providing responsible answers to the call for adequateness made by Schumacher forty years ago.

6   Conclusion

As was pointed out by E.F. Schumacher in all his works, the only outlet for contemporary capitalism relies on a deep ethical and cultural change, consisting in the abandonment of a short-term, utilitarian, subjectivist and hedonistic thought that originated in the Enlightenment and was emphasized recently by contemporary postmodern culture. According to him, a sustainable economic order should put aside the unrealistic and destructive idea that each individual can become an absolutely independent self, to the point where his or her subjective desires or preferences can be considered absolute requirements regardless of their consequences for their fellow men, society or nature. It is no longer possible to continue thinking of society merely as a utilitarian contract and of nature as raw material whose only purpose would be to meet people's selfish individual goals.

In fact, Schumacher's call for 'adequateness' and responsibility means to overcome the false cultural pattern through which we have thought that it was possible to be efficient and economically competent regardless of the moral purpose or the values implied in our actions. Such value free efficiency is false. We are always choosing the means that explicitly or implicitly point to a value. In this sense, especially after the crisis, we can clearly perceive that instrumental rationality in the activities of financial agents, borrowers and economists must be a topic of open discussion in order to make explicit the implicit values and purposes in play.

Finally, I think it will be impossible to make a change in the direction shown by Schumacher unless we recover the sense of reality understood as a created order, endowed with meaning, mystery and beauty that cannot be ignored or manipulated at will. This implies that reality is not a human product and it will never be completely replaced by artificial systems. The financial system collapsed due to a lack of respect for and adequateness to the order of being that was somehow violated by the claims of omnipotence of man. Only a spiritual conversion that leads us to concrete actions put into practice in the above areas and in many other ones not mentioned in this short paper will prevent us from falling into a similar or even a worse crisis in the future.

References

Alford, H. (2009). 'Crisis and Incentive Systems', *Cultura Económica*, 73–4, 22–7.

Bauman, Z. (2006). *Vida Líquida*. Barcelona: Paidós.

Bouckaert, L. (2009). 'The Financial Catharsis', *Cultura Económica*, 73–4, 10–16.

Crespo, R. (2009). 'On the Causes of the Crisis', *Cultura Económica*, 73–4, 28–30.

Frey, B. (1997). *Not Just for the Money. An Economic Theory of Personal Motivation*. London: Elgar.

Greenspan, A. (2008). *The Age of Turbulence: Adventures in a New World*. New York: New York.

Gregg, S. (2009). 'No Morality, no Markets', *Cultura Económica*, 73–4, 48–51.

Lasch, C. (1991). *The Culture of Narcissism: American Life in an Age of Diminishing Expectations*. New York: Norton.

Naughton, M. (2009). 'A Great Opportunity for Moral Reform', *Cultura Económica*, 73–4, 34–8.

Schumacher, E.F.(1978). *A Guide for the Perplexed*. London: Abacus.

Schumacher, E.F. (1980). *El buen trabajo (Good Work)*. Buenos Aires: Debate.

Schumacher, E.F. (1983). *Lo pequeño es hermoso (Small is Beautiful)*. Buenos Aires: Orbis.

Stiglitz, J. (2010). *The Stiglitz Report, Reforming the International Monetary and Financial Systems in the Wake of the Global Crisis*. New York: The New Press.

Stiglitz, J., Fitoussi, J.P., and Sen, A. (2010). *Mismeasuring Our Lives: Why GDP Doesn't Add Up*. New York: The New Press.

Zamagni, S. (2008). 'La Lezione e il Monito di una Crisi Annunciata', *Working Paper, Università degli Studi di Bologna, Dipartimento di Scienze Economiche*, pp. 1–23. Bologna: University of Bologna.

MICHAŁ A. MICHALSKI
ADAM MICKIEWICZ UNIVERSITY POZNAN

11 Economics as if the Family Mattered

1 Introduction

In this chapter I would like to examine the importance of the institution of the family from the perspective of the work of E.F. Schumacher. Especially I would like to concentrate on *Small is Beautiful. A Study of Economics as if People Mattered*, as can be seen from the title of my paper. I think it is justified to say that Schumacher was one of these thinkers who understood the meaning of the family well, although it was not one of his central topics. In *Small is Beautiful* we read that, 'next to the family, it is work and the relationships established by work that are the true foundations of society. If the foundations are unsound, how could society be sound? And if society is sick, how could it fail to be a danger to peace?' (Schumacher 1993: 23).

In my opinion the contribution of family life to market and management domains is still not sufficiently being discussed and understood. Although there are examples of theories that stress the role of a family in creating so-called 'human capital' (Becker 1993), there is still much to be done in this field. One of the things that can be seen as a proof of the diagnose I offer is the problem of the individual vs. the familial paradigm in the economy. Reinhard Marx recently remarked that the shift from an individualistic to a familial perspective in economic activity is the necessary condition of justice (Marx 2009: 105–6). What's more, it can be supported by the point that Schumacher makes in *Good Work* when he criticizes a quantitative and strictly individualistic attitude to human beings. He writes that the census 'treats people as if they were units, whereas they are not. Each is a universe' (Schumacher 1979: 145).

His approach in this matter – although it may seem solipsistic – should be rather qualified as personalistic, since it respects the uniqueness and relational nature of man – with reference to both the natural world and society, with the family as its basic community. The difference between the perspectives discussed above is presented in the following graph. The 'Individualistic' perspective is divided into a radical 'Atomized Vision of Society' and a moderate 'Together-Alone Vision of Society'. They both fail to respect the dual nature of the human being as the unique person ('a universe') and social being that Schumacher finds equally fundamental. This graph will also be useful in understanding that only in the third perspective is there a ground and space for responsibility. While in the first case there is a distance that makes the responsible approach problematic, in the second vision there may be not enough space for a free and responsible attitude (which is paradoxically similar to the situation in a collectivistic vision of society).

Atomized (Radically Individualistic) Vision of Society	Together-Alone (Moderately Individualistic) Vision of Society	Personalistic Vision of Society as Multidimensional Community of Communities (e.g. Families) of Persons
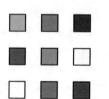		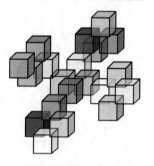
– no or not enough of common ground for free responsible attitude	– no or not enough space to perform free responsible attitude	– common ground and enough space to perform free responsible attitude

Another point of interest is the 'family experience' – which is somehow a universal human experience – and which should be seen as a fundamental preparation for our professional and civic activity. It is well known that one of the important functions of a family is to socialize its members. Nowadays this truth seems to be forgotten, and companies spend serious amounts of money on training and development of what is called 'soft skills'. If we think of it thoroughly we will see that it is in the family that we learn these skills, which are necessary to exist and cooperate in different social groups, including professional ones.

Among these attributes trust and responsibility play the key role. It is the family that is the first school of these abilities. Trust and responsibility are not inherited but have to be developed through a very unique process that takes place in a family, as Jennifer Roback Morse in her *Love & Economics* convincingly shows. Parents are the first teachers of these attributes. I stress here the importance of personal testimony of the couple as their responsible attitude towards each other and their children shapes the climate where responsibility has a more favorable environment in which to develop. It is confirmed by the fact that human beings learn not only through verbal transmission of knowledge but also through observation and action.

Engaging with the contribution of E.F. Schumacher in this analysis of the role of family life as the crucial factor in shaping the economic domain in my opinion can be helpful in – firstly – deepening awareness of the social importance of the family and – secondly – popularizing Schumacher's ideas which – at least in Poland, where I come from – are yet to be further discovered.

In the course of this chapter I will engage with the contributions of authors representing different disciplines, not necessarily to connect their findings together but rather to illustrate the wide range of problems and perspectives that Schumacher embraced in his work.

2   To be responsible, or not to be...?

> The theme of *Small is Beautiful* is that people matter. And if people
> matter, so do all other forms of life. Humanity is part of an integrated
> and ordered living creation and cannot exist in isolation from the bio-
> sphere that sustains it. If we destroy life on our planet we are ultimately
> destroying ourselves. Biocide is suicide.
>
> — PEARCE 2006: 279

It is worth examining the question of responsibility as one of the basic
aspects of the human condition. It can be expressed by saying that to 'be'
authentically means to 'be responsible'. (See: de Saint-Exupéry 1964: 117,
cited after Filek 2003: 15). Throughout the twentieth century responsibility became an issue of great interest and this resulted in the development
of knowledge in this field. Although 'responsibility' was not a new term,
it turned out that there is still not much known about it. It is related to
the fact that the *retrospective* way of understanding responsibility was most
common, while *prospective* responsibility was still to be promoted (Zsolnai
2000: 71).

The philosophy of responsibility was developed by such authors
as Martin Buber, Eberhard Grisebach, Wilhelm Weischedel, Dietrich
Bonhoeffer, Hans Jonas, Dieter Birnbacher and Emmanuel Levinas. They
helped to see the human embeddedness of responsibility. This means that
the natural existential situation of man points to the need for a non-reciprocal kind of relation which is responsibility (Jonas 1984: 38–9). These philosophers – defined most often as the philosophers of dialogue – underline
that the ability to become responsible is based on the innate necessity of
being in relation to other human beings which can be defined as the expectation of response. If responsibility is a potential predisposition inscribed in
human nature, then it rather needs to be discovered than achieved. What's
more, responsibility is a uniquely human attribute, because no responsibility is expected from other species.

This 'discovery' of responsibility is somehow related to the transformations that humanity experienced throughout the twentieth century and still experiences in the beginning of the twenty-first century. It was Hans Jonas who was convinced that the new character of human action demands a new ethics of responsibility. He wrote that in the past 'all dealing with the nonhuman world, that is, the whole realm of *techne* [...] was ethically neutral. [...] Ethical significance belonged to the direct dealing of man with man, including man dealing with himself: all traditional ethics are *anthropocentric*. [...] the entity of "man" and his basic condition was considered constant in essence and not itself an object of reshaping *techne*' (Jonas 1984: 4–5). This means that the contemporary challenges that are related to technical and economical aspirations of human beings become the source of possible harm and disaster on an unprecedented scale. In this context, the call for development of responsibility can be seen as the necessary consequence of the claims for realizing one's freedom and rights.

Here the great similarities between Jonas and Schumacher are to be found. They both indicate that the scale and possible consequences of human activity – which are so evident within the economic domain – are in fact something that the past generations did not face and thus twentieth- and twenty-first century mankind is not prepared to deal with. They both put stress on the need to predict and foresee the possible consequences of human decisions and only then the choice can be made. What may be different in their approaches is a matter of emphasis: Jonas puts stress on the transformation of ethics in order to embrace and tackle new issues, while Schumacher believes that prudence and moderation are the virtues necessary in the face of changing reality. The first 'argues that the nature of human action has changed so dramatically in our times that this changed nature of human action calls for a radical change in ethics as well' (Zsolnai 2000: 74), while the latter states that 'only on the basis of this magnanimous kind of prudence we can achieve justice, fortitude and *temperantia*, which means knowing when enough is enough. [...] What, therefore, could be of greater importance today than the study and cultivation of prudence, which would almost inevitably lead to a real understanding of the three other cardinal virtues, all of which are indispensable for the survival of civilization?' (Schumacher 1993: 251).

In this chapter special emphasis is put on responsibility in the sphere of economic activity and the unique role that the family plays in the development of this attribute. It is also useful to describe the family contribution to the functioning of this domain in general.

3   Family and Economy

> I was brought up on an interpretation of history which suggested that in the beginning was the family; then families got together and formed tribes; then a number of tribes formed a nation; then a number of nations formed a 'Union' or 'United States' of this or that [...].
>
> — SCHUMACHER 1993: 47

When it comes to the reason why it is necessary to underline the extraordinary role that a family plays in the functioning of any economic system one has to start by seeing the family as *conditio sine qua non* of society. The understanding of a family as 'a social unit consisting of parents and the children they rear' (Neufeldt & Guralnik 1991: 489), means that the society develops through the development of the family. Firstly, this means that a family as a sphere of procreation is the only place where new members of the society are born. Secondly, it is there that they are socialized. As Jennifer Roback Morse writes, 'the family performs a crucial and irreplaceable social function. Inside a family, helpless babies are transformed from self-centered bundles of impulses, desires, and emotions to fully socialized adults. The family teaches trust, cooperation, and self-restraint. The family is uniquely situated to teach these skills because people instill these qualities in their children as a side effect of loving them' (Roback Morse 2001: 5).

Before I turn to other issues, I want to explain why I think that defining the family in the way I do is crucial. First of all my definition of 'family' is conventional because 'family' is a natural group. Although – and I am aware of it – there are different theoretical perspectives which deny the universal nature of family, we find confirmation of this fact in many sources. As we read in the Article 16, paragraph 3 of the Universal Declaration of Human Rights, 'The family is the natural and fundamental group unit of society and is entitled to protection by society and the state'. This statement expresses the fact that it is fundamental within social and cultural identity of the West. This is also reflected in a large body of knowledge from different disciplines (Zimmermann 2008: 1; Malinowski 1913: 299, 303–4; Firth & Djamour 1956).

There is one more – methodological – reason why a clear definition of 'family' is necessary. If one decides to call 'families' those groups that do not consist of parents and their children, then in my opinion one blurs or distorts the meaning of the term. In consequence this must cause problems for the research that is done in this field. If many different realities were called a 'family', in the end it would be problematic to know what one exactly talks about. What's more, there is a quite useful term – 'quasi-familial groups' – that serves well to describe what is not a family, but somehow resembles this group or fulfils similar functions.

Coming back to our point, it is also important to look at the family from the perspective of the economic function that it has performed in societies throughout the ages. In fact, families can be seen historically as the basic institution of economic development. This is reflected in the origins of the word 'economy' which is derived from the Greek terms *oikos* (οἶκος), which means 'house', and *nomos* (νομος), which means 'law', 'rule'. It is reasonable then to ask about this relation between economy and family today. In different parts of the world – depending on the character of the transformations and their pace – the family either is still the basic economic unit or it is no longer perceived as such. When we look at the Western culture, we see that the family is not understood as an economic unit anymore. Unfortunately, as a result of this change the family seems to be no longer treated as an institution which is economically important. Indeed, this opinion has changed slightly in recent years thanks to the researchers from the field defined as economics of the family, with the contributions of such authors as Becker, Schultz, Lecaillon, Ermisch and Pollak. The following fragment from Becker's *Treatise on the Family* is a good example of how family and economy are related:

> The family in the Western world has been radically altered – some claim almost destroyed – by events of the last three decades. The rapid growth in divorce rates has greatly increased the number of households headed by women and the number of children growing up in households with only one parent. The large increase in labor force participation of married woman, including mothers with young children, has reduced the contact between children and their mothers and contributed to the conflict between the sexes in employment as well as in marriage. The rapid decline in birth rates has reduced family size and helped cause the increased rates of divorce and labor force participation of married woman. Conversely, expanded divorce and labor force participation have reduced the desire to have large families. (Becker 1993: 1)

Although economics of the family lays stress on the importance of family life in relation to the economic system, its approach is limited to the economic perspective and that means that it is unable to address all the crucial issues fully.

Another thing that can be discussed in the context of the family's influence on the economy is the issue of social security systems. This is mainly related to the pension that people get when they retire. Commonly, there are two alternative sources of pension proposed: first is the public sector, and second the private sector. In different countries there are different possibilities and combinations of these two sources available to choose from. In fact, there is a mistake underlying this discussion. The only real source of the pension system is the family, since public or private sectors are nothing more but a means of redistribution of the wealth produced by the workers and consumers born and raised in families. It may sound surprising, but if one thinks about it, the real relation is to be found there. To help analyse this issue, it is worth observing the demographic decline in many countries which points at this problem and puts in doubt the future existence of contemporary pension systems. One of the aspects of this issue is the question of intergenerational responsibility, which is also noticed by Becker when he writes that 'conflict between generations has become more open, and today's parents are less confident than those of earlier years that they can guide the behaviour of their children' (Becker 1993: 1). It means that contemporary man is not sure about the direction he should follow, so in consequence how can he know what advice he should give to his children? This touches the real problem of the responsibility for the generations that are to come and is connected – among other things – with the problem of pensions that has been discussed already. In this context Schumacher's intuition about permanence as the central concept of wisdom necessary for an economic perspective is accurate. This means, firstly, the reduction of needs, and secondly the 'new orientation of science and technology towards the organic, the gentle, the non-violent, the elegant and beautiful' (Schumacher 1993: 20).

Here one can ask how a reorientation of the whole economy can be achieved. If this is to happen, all the economic actors need to be transformed. We can wonder whether they are exactly as the dominating economic paradigm tells us, or if, while they enter the economic domain, they 'take with them' only the *homo oeconomicus* part of their personality. I would rather opt for the second possibility. This means that one part of a person – let us call him the *homo familiaris* – stays at home while at the same time the second part – which is the *homo oeconomicus* – goes to work or shopping. In consequence, a large part of the human personality, his attitudes and actions is absent or invisible in the market sphere, because it stays outside of it or is not appreciated there. The shortest explanation of this fact that Schumacher would give is probably the statement: 'it's uneconomic' (Schumacher 1993: 27–30).

The fact that the existence and proper functioning of the economic system depends to a large extent on socio-cultural institutions and elements is nowadays rarely questioned. It means that certain attributes of human actors necessary as catalysts of market processes – among which we find responsibility – cannot be produced by the market itself. This is clearly expressed by Buttiglione, who writes: 'Free market society needs not only consumers but also responsible individuals, capable of hard work and creative action. Strong, responsible, and reliable individuals are not produced, for example by sexual revolution, but rather are born and educated in morally healthy families' (Buttiglione 2000: 27).

This can be followed by the – in its manner strict – argument of Schumacher, who describes market in its current shape as the sphere where responsibility is not likely to develop: 'The market therefore represents only the surface of society and its significance relates to the momentary situation as it exists there and then. There is no probing into the depths of things, into the natural or social facts that lie behind them. In a sense, the market is the institutionalisation of individualism and non-responsibility. Neither buyer nor seller is responsible for anything but himself' (Schumacher 1993: 29).

In this fragment responsibility is described as if it were a 'fuel' that determines and supports the existence of the economic system. If the market is seen as the close-to-surface sphere of human action, then family can be seen as the deeper layer of society, where the 'fuel' of responsibility comes from. It harmonizes with the conviction that was expressed before, that the family can be seen as the basic source of economic development of society. What's more, when Schumacher discusses the problem of capitals and discusses human substance as one of them (Schumacher 1993: 8), we can understand it as the emphasis put on the family way of life as the fundamental part of human nature. It corresponds with concepts of 'human capital' and 'social capital' which were developed sometime around the years when Schumacher was working on *Small is Beautiful*. These theories confirm Schumacher's conviction that it is human beings and their different abilities that are the foundation of any development. If this is the fact, then it must be discussed if the exploitation of family in such shape as it is observed today should not be alarming. If there is nothing surprising these days in the respect and care for animals and plants, then it should be even more justified to call for human ecology. This is present in Jonas' reflection, when he writes that an imperative responding to the new type of human action might run thus: 'Act so that the effects of your action are compatible with the permanence of genuine human life'. Or expressed negatively: 'Act so that the effects of your action are not destructive of the future possibility of such life'. Or simply: 'Do not compromise the conditions for an indefinite continuation of humanity on earth'. Or, again turned positive: 'In your present choices, include the future wholeness of man among the objects of your will' (Jonas 1984: 11). When it comes to Schumacher, we can find a similar approach in his work. He pointed out that 'there is overwhelming evidence that the great self-balancing system of nature is becoming increasingly unbalanced in particular respects and at specific points' (Schumacher 1993: 17). When we recall the fact of the natural dimension of human procreation and family role, we can agree that the fertility transition that transforms seriously our current context is a proof of the lack of balance that Schumacher talked about.

This means that if the economy is expected to serve real development of a man, it has to stop ignoring man's dependence on the natural world (Schumacher 1993: 29), especially in the context of different experiments – presented often as market choices – in the field of human procreation and family life as well, which put these essential aspects of our human nature at risk.

4 Family and Responsibility Development

> It is the distinction between natural responsibility, where the immanent 'ought-to-be' of the object claims its agent *a priori* and quite unilaterally, and contracted or appointed responsibility, which is conditional *a posteriori* upon the fact and the terms of the relationship actually entered into. In the latter case, even the requisite power, without which there can be no responsibility, is typically generated by the contract itself together with the duty; in the natural case, it is there to begin with and underlies the object's sovereign claim on it. Evidently, in moral (as distinct from legal) status, the natural is the stronger, if less defined, sort of responsibility, and what is more, it is the original from which any other responsibility ultimately derives its more or less contingent validity. This is to say, if there were no responsibility 'by nature' there could be none 'by contract'.
> — JONAS 1984: 95

In this section some aspects of the contribution of the family to the existence and functioning of the market are discussed. In the above fragment we see how Jonas describes different kinds of responsibility and their hierarchy. He distinguishes between natural and contractual responsibility, and shows that the first is prior to the second. In the context of our analysis it is necessary to point out that while the family is the sphere where natural responsibility dominates, the market operates mainly by contractual responsibility. If then – according to Jonas – contractual responsibility builds on natural responsibility – this means that the family is the real foundation of the market, and consequently, the well-being of the family is the precondition of the market's well-being.

The most evident situation which points at the necessity of responsibility is the child-parent relation, which is defined by Jonas as the archetype of the responsibility (Jonas 1984). The family experience tells us that responsibility is not fully embraced and understood if seen only from an individual perspective, because responsibility can be described as the bond that reaches beyond an individual. The responsibility of one person overlaps that of another person and vice versa. Here we encounter an important aspect of responsibility, which is asymmetry. It deals with the question if responsible relations are in force when there is no equivalence between persons. Our human nature tells us that the most important relations in human life in fact are not symmetric. The facts of conception and birth, which can be seen as a kind of breakthrough in a human person's lifetime, are in fact situations where symmetry cannot be found, and if so, responsibility is indispensable. Here it is evident that the natural helplessness of a baby is a call for response, and it is responsibility that is the adequate answer. The asymmetry between parents and children is a situation that calls for such kind of reciprocity that would reflect the uneven nature of family relations. In this context responsibility appears to be a non-reciprocal duty to support and protect other human beings (Jonas 1984: 38–9).

That is why it is worthwhile to stress the procreational role of the family, which was mentioned earlier as the condition of the development of a society, because it is in this continuous process of transmission of life where the responsibility within the society is reproduced over and over. If this process is interrupted it must influence the potential of responsibility that is available in society. This means that if married couples do not undertake their responsibility of conceiving and raising children, not only the future of the economic system but of society as a whole is put at risk.

In this context it is worth to show how Schumacher understood the position of the family. Firstly, it can be assumed that he saw it as an integral part of social structure, which in his opinion was endangered by degradation by improper use of science and technology (Schumacher 1993: 20). This can be supplemented by the notion of 'psychological structures', which according to Schumacher are of great importance. He illustrates this problem by the transmission of knowledge and skills within the parent-child relation and warns that economic transformation and development cannot ignore these vulnerable 'psychological structures'. This is of great importance if such attributes necessary for economic activity as 'social cohesion, cooperation, mutual respect, and above all self-respect, courage in the face of adversity, and the ability to bear hardship' (Schumacher 1993: 159) are to remain present.

The last aspect of the development of responsibility within the family is connected with the natural orientation towards setting limits on individual needs and wants of the family members. This can be called the tension between hedonism and self-limitation (Pearce 2006: 297). It means that every-day family life offers challenges to personal formation. Every member of the family does not cease to be an individual, but his or her individualism is constantly confronted with individual needs and wants of others and the common good of the family as well. This process aims at preparing a person to live in a larger society with other people. An important byproduct of this formation and socialization is the development of the awareness of responsibility for the impact of one's individual choices on other people, and it should gradually lead to practical implementation of a responsible attitude towards one's own life and the lives of other people.

5 Conclusion

Since Schumacher's time we have seen the increasing atomization of society in the direction of self-centered individualism. The so-called 'rights' of the individual have trampled on the rights of the weak and defenseless. In the past thirty years we have also seen a concerted attack on the family itself and on the traditional understanding of marriage. Schumacher would have been horrified by these developments. He understood that families form the smallest and most beautiful part of any healthy society – that they are, in fact, the building blocks upon which all healthy societies are erected. Take away the family from the heart of society and you are left with a heartless hedonism. And since hedonism is selfishness without limits, it is the very antithesis of the self-limitation necessary for the restoration of economic and political sanity. In short, small is still beautiful because families still matter!

— PEARCE 2006: XVI

> [...] to be wise in the fullest sense of the term one has to be so in regard to
> one's personal life (one's work, one's leisure), family, friends, environment,
> and community, whether local, national or international.
>
> — MOSS 2011: 23

In this paper an attempt was made to discuss the role that the family plays in the functioning of economic systems. As our discussion made clear – and this has to be underlined – it is the family where trust, the ability to co-operate, self-restraint and responsibility are developed. As Roback Morse writes, 'contracts and free political institutions, the foundations of a free society, require these attributes that only families can inculcate. Without loving families, no society can long govern itself' (Roback Morse 2001: 5).

Although Schumacher did not concentrate on the family, his contribution can serve well to improve our understanding of the role that this institution plays in the well-being of a society. This is evident when he discusses our attitude towards the natural world and the dilemmas of scale and calls for a revision of the relation between individually oriented economics and real human development. Schumacher's important observations are still helpful because today we discuss the proper shape of our societies and economic systems. When he wrote that 'in the market place, for practical reasons, innumerable qualitative distinctions which are of vital importance for man and society are suppressed; they are not allowed to surface' (Schumacher 1993: 30), he invites us to engage in and take responsibility for transforming the dominant ways of performing economic activities, which in their deepest sense are human and social activities.

The role that the economic system can play in supporting the well-functioning family – which can be seen also as the source of human attributes described as 'soft skills' that are indispensable for economic prosperity – is crucial. It means that the awareness of the impact that the family has on the economy can serve as a useful criterion for making economic choices.

A responsible approach to economic actors and organizations in the context of the family in fact should be seen as a rational choice. If the market is designed and coordinated in such a way that it rewards family-supportive products, services and behaviors, then this proves that it operates in a long-term perspective that is oriented towards permanence.

To conclude, it can be said that a responsible economy should take care of the sources it builds and depends on. If the family is the basic source of existence of the economic system, then the economy should responsibly care for the family. If the existence of responsible actors in the economic system depends on the family, then the first responsibility of the economy is to serve the development of a person and the family he or she lives in and for. In the end, it is worth coming back to Schumacher's idea that small is beautiful. This is so – according to him – because man is small (Schumacher 1993: 131, 57). Family life then is a continuous experience of this actual size of man: from the day of his birth to the day of his death – although in a different way – man relies on responsible love of others and gradually learns to love them responsibly through different – also economic – activities.

References

Becker, G.S. (1993). *Treatise on the Family.* Cambridge & London: Harvard University Press.

Buttiglione, R. (2000). 'Behind Centesimus Annus'. In M. Novak, W. Brailsford and C. Heesters (eds), *A Free Society Reader.* New York: Lexington Books.

Filek, J. (2003). *Filozofia odpowiedzialności XX wieku.* Kraków: Znak.

Firth, R.W. and Djamour, J. (1956). 'Kinship in South Borough'. In R.W. Firth (ed.), *Two Studies of Kinship in London.* London: Athlone Press.

Jonas, H. (1984). *The Imperative of Responsibility; In Search of an Ethics for the Technological Age.* Chicago & London: University of Chicago Press.

Malinowski, B. (1913). *The Family Among the Australian Aborigines.* London: University of London Press.

Marx, R. (2009). *Kapital,* transl. J. Serafin CSsR. Kraków: Homo Dei.

Moss, W.G. 'The Wisdom of E.F. Schumacher', <http://www.wisdompage.com/SchumacherEssay.pdf> accessed 28 May 2011.

Neufeldt, V. & Guralnik, D.B. (eds) (1991). *Webster's New Word Dictionary of American English.* New York: Prentice Hall.

Pearce, J. (2006). *Small is Still Beautiful: (Economics as if Families Mattered).* Wilmington: ISI Books.

Roback Morse, J. (2001). *Love & Economics: Why the Laissez-Faire Family Doesn't Work*. Dallas: Spence Publishing Company.

Schumacher, E.F. (1979). *Good Work*. New York: Harper & Row.

Schumacher, E.F. (1993). *Small is Beautiful. A Study of Economics as if People Mattered*. London: Vintage Books.

Zimmerman, C.C. (2008). *Family and Civilization*. Wilmington: ISI Books.

Zsolnai, L. (2001). 'The Idea of Responsibility', <http://www.lib.uni-corvinus.hu/gt/2000-4/zsolnai.pdf> accessed 26 May 2011.

LUDO ABICHT
UNIVERSITY OF ANTWERP

12 Who Really Needs Frugality?

1 Introduction

In *A Guide for (to, of) the Perplexed (Moreh nevukhim)* the medieval Spanish medical doctor, theologian and philosopher Moses ben Maimon (Maimonides, 1135–1204) showed the 'perplexed' Jews of his time how modern, i.e. Aristotelian science and logic could and should be reconciled with their traditional Talmudic and Kabbalistic wisdom. Thus he, and some of his great Muslim colleagues, not only paved the way for the thirteenth-century synthesis by Thomas Aquinas, but also prepared the foundations for what a few centuries later would be known as the Renaissance and, from there, Modernity. And though there is neither circumstantial nor textual evidence to suggest that Ernst Schumacher consciously referred to Maimonides by calling his 1977 essay *A Guide for the Perplexed*, in many ways it is an uncanny coincidence. Maimonides and his followers had defended the autonomy of logic and science, without abandoning their religious worldview. Schumacher, writing about a century after the triumph of positivism, of course doesn't reject science, but warns against its hegemony and usurpation of all other paths to knowledge. To a secular humanist and materialist his attack on 'materialistic science' is a challenge, for while accepting the bulk of his criticisms, I maintain that there is room for a secular, atheistic approach to the central problems he raises in most of his work. In this paper I've attempted to deal with 'frugality' from a perspective that is avowedly different from that of Schumacher, though demonstrably not so different in its outcome.

Whenever my four-year-old granddaughter noticed a toy or other colourful object in a supermarket, she would grab it from the shelf and put it in the shopping cart. 'Why do you take it?' – 'Because I want it'. – 'But why do you want it?' – 'Because I need it!'. Occasionally she would reverse the order: 'I need it because I want it'. It's an obviously childish but clever ploy: if I can convince the grownups that I really *really* need this, they'll understand. But is our adult behaviour that much different? Aren't we as well convinced, or don't we convince ourselves that we want something (and take it if we can) legitimately, simply because we perceive a strong need to possess it? And isn't this conviction constantly reinforced by our observation of the way most of the others, be they individuals, corporations, political parties or governments, do in fact behave? Within the limits of the law if possible, outside of them if and when we can get away with it. Why aren't we surprised when we are informed by the evening news that in the wake of some major natural disaster single citizens and entire mobs have already started looting houses and shops, way before the last wounded victims have been rescued from the mud or the rubble? One of the indelible childhood memories that made me wonder about human nature was the looting that took place in my neighborhood in September 1944, in the political and social vacuum between the chaotic flight of the last German soldiers and the arrival of our Canadian liberators. Ordinary citizens were literally fighting in the streets over boxes with coat hangers and picture frames stolen from an abandoned store. No doubt they wanted these rather ludicrous objects very strongly and were ready to hurt their competitors, but even then I doubted they really needed them. I would have dismissed this display of public frenzy more easily, if I had not found out that similar scenes were taking place all over town. Possibly they did not want these things as much as they wanted the others *not* to have them. Slavoj Žižek (2008) refers in this respect to a Slovene peasant tale, in which a peasant is given a choice by a good witch. She will either give him one cow and two to his neighbor, or she will take away one of his cows and two from his neighbor. Without any hesitation the peasant chooses the second option. Thus we seem to be willing to contain our greed and curtail our needs, if this means that other people will suffer more as a result of our sacrifice. Such a perverted form of voluntary 'frugality' is certainly not unusual among children and adults, but it has everything to do with *ressentiment*, a common but forceful human impulse, rather than with a genuine search for a more noble, spiritual life or a more equitable world.

2   What Are Human Needs For?

Within the dominant Western, Judeo-Christian and humanistic discourse, however, frugality is not defined as an expression of this *ressentiment*, but as a positive virtue inherent in the care-for-oneself, the *epimeleia* of Socrates and the Stoics, and the care for the others, as in the Jewish *tsedeka*, a combination of both justice and charity, the Christian *caritas* and the modern concept of *solidarity*. In order to develop their own potential and at the same time function as useful members of a community, people are supposed to transcend the fulfilment of their immediate needs and, if necessary, suppress or transform them. Even while our own postmodern society appears to be dominated by an unrelenting search for instant hedonistic gratification and so-called 'leadership status', we are still repeating the ideological phrases of the past In his insightful analysis of fascism Wilhelm Reich (1969) demonstrated that ideologies often survive for decades and ages the historic circumstances that inspired them. This might explain the discrepancy between the real forces at work in our globalized consumer society and the way the representatives of our political, cultural and even economic institutions are still paying lip service to the values and norms of the past. This survival of the best and the brightest (ideas) in fact enables us to develop an adequate criticism of the really existing rat race and productivism of our present-day society. In order to do this adequately, however, we owe it to ourselves and the future generations to be unambiguous and candid. This means that we cannot simply repeat the noble mantras of the Christian or the Enlightenment variety, lest we appear ignorant or hypocritical, for so much has gone wrong in the name of these lofty ideals that we cannot simply ignore it. Furthermore, since time is running out fast, we can no longer afford any misunderstandings or ambiguities which might delay action and postpone the necessary confrontation with the real and imminent social, economic and ecological dangers threatening all of us. So what do we mean when we say that the concept of frugality is intrinsically linked with that of 'needs'? Of course we realize that those needs are neither universal nor unchanging, but are clearly shaped and to a large extent determined by the social and historical circumstances. Thus I remember several frustrating discussions between proponents of special social and educational measures for non-white minorities in the US, who advocated such governmental programs as *Headstart* and *Affirmative Action*, and their opponents who kept comparing the objective social status of e.g. American blacks with that of black people in Sub-Saharan Africa. The problem was that the black residents of an American urban ghetto rightly compared their situation with that of their white fellow citizens in the same democratic and prosperous state. They indeed 'needed' more than e.g. the inhabitants of a poor neighbourhood in Dar-Es-Salaam. One can argue that all human beings need (or are entitled to) 'life, liberty and the pursuit of happiness', but these wonderful terms ought to be properly explicated, that is contextualized.

In a culture that has thoroughly been informed by both Platonic, neo-Platonic and Christian metaphysics it is nearly impossible to escape from the dualism that has characterized our commonwealth from the onset of the Middle Ages. We all agree that there are material as well as spiritual needs: to survive physically is not the same as to satiate one's 'hunger' for knowledge, culture and the arts, not to mention philosophy, religion and mysticism. But not unlike the black silk sash that separates the 'higher' parts of a pious Hassidic Jew's body from the 'lower' parts, and we're not just talking about the location here, we tend to sharply distinguish between so-called higher and lower needs. Those individuals who give priority to their 'higher', spiritual needs are considered superior to the ones who restrict themselves to their mere material needs. This Platonic heritage is far from innocuous, for this dualistic approach tends to distort both categories of needs. As a result, material needs are looked upon as rather primitive and animalistic – food, sleep, shelter, safety and sex – whereas the spiritual needs distinguish us from those with less culture and refinement. In this essay I propose a different approach, which should less disparage the material needs and less exalt the spiritual ones. As to a general definition of needs, we can start with a quote from Roger Scruton (1982): 'Needs form a special class of interests. I have an interest in anything that I would, on rational consideration, desire, but not every such thing is necessary to me. I need only that without which I would cease to exist or cease to flourish in accordance with the norms of my nature'. He then expands this definition with the notions of artificial and relative needs, two concepts that will no doubt play a role in the discussion about the limits of frugality. Before we proceed, however, I ought to clarify why I opted for a 'materialistic approach' to the problem. Against metaphysical idealism, the materialism proposed here posits the primacy of matter over spirit, but rejects the extreme Enlightenment definition of matter as the only thing in existence, thus reducing mental processes to material ones. According to Ernst Bloch (1972) 'The new materialism would be one that would not only understand man as a question and the world as the pending answer, but above all also the world as a question and man as a pending answer'. This concept of matter, out of which the spirit evolved, is not static but dynamic and culminates in the transformation of the world by man and the permanent development of humanity. It is neither dualistic nor 'vulgarly' materialistic, but monistic (there is only one reality) and open toward a future which only humans can bring about. Human beings are neither totally determined by their genetic or social structure to realize such a future, nor can they escape matter altogether by relocating the fulfilment of these goals to a non-material supernatural reality or an afterlife. The existence or non-existence of such a reality cannot be proved, that is to say verified or falsified scientifically, which entails that such a materialistic (and thus atheistic) worldview is as much the outcome of a choice as is religious faith. This is not a question of polemics, but an invitation to an open dialogue between the proponents of either viewpoint, provided both sides accept the same scientific criteria and are self-critical enough to acknowledge the gaps and shortcomings of their own theories.

As will be demonstrated, such a materialistic approach will by no means ignore or even belittle the spiritual needs, but it will proceed from the bottom up, for to speak of these 'higher needs' before we have properly addressed the material needs of a very large percentage of humanity may very well appeal to people whose material survival and in many cases comfort and luxury have been secured for generations, be it in a neo-liberal or in a social-democratic society, but it once again leaves those barely surviving in the lower social strata behind. After the Second World War the German philosopher Max Horkheimer wrote: 'One cannot seriously speak of fascism without mentioning capitalism'. In the same vein one might say: 'To speak about the rather abstract idea of frugality without mentioning the very concrete realities of poverty and destitution is intellectually and ethically dishonest'.

3   Agnes Heller and the Marxist Theory of Needs

During the 1970s a remarkable group of Hungarian social philosophers, most of them former students of the somewhat unorthodox Marxist Georges Lukács, started to publish insightful and critical essays and books on e.g. ontology (György Markus), literature (Ferenc Feher), epistemology (Mihaly Vajda), ethics and social theory (Agnes Heller), in which they not only incorporated their critique of the official Party doctrine, but related works of their contemporary colleagues in the West as well and, most importantly, their renewed understanding of social *praxis* in a country that had been traumatized by the upheavals of 1956. The bitter polemics with the authorities of those days are definitely over, and so is the socialist experiment their country had been coerced into after the Second World War, but their reflections remain nevertheless very useful, since they illustrated almost *e contrario* how little Eastern European 'really existing socialism' had in common with the ideas of Marx and Lukács, especially in regard to genuine human needs. Oh yes, there certainly was more frugality, or rather shabbiness, in their society than in the West, but that made the slightly idealized decadent Western luxury all the more attractive to the majority of the citizens: 'if we only were so lucky to experience your particular brand of capitalist exploitation!' The members of the so-called Budapest School, on the contrary, were aware of the shortcomings in both competing systems and used this knowledge to pay renewed attention to key Lukácsian categories such as *reification* and, more generally, what they called 'the restructuring of everyday life'. Since they had to constantly struggle against the attempts of petty party officials to denounce and persecute them as bourgeois and even subversive intellectuals, many of them were forced into exile, a move that eventually led to the demise of the Budapest School. Ten years later, the collapse of the Eastern European regimes almost obliterated their important contributions to philosophy and social theory. In the light of the ongoing discussions about frugality and human needs particularly the work of Agnes Heller cannot be ignored. In 1976 she published *The Theory of Need in Marx*, a compact essay in which she not only elaborated the theoretical categories of Lukács, but developed a new interpretation of the social philosophy of Marx, based primarily upon such key texts as *Die Frühschriften* and *Grundrisse der Kritik der politischen Oekonomie*. The bulk of Marx' early writings, from 1843 to 1848, had been published as late as 1932 and the *Grundrisse*, written in 1857–8, now regarded as one of his major programmatic texts, were not available in print until 1953. It is interesting to note, although not really surprising, that the ideologues and organic intellectuals of the leading Marxist regimes largely ignored the message of these works, as it contradicted their dogmatic approach of 'Marxism' to an embarrassing degree and turned into a powerful weapon against their usurpation of power in the name of socialism and democracy. Their Western counterparts, the apologetic academics and editorialists of the capitalist world system, were just as little interested in a discussion that could put Marx back on the intellectual agenda. Therefore these writings were explored and cherished by only a handful of independent leftist thinkers in East and West, from Erich Fromm to Agnes Heller.

In dealing with the 'quality of everyday life', Heller starts out from the following observation: 'Marx rejects a society that is based upon private ownership from the viewpoint of the value of "rich human needs". Such a society is unable to transform "elementary needs" into "rich human demands", regardless of the material wealth it produces'. Here some remarks are in order:

First, these 'elementary' or natural needs are, of course, nothing but the concept of a 'lower limit', beyond which mere survival can no longer be guaranteed. She therefore refuses to call them 'natural needs', but rather *the existential boundary of the satisfaction of our needs*. It is furthermore significant that 'riches' is defined here in non-material terms, or at least as a combination of both material and spiritual needs: only a person who is stimulated by these needs may be called 'rich'. Neither King Midas with all his sterile and potentially lethal gold, but Socrates who at least 'knew that he didn't know a thing' and hence could embark upon a journey to uncover the hidden truth of reality, nor a frustrated Tantalus condemned to always desiring while never being satisfied, but rather Sisyphus, surely in the reinterpretation by Camus, a convicted man who succeeds in taking control of his own absurd destiny. And thirdly, we should always be aware of the difference between 'private' and 'individual' property: in a future society, once we have been able to overcome the alienation of the present one, human needs and faculties will have a *qualitative* nature, and that which is qualitative can only be 'exchanged' for something qualitative, that is to say something possessing the same quality. This means the *positive suppression of private property* and the emergence of *the world of individual property*. We have to keep in mind that 'private property' (of the means of production) is the very definition of the existing capitalist system, much more than the misleading concept of a 'free market', whereas 'individual property' has to be situated in a post-capitalist, one could say 'concrete utopian' society that has not yet been realized.

Redirecting her attention to the various 'needs' in our present society, Heller agrees with Marx that the unrelenting extension of products and needs turn us into *a creative and always calculating slave of inhuman, sophisticated, imaginary desires that are contrary to nature*. There is in fact no limit to the amount of material goods and services we might want to possess, as our desire will never be satisfied. The tragedy is that for that reason we become unable to develop new and varied needs of a different quality. This dependency truly alienates us from our true human nature, as it amounts to 'the quantification of that which can never be quantified', such as esthetic pleasure, friendship, love and disinterested social interaction in which the relationships between people, once the basic needs of all the members of a society have been taken care of, vastly transcend the relationships between things. As this quantification (and alienation) cannot be separated from the existing industrial and economic system, a radical critique of that system ought to be developed. This critique is based upon the notion of *radical needs*, meaning needs that the present system cannot but produce, but which it cannot possibly satisfy for a majority of the people without destroying itself. Although Heller doesn't mention it, this situation can be compared to the radical needs a colonial system produces in the hearts and minds of its subjects, e.g. the much vaunted values of Western modernity, the realization of which will inevitably lead to a revolt by their educated subjects against colonial oppression and injustice and eventually destroy it. From Marx' historical vantage point, the carrier of these radical values and thus the agent of radical change could only be the newly emerging industrial working class. For Heller, writing in a drastically (yet not fundamentally) altered society, this is no longer the case, but the notion of radical needs has not in the least been invalidated.

As capitalist production and productivity keep expanding, this could lead in the future to a point of 'saturation', a situation in which the human needs could, but will not automatically lead to a decreasing orientation toward material consumer goods. This 'restructuring of the needs', as Heller calls it, would amount to a relative reduction of material needs and the expansion of non-material, e.g. social, esthetic, affective and spiritual needs that would contribute to true 'human riches', for 'the real human riches is man himself'. Hardly anybody, let alone a democratic humanist, would disagree that the full development of each and everyone's human potential ought to be the main goal of any just society. Heller is no exception, but she links this concept to one of the key formulas in Marx' major works, from *Grundrisse* to *Capital III*: 'the essence of a capitalist society doesn't reside at all in the [appropriation of] extra labour [*Mehrarbeit*], but in the conversion of this extra work into capital'. In other words: as long as the existing system enables the economic decision makers to convert this extra labour into investment or, increasingly, financial capital, all attempts at creating new forms of ethically or ecologically responsible forms of capitalism are doomed to remain marginal, whatever the good intentions. There is absolutely no structural guarantee that the wealth created by this extra labour will be used to enhance true human riches for the vast majority of the world's population.

This development of human riches can only be realized within the 'reign of freedom', but this realm can only be expanded upon the foundations of the 'reign of necessity'. Both realms are intrinsically linked, for if we neglect the sphere of material production, our entire economic, social and political system will collapse. If, however, we remain within the logic of this realm of necessity, we condemn ourselves to an indefinite future of quantitative accumulation, adequately depicted as the unrelenting spiral of Science, Technology and Capital that has shaped the West and increasingly the rest of the world up to this day. In order to overcome this spiral of continuous alienation, Heller proposes to complete and correct Friedrich Engels' characterization of socialism as 'the journey from a utopian to a scientific approach' by once again incorporating concrete utopianism as a norm that most probably will never be fully attained, but should serve as a standard measure 'that expresses the highest aspirations of mature humanity which, as a tendency, are part of our very being'.

4   Genuine Frugality Can Only Be Universal

One of the most compelling reasons to promote frugality is the ecological concern for 'the preservation of the planet'. If we want to 'save the earth', it is argued, we had better change our insanely consuming way of life before it is too late. This sounds reasonable, but from a purely scientific viewpoint it is not. Leading natural scientists such as the late American paleontologist Stephen Jay Gould (1989 et al.) and the French geneticist Albert Jacquard (2009) remind us, that it is not so much (or in fact not at all) 'the planet' that is endangered, but human life on earth. This is an important distinction, for it takes away the aura of pure selflessness from so-called eco-centrists and other opponents of Christian and humanistic anthropo-centrism: what really is at stake is our survival as the latest and most predatory species on a planet that in all probability will continue its course for another four billion years, long after we have managed to extinguish ourselves. This long-term scientific prediction, while it may teach us some modesty about our self-image as kings of the universe, doesn't in the least diminish our responsibility toward ourselves and mankind in general, on the contrary, for we stand before crucial choices regarding the quality of human life and, to a certain extent, of the part of non-human life we do have a real impact upon.

In a similar way, when we talk about the need for a more frugal life, we ought to remember who 'we' really are and who will most likely benefit from a substantial increase in frugality. The answer to these questions is not difficult: as Westerners, 'we' are the heirs to those generations of Europeans and North-Americans who almost from the beginning of our civilization and especially since the development of our worldwide economic expansion in the sixteenth century have exploited the earth's resources and the majority of the non-Western populations in demonstrably careless and at times utterly greedy and cruel ways. Anybody even superficially familiar with the works of world historians such as Fernand Braudel (1967, 1979) or Immanuel Wallerstein (1974, 1980, 1989) is aware of this history that accompanied and to a large extent even enabled our fabulous economic, technological, scientific and political development. Thus when we finally, after the dire warnings by our own Romantic poets in the nineteenth century and the occasional protests by bewildered native Americans, Asians and Africans, have come to realize the damage we have done and still might do, we are struck by the dangers that are increasingly threatening our own well-being and even survival. *Nam tua res agitur*, as Horace rightly said. Once again, there is nothing wrong with this concern for our own quality of life, as long as we realize that we are not alone in this world. To put it differently: even though we know for sure that the adoption of frugality is bound to improve the lives of people in, say, a developing or impoverished country – if only by helping them to avoid making the mistakes our ancestors made in abusing natural resources or in becoming mindless and uncritical consumers – how do we propose to convince them? When we tell them that the acquisition of a comfortable amount of wealth and the lives of luxury that we enjoy in their eyes don't necessarily make us happy, will they not respond that they'd rather be overfed and unhappy than hungry and unhappy? By now these people have realized how much we have profited from their land and cheap labour, some of them may even quote to us the exact figures out of the college textbooks they share with us, and all of a sudden we seem to imply that they should never hope to reach our level of material wealth, for if they did, all the available resources would be depleted within a couple of decades? Basic mathematics are the same in Swaziland and Sweden: either we discover new raw materials or produce manufactured substitutes for them, and that is a question of time, money, scientific skills and an uncertain percentage of luck, or we have to deny the majority of the earth's growing population even the prospect of attaining the standard we have set for ourselves for over a century. And who is going to stop the populations of China and India from revolting against such arrogant callousness and injustice? From a historical and geo-political perspective there is more self-preservation than genuine altruism to be found in our present campaign for frugality, which is not to say that the same measures might not be beneficial to non-Westerners as well, as all of us are in fact in the same global predicament, though not necessarily in the same state of mind.

Once we have realized and admitted the ambiguity of this campaign for frugality, we may now return to the discussion on the continuity and discontinuity between 'natural' or material and 'higher' or spiritual needs. While it is true that exceptional individuals (e.g. Hindu yogis, Buddhist monks, philosophical Stoics and Cynics in ancient Greece and Rome, Christian ascetics, religious fundamentalists and social revolutionaries today) may be so utterly devoured by their commitment that they put almost all the emphasis on the fulfilment of the spiritual needs (from the achievement of inner enlightenment and the spreading of the Gospel to the furthering of the social and political liberation), this is certainly not the case for the majority of mankind. In most cases, the satisfaction of basic (material) human needs seems to create the conditions for the emergence of so-called higher or spiritual needs. Granted, it is a double-edged kind of argumentation, for it has been seen in the past that this satisfaction didn't open the gate to higher yearnings, e.g. for more democracy, political autonomy, access to culture or even plain freedom, but on the contrary lured people into the *false infinity* Kierkegaard discussed in *Either-Or* (1843), that is to say into the craving for more of the same quantitative goods, honours and services. Though I have never read any conclusive proof of

it, there exists a persistent rumor that in good old Christian rural societies the clergy opposed industrialization, lest the people became better off
materially and neglected the higher needs of their immortal souls. Even
if this is just an example of anti-clerical slander, it illustrates the dilemma
of spiritual reformers and activists very well: do we want to run the risk of
losing our followers once they have gotten a taste of the fleshpots of Egypt?
The answer to that question is a resounding 'yes!', for only people who
have had the choice between both aspirations can be authentic. Instead of
making a virtue out of necessity through self-denigration and self-denial,
they possess the genuine freedom to transcend the already achieved level
of material satisfaction and explore the world of spiritual needs. The choice
for individual and collective frugality can only be convincing, if it is made
consciously and out of free will. This means that its proponents should be
staunch advocates of social justice and of a society that at least strives to
provide enough material goods to all its citizens, 'to each according to his
or her needs'. Frugality is not a sober biological dinner party served to the
enlightened happy few in 'a villa in the middle of a jungle', to borrow and
mix two (in)famous twentieth-century metaphors.

5   No Frugality without Spirituality

It ought to be possible to elaborate a credible defense of spirituality without
reverting to the Platonic dichotomy of body and soul that has informed and
deformed Western civilization ever since the fifth century BCE. We know
how this distinction between the perfect world of forms (ideas) and our
miserable earthly reality has influenced Christianity and has resulted in a
disregard for our material, physical and sexual needs that goes way beyond
the teachings of Christ himself as they were recorded in the Gospels. In two
of his recent essays (2007 and 2009) the French philosopher and director
of *Le Monde des religions* Frédéric Lenoir has successfully deconstructed
this erroneous image of Jesus as an ascetic and other-worldly preacher, and
portrayed him rather as a philosopher in the sense of the radical definition

by Michel Foucault (2008), a *parrèsiastès* or 'speaker of the truth', someone who refuses to distinguish between his practice and his teachings, is not disdainful of the good material things, but willing to renounce all of this and even to risk his own life for the truth he holds. Fortunately, Lenoir is respectful enough of the historical record not to try to reconstruct the figure of Christ as a present-day secular humanist, even though the evidence for establishing a crucial link between the Gospels and the Enlightenment is compelling. His work, together with that of his colleague and contemporary French philosopher André Comte-Sponville (2006), casts a new and revealing light on our understanding of spirituality: is it possible to imagine a non-religious yet authentic form of spirituality or is this term inextricably linked to religion in the traditional sense, as the belief in a god and other forces that transcend our empirical and even scientific reality? Both fundamentalist believers and their secularist counterparts tend to agree that to speak of e.g. an 'atheistic spirituality' is blurring the lines, for faith is faith and atheism is atheism and the twain are never meant to meet. They are absolutely right, as long as the former espouse an integrist form of religion and the latter stick to positivism, but haven't we moved beyond these nineteenth-century positions by now? There is little doubt that spirituality has for the longest time been associated with religion, organized or other, but couldn't we reasonably argue that, once we have reached the limits of a materialist world view, we have no choice but to develop a genuine form of spirituality? Our predecessors were probably right in distrusting the preachers who told them during mass that 'man doesn't live by bread alone' and who afterwards enjoyed a substantial meal with a deeply Christian but, more important, filthy rich patron, but this doesn't mean that the statement itself was erroneous. On the contrary: it is only after we have done everything in our power to defend the access of, in principle, all the people in the world to food, clothing, shelter, healthcare and education that we may realize in all honesty how little we have achieved. At that point we no longer have an excuse for hiding behind our social responsibilities, but we have to face the urgency of the fulfilment of these spiritual needs. Spiritual yet immanent, such as the need for mutual trust and solidarity, the need to risk one's own well-being and security in order to support and comfort others, the need for beauty, silence and awe, for friendship and solitude, the need to be taken into account and consideration and, at other times, to be left alone. The need to grieve at the loss of somebody close to me and at the same time the need to accept the mystery of death without consolation or explanation, for there is none. All of these needs are immaterial (i.e. 'not material'; isn't it a little disturbing that it also means 'unimportant'?) and thus cannot be quantified. On the contrary: we have realized that the fulfilment of these spiritual needs can be severely impeded by too large an accumulation of quantifiable material goods and services, and this is exactly where frugality will play a central role, for without the adoption of a frugal lifestyle-cum-mentality these spiritual needs can neither be fully perceived nor attended to. *No authentic spirituality without frugality.* Cum-mentality, for frugality consists of much more than outward behaviour. It requires an altered state of mind, of inner detachment, lest we fall prey to arrogance and/or hypocrisy, the twin evils of a resentful asceticism. Thus internal as well as external frugality is the precondition for true spirituality, the receptiveness to and permanent expansion of the truly qualifiable 'needs' that constitute full human wealth. When this spirituality is lacking, human life, frugal or not, once again reverts to its mechanical and material foundations, the necessary but cold skeleton of which spirituality is the warm and living body: *no frugality without spirituality.*

References

Bloch, E. (1972). *Das Materialismusproblem, seine Geschichte und Substanz.* Frankfurt am Main: Suhrkamp Verlag.

Braudel, F. (1967). *Capitalism and Material Life 1400–1800.* New York: Harper & Row.

Braudel, F. (1985). *The Wheels of Commerce*, London: Fontana Paperbacks.

Braudel, F. (1984). *The Perspective of the World.* London: Fontana Paperbacks.

Comte-Sponville, A. (2006). *L'esprit de l'athéisme. Introduction à une spiritualité sans Dieu.* Paris: Albin Michel.

Foucault, M. (2008). *Le gouvernement de soi et des autres. Cours au Collège de France. 1982–1983.* Paris: Gallimard.

Foucault, M. (2009). *Le courage de la vérité. Le gouvernement de soi et des autres II. Cours au Collège de France. 1984.* Paris: Gallimard.

Gould, S.J. (1989). *Wonderful Life. The Burgess Shale and the Nature of History.* New York: W.W. Norton & Company.

Heller, A. (1978). *La théorie des besoins chez Marx.* Paris: 10–18.

Jacquard, A. (2009). *Le compte à rebours a-t-il commencé?* Paris: Stock.

Lenoir, F. (2007). *Le Christ philosophe.* Paris: Plon.

Lenoir, F. (2009). *Socrate, Jésus, Bouddha.* Paris: Fayard.

Marx, K. (n.d). *Grundrisse der Kritik der politischen Oekonomie.* Frankfurt am Main: Europäische Verlagsanstalt.

Marx, K. (1964). *Die Frühschriften.* Stuttgart: Alfred Kröner Verlag.

Reich, W. (1971). *The Mass Psychology of Fascism.* New York: Farrar, Straus & Giroux.

Schumacher, E.F. (2010, first edition 1973). *Small is Beautiful. Economics as if People Mattered.* London: Harper Perennial.

Schumacher, E.F. (2004, first edition 1977). *A Guide for the Perplexed.* London: Harper Perennial.

Scruton, R. (1983). *A Dictionary of Political Thought.* London: Pan Books.

Wallerstein, I. (1974). *The Modern World-System I. Capitalist Agriculture and the Origins of the European World-Economy in the Sixteenth Century.* San Diego: Academic Press.

Wallerstein, I. (1980). *The Modern World-System II. Mercantilism and the Consolidation of the European World-Economy. 1600–1750.* San Diego: Academic Press.

Wallerstein, I. (1989). *The Modern World-System III. The second Era of Great Expansion of the Capitalist World-Economy. 1300–1840s.* San Diego: Academic Press.

Žižek, S. (2008). *Violence. Six Sideways Reflexions.* New York: Picador.

13 Responsibility in Technology

Practical Action, formerly known as the Intermediate Technology Development Group, was founded by Fritz Schumacher in 1966 with a mission to help poor people in the developing world use technology to fight poverty and transform their lives. Today we work across ten countries in South Asia, Sub Saharan Africa and Latin America helping people improve food production, establish sustainable livelihoods and gain access to basic services such as water, sanitation, energy, housing and transport. Our work touches the lives of around 1 million people each year. Given my organisation's interests a lot of my remarks will relate to the technology in the context of the developing world, but I believe that the general principles I will discuss have wider relevance.

The pursuit of modernisation through the access to ever more sophisticated levels of technology has, together with economic growth, underpinned ideas of development for the last half century. In his book *Science & Technology for Development* the Edinburgh based academic Professor James Smith traces the way views of how this is supposed to happen have changed over the years. In the 1960s one school of thought saw development in terms of a linear process of modernisation, whereby countries pass through a five-stage model from 'traditional society' via industrialisation to an 'age of mass consumption' with 'widespread affluence, urbanisation and the consumption of consumer durables'. More recently the alternative idea of 'technological catch-up' whereby countries can develop their skills base and use new technologies to leapfrog stages of the linear model and catch up or even overtake richer 'leader' countries has been an idea 'that many countries aspire to' (Smith 2009: 14–17).

Schumacher challenged this received wisdom on growth and technological progress more than forty years ago, essentially on both environmental and human grounds and it's his views on technology that I would like to begin with.

Schumacher started off *Small is Beautiful* with the environmental argument that the traditional discourse on economics is fundamentally flawed because it is based on the idea that development relies on perpetual economic growth which, in turn, relies on ever increasing consumption of material resources. He introduced the concept of 'natural capital', talked about the finiteness of natural resources and used the field of energy to demonstrate how the consumption patterns of Europe and North America could never be replicated on a global scale. His conclusion was that humanity was on a collision course with nature and needed to take action quickly. Schumacher identified technology as one of the areas in which we needed to take action to avoid environmental catastrophe, on the grounds that 'the technology of mass production is inherently violent, ecologically damaging, and self-defeating in terms of non-renewable resources'. But Schumacher made it clear the he believed the prevailing model of development is not only inherently violent to the environment but also to the human spirit. In *Small is Beautiful* he argues that traditional economic thinking fails to get beyond its vast abstractions of: 'the national income, the rate of growth, capital/output ratio, input-output analysis, labour mobility, (and) capital accumulation'. And that because of this it fails to make, in his words, 'contact with the human realities of poverty, frustration, alienation, despair, breakdown, crime, escapism, stress, congestion, ugliness and spiritual death'. Again he identified the nature of technological progress as being partly to blame. He claimed that the technology of mass production is 'stultifying for the human person' and that modern technology, 'has deprived man of the kind of work that he enjoys most, creative, useful work with hands and brains, and given him plenty of work of a fragmented kind, most of which he does not enjoy at all'.

In his second book, *Good Work*, Schumacher expanded his critique of technology, suggesting that it was not ideologically neutral but something that bore the hallmarks of the society that developed it. As such, he saw technology development and transfer as a fundamental formative force in society. The technology choices we make, he believed, can shape the values, norms and culture of the society we then get. In *Good Work* he used a quote from the Prime Minister of Iran who, in 1976, said, 'There are many aspects of the West we particularly wish to avoid in the industrialisation of Iran. We seek the West's technology only, not its ideology' (Schumacher 1980: 42–4). To which he (Schumacher) then responded:

> The implicit assumption is that you can get a technological transplant without at the same time getting an ideological transplant, that technology is ideologically neutral; that you can acquire the hardware without the software that lies behind it, that's made it possible, that keeps it moving. Isn't that a bit like saying I want to import eggs for hatching, but I don't want chicks from them but mice or kangaroos?

Schumacher went on to suggest that:

> It's a great mistake to under-estimate the effect of [technology] on people's lives, not just their standard of living [but]:
> • How they produce, what they produce
> • Where they work, where they live, whom they meet
> • How they relax or 'recreate' themselves; what they eat breathe and see
> • And therefore what they think, their freedom or their dependence.

Schumacher's argument was that some technologies are so inherently ideological that they can cause society to reorganize itself to accommodate them. For example, if society chooses a form of agriculture based on mechanisation, fertilisers, pesticides, herbicides and hybrid seeds, that can in turn determine a whole range of societal outcomes because we have to organize ourselves in a way which allows that technology to operate (on its own terms) 'efficiently'. Choosing such technology can then determine 'optimum' farm size, agricultural labour force size, and therefore the size of population that can be sustained in rural areas, the quality of life there and the rate of urbanisation, the ecology of the countryside, the economics of food distribution system, what we eat (and therefore our health), how much of our income is spent on food, the size and location of our shops etc etc.

Schumacher's solution to all of this was, of course, a new form of 'economics as if people mattered', which he called 'Buddhist Economics'. The central purpose of this new economics, in his view, would not be to create

growth per se, but to create 'right livelihoods' – jobs which bring meaning to people's lives, which do no violence to the environment and which
allow them to produce goods that are consumed within the community in
which they live (so as to strengthen societal relations and build a sense of
community). In order to establish 'right livelihoods' Schumacher believed
that technologies were needed that were human in scale and which could
be owned, understood and managed by those who used them; technologies
'with a human face'. He also argued that a theory of economics that put
the creation of employment at its heart had to consider the cost of establishing each new workplace as more important than a crude calculation of
the productivity of each worker. From this he came up with the concept of
a different form of technology which he sometimes called 'Intermediate
Technology' 'to signify that it is vastly superior to the primitive technology of bygone ages but at the same time much simpler, cheaper, and freer
than the super-technology'. And sometimes called 'democratic or people's
technology – technology to which everybody can gain admittance and
which is not reserved to those already rich and powerful' (Schumacher
1974: 126–7).

So was Schumacher right to be so concerned about the use and
development of technology? In my view the answer to that question is
a definite 'Yes'. Human development has gone hand-in-hand with technical change. Technology development and adaptation enables people
to achieve well-being with less effort and drudgery, or at lower cost and
with fewer resources. Innovation is essential for people to be able to make
more effective use of the resources available to them and to respond to
social, economic and environmental changes. Improved technologies can
make a huge difference to people's lives – providing access to basic services
such as water, energy, transport and housing; helping in the development
of sustainable livelihoods and providing for reliable and sufficient food
supplies; providing the platform from which improvements in health,
education, income and well-being can be achieved. In short, though the
development and use of technology has not always been for the good of
all, we know access to improved technology can be an effective lever out
of poverty and that conversely, its absence is almost always a key feature
of living in extreme poverty.

Schumacher was not only right to point out the fundamental importance of technology choice in development but also to highlight that fact that, although we know improved technology can make a huge difference to people's lives, it is clear that technology has not solved the problems faced by a large part of the World's population so far. The consequences of this failure can only be classified as a great injustice. Access to the basic services that are taken for granted in the developed world is far from universal in the developing world, for example. 1.6 billion people do not have access to electricity; 2.4 billion people still depend on traditional biomass for cooking; 1.5 billion people still live in inadequate shelter; 1.3 billion people still have no access to safe water; and 2.6 billion have no sanitation. Technology is clearly critical to filling this gap and ensuring access to basic services for all, but has failed to do so to date. You could easily make the similar points, for example, in the field of health or agriculture and food production.

Why is this the case? Why has technology largely failed to work for the poor to date?

One answer to this question is that the withdrawal of the public sector from research and development over the past few decades has meant that research agendas are now driven largely by commercial concerns and that, as a consequence, the vast bulk of technology innovation now occurs around issues that are irrelevant to tackling the problems of the poor. In the health sector, the Global Health Forum has estimated that only about 5 per cent of the world's resources for health research are being applied to the health problems of low- and middle-income countries, where 93 per cent of the world's preventable deaths occurred (Global Health Forum 2008). Bill Gates probably summed the problem up most concisely when he claimed that we live in a world today where more money is spent each year on researching a cure to male baldness than on finding a vaccine for malaria (Gates 2009).

This disparity in application of funding for research can be seen across many other sectors too. In the agricultural sector, for example, Professor James Smith of Edinburgh University argues that we are currently witnessing an enormous shift in the balance of power in research and development from the public to the private sector. He notes that 'the five largest technology-led multinational companies – Bayer, Dow Agro, Dupont,

Monsanto and Syngenta spend $7.3 billion per annum on agricultural research' (Smith 2009: 83–4), twenty times the budget for the world's largest publicly funded agricultural R&D system for developing countries (CGIAR). Smith believes that this shift to private funding of research is problematical in that in the area of R&D 'the market does not and indeed cannot respond to the needs of the poor'.

The lack of a pro poor technology development agenda however is not the only reason poor people lack access to the technologies they need to achieve a reasonable basic standard of living. Interestingly, much of the technology that is needed to address these problems already exists, which leads to some puzzling questions. For instance, the health benefits of clean drinking water and sanitation facilities have been understood for centuries: the Romans had piped water for their public baths and the Victorians in Britain had their sewerage systems. So why have the basic technologies needed to provide clean water and sanitation not yet been spread to everyone? Edison invented the electric light in 1880, so why is it that almost a quarter of humanity still has no access to electricity?

The answer to these questions is that, in many cases, the issue is often less to do with the need for further technology development and more to do with poor people's lack of rights of access to existing technologies.

The slum settlement of Kibera in Nairobi is home to several hundred thousand people. Although the situation is beginning to improve, historically the citizens of Kibera have had no access to mains water. This is not because the technology is unavailable – many of the residents of Kibera live within a few metres of a water main. Neither is it because of their inability to pay – most households in Kibera buy water from water vendors at a price per litre that is several times that paid by the middle class Nairobi consumers who are connected to the city's water supply. It is because the residents of Kibera do not officially exist, they have no formal rights of tenure to the land their slum occupies and no power or voice to argue that they should have a fundamental right to access a service that is critical to life.

Another explanation also exists. For some, a lack of right of access to technology can be explained as a consequence of an economic model of development that still prioritizes growth of GDP over everything else and which is still tied to a trickle down approach to poverty eradication. In sub Saharan Africa 60 per cent of the population rely on small scale subsistence farming for a living. However official aid for agriculture by and large deliberately ignores small farmers on less fertile lands and instead focuses on commercial farmers on the most productive areas and on the use of large scale industrial technologies – fertilisers, pesticides, mechanisation, and on production for export. This myopic view of development not only denies technical support to improve the efficiency of the cultivation techniques used by the 60 per cent of the population, but also often promotes industrial technologies that compromise soil fertility and the conservation of water and which are potentially environmentally unsustainable.

We live in a world where the gap between those who have access to the technologies they need to live a decent quality of life and those who don't is growing into a yawning chasm and where the developed world's attention has largely moved on to meeting the 'wants' of consumers rather than the 'needs' of the poor.

We live in a world that is fundamentally, technologically unjust. And that technology injustice is not just manifest in the gap between poor and rich countries. It also now manifests itself in an intergenerational injustice. Our own addiction to fossil fuel based technologies in the developed world for example will leave a very difficult legacy for our children and grandchildren to deal with in the form of climate change.

Schumacher's Buddhist Economics was, I would argue, fundamentally about two things: Firstly it was about putting human well-being and not growth as the central concern of development. Secondly it was about finding a path to a new equilibrium – a rebalance of our efforts at technological innovation away from meeting the 'wants' of consumerism towards meeting the basic needs of the 2 billion people in this world who still live in abject poverty as well as a better recognition of the rights of future generations alongside those of our own.

Those ideas have stood the test of time and are as relevant today as they were forty years ago. Our responsibility to current and future generations must be to put human well-being back as the central purpose of economics and development. But in doing this we need to heed Schumacher's challenge to create an economics that makes contact with the human realities of poverty, frustration, alienation, and despair. We therefore need to make sure that our definition of well-being goes beyond people's material concerns (for food, shelter, access to basic services such as water and energy, education and health, and an income to pay for all of this) and includes also critical relational aspects of well-being (a sense that you as an individual have a degree of control and power over your own life, that you can be a part of decisions that have a major impact on the way you live, that you can live in dignity, that you have the respect of your fellow citizens, and that you can live in peace with your neighbours).

If we are to do this we will need, again as Schumacher suggested, to re-think our very relationship with technology. The choices we make in our development and use of technology play a huge role both in shaping our society today and in determining whether mankind has a sustainable future. Our governance of technology is therefore a critical issue requiring much thought. It is Practical Action's belief that to ensure equity for current and future generations our governance of technology will have to be founded on a principle of Technology Justice. This principle would combine a right – that all people should be able to choose and use technologies that assist them in leading the kind of life they value – with a corresponding responsibility – that this right could be enjoyed only so long as that choice does not compromise the ability of others and future generations to do the same. Our challenge locally and globally is to find a way to govern the development and use of technology so that it better meets the principle of Technology Justice in the future.

References

Gates, B. (2009). <www.ted.com/talks/bill_gates_unplugged.html> accessed 1 May 2013.

Schumacher, E.F. (1999). *Small is Beautiful*. Vancouver: Hartley & Marks.

Schumacher, E.F. (1980). *Good Work*. London: Abacus.

Smith, J. (2009). *Science & Technology for Development*. London: Zed Books.

The Global Forum for Health Research (2004). *10/90 report 2003–2004*, Data on R&D for health investments, p. 15.

PART III

Responsibility in Economics

LUK BOUCKAERT

K.U. LEUVEN & SPES ACADEMY

14 Schumacher and the Principle of Responsibility in Economics

1 Introduction

Reading Schumacher today is different from reading him in 1973 when *Small is Beautiful* was first published and became one of the cult books of the 'limits to growth' movement. *Small is Beautiful* was at that time an attractive alternative for the large-scale industrial growth obsession. It argued in favour of local economy, intermediate technology and new patterns of democratic ownership. Schumacher stood for a non-conventional economics inspired by Tolstoy's and Gandhi's democratic anarchism.

Re-reading Schumacher for this conference was an opportunity for me to rediscover his message. But in the context of today, it was not *Small is Beautiful* but the *Guide for the Perplexed*, published in 1977 just before his death, that was the eye-opener. However, in this *Guide* we do not find any adulation of small-scale economics but only a genuine case for wisdom. Hence, a puzzling question has to be solved: how to relate in an intellectually consistent way Schumacher's small-scale economics with his search for wisdom?

The question of bringing wisdom to small-scale economics is not trivial. Both concepts have their own logic. While wisdom requires a philosophical and theoretical effort, small-scale economics is a matter of practice and organization. Wisdom implies a logic of truth while small-scale economics is related to a logic of efficiency in social engineering. Most of us know the quote of Karl Marx that philosophy has to change reality and not just explain it. Probably Schumacher would reply that to change reality in a sustainable way we need an adequate philosophical framework. We believe that responsibility is the key notion in a theoretical framework that links wisdom to small-scale economics.

The aim of this contribution is to complement Schumacher's philosophical map by elucidating the notion of responsibility which remains underexposed in his *Guide* while it was the cornerstone of his ideas about economic democracy. Focusing on responsibility narrows the gap between the logic of *making a map* that explains reality and the entrepreneurial ambition of *making history* that changes reality. Moreover it sustains the claim for a charter of universal responsibilities and its implementation in the business world.

2   Schumacher Re-discovered

Let me start with a personal note. I recall very well my first reading of Schumacher's books during the seventies. As an assistant at the Faculty of Economics in Leuven, I lived in two different worlds. During the day as a researcher I lived in the Keynesian world of macro-growth models where multinational investors and governmental policy makers were the central players of the game. At the same time, this macro world was publicly challenged by one of the most influential reports since the Second World War: *Limits to growth*, published in 1972 by the Club of Rome, a year before the oil crisis. This report and a lot of other anti-growth books predicting ecological and demographic catastrophes were read and discussed in alternative circles, after working hours, in the evening and even at night. In this polarized world of pro and anti-growth believers, Schumacher's book was a relief.

Schumacher did not solve the growth dilemma but he changed the perspective (which as he later explained is the adequate method to solve divergent problems). Instead of launching a new predictive macro-economic model, he focused on the micro-world of people looking for opportunities to develop themselves as free and responsible actors. While macro-economic models for or against growth reduce people to dummies in a game they do not define, Schumacher's starting point was to disclose economics as a game by and for people. His work created a warm glow effect.

However, when I read Schumacher's *Guide for the Perplexed* during the late seventies, I was disappointed. I did not realize the point of his common sense philosophy, inspired by Aristotle and Saint Thomas and mixed with some Indian wisdom. In my view Schumacher's philosophical map missed a dynamic philosophy of time. My disappointment did not concern his strong criticism of evolutionary materialism but the fact that he did not succeed in disclosing a concept of 'creative evolution' in the line of philosophers such as Nietzsche, Bergson, Heidegger or Whitehead. His focus on the hierarchic structure of being (his 'four levels of being') and the idea of truth as *adequatio* reduced philosophy to the activity of 'making a map'. A map tends to visualize reality as a space at a fixed moment and this is far remote from viewing reality as a process or a function of time. According to Heidegger, time is not a level of being, nor a 'progression' within a certain level, it is being itself. Therefore, at that time I did not consider Schumacher's *Guide* a very progressive book.

After the oil crisis of the seventies and the short-lived breakthrough of the limits-to-growth awareness, the economic climate changed again. Ronald Reagan and Margaret Thatcher sympathized with the monetarist and neoliberal models of globalization. A strong belief in the self-correcting mechanism of global markets fuelled the new policies of unrestricted growth. The voice of Schumacher and other prophets of the limits-to-growth economy were pushed away from the public stage. The plea for self-restriction turned into material for academic articles or was adopted by small, idealistic, grassroots organizations. Schumacher's economics was not able to bridge the gap between soft thinking and the real game.

The scene of today once again has changed. After the neoliberal euphoria we are faced with a complex chain of crisis phenomena: increase of oil price in 2008, climate crisis, banking crisis and an international debt crisis. The self-correcting mechanisms of financial markets have failed. And it is not clear at all if the visible hand of governments will be able to correct the system failures. Governments themselves are part of the problem by supporting unsustainable credit and debt systems. The questions of limits-to-growth, self-constraint and frugality are once again questions of 'to be or not to be'. But even for those who realize the questions, it remains very difficult to implement the solutions. Why should I limit myself if others do not? Is a free and democratic choice for frugality possible? When we are always driven by the mimetic desire to grow a bit more than the other, how to refrain a system substantially?

Re-reading the *Guide for the Perplexed* in the context of today, I realized that I probably missed the point of Schumacher's effort during the seventies. Still I believe that Schumacher's space-oriented concept of a 'reality map' needs to be complemented by a more time and history-oriented philosophy of being. However, his 'map making' approach expressed a deep intuition: we will never respect outer and physical limits to growth if we do not previously respect the immaterial and metaphysical limits of reality. Only the awareness of limits at the level of being makes it possible to introduce limits at the level of doing. Moreover, by a more accurate reading of Schumacher's text, I discovered an embryonic philosophy of creative evolution. In the last chapter, when speaking about divergent problems, Schumacher provides a very interesting dynamic of history and development. He interprets history or at least human history as a process of creative divergence which opens a space for unexpected events, social creativity and being as a way of making history.

The distinction between convergent and divergent problems in the *Guide* is probably Schumacher's most original contribution to the development of a spiritual-based or wisdom-based social science. Convergent problems are problems that can be designed and solved as technical or rational problems. At the end there is one optimal solution. A bicycle e.g. turns out to be the most adequate solution to make a two-wheeled, man-powered means of transportation (Schumacher 2004: 121). Not only technical science but even social science tends to design all problems as convergent choice problems which can be solved by a cost-benefit analysis or by other optimization procedures. This tendency creates a blind spot for the nature of divergent problems, which are problems that lead people to different and opposite answers. Schumacher illustrates this with the case of education where those who are primarily committed to *freedom* will defend non-authoritarian answers to educational problems while people primarily committed to *order* will always argue in favour of discipline and obedience on the part of pupils. Such divergent positions cannot be solved on logical grounds or by optimization procedures. They are based on different value-commitments and to be solved, they require a capacity to engage in an existential and empathic dialogue in order to disclose common ground for action. To quote Schumacher:

> Divergent problems cannot be solved in the sense of establishing a 'correct formula'; they can, however, be transcended. A pair of opposites – like freedom and order – are opposites at the level of ordinary life, but they cease to be opposites at the higher level, the really *human* level, where self-awareness plays its proper role. It is then that such higher forces as love and compassion, understanding and empathy, become available, not simply as occasional impulses (which they are at the lower level) but as a regular and reliable resource. (Schumacher 2004: 126)

It may be clear that 'managing' divergent problems requires well-trained capacities of self-reflection, dialogue and understanding: 'so to speak a strain-and-stretch apparatus to develop the Whole Man, and that means a discipline to develop man's supralogical faculties' (Schumacher 2004: 128). Without the help of our supralogical faculties we will never succeed in transcending opposite positions or disclosing a more foundational value commitment. In this sense, Schumacher's *Guide* is a strong plea for introducing methods of spiritual knowledge such as introspection, intuition, dialogue and contemplation into the field of social science and practice. Not spirituality in its more esoteric or mystical forms but spirituality as a *method of disclosing reality in its immaterial aspects*. He expected that a spiritual disclosure of reality would enlarge the concept of social science from an instrument for social manipulation into a comprehensive method for understanding human life in all its aspects.

But saying that a more foundational value commitment is needed to solve or to overcome divergent problems, is not yet saying what *kind* of value commitment is involved. I believe that the *principle of universal responsibility* is the key factor in this value commitment. The characteristic of universality stresses the fact that the principle of responsibility is not confined to national or international borderlines. Neither is it confined to

existing persons. It involves all persons including future and past generations, marginalized groups and embryonic persons.

Why focus on responsibility? Because responsibility as a spiritual
commitment has the potential to stimulate self-reflection, to mobilize our
higher capacities such as empathy and compassion and to keep polarized
values such as freedom versus order, freedom versus equality, growth versus
frugality, individualism versus community, in a productive and viable balance. It would be interesting to disclose how the notion of responsibility
has developed throughout Europe's cultural history. But this would take
us too far. I will restrict myself to elucidating in the next section the distinction between a spiritual and a political interpretation of the principle
of universal responsibility.

3   Responsibility as a Spiritual Commitment

One of the aims of this conference is to support a 'charter of universal
responsibilities'. Why do we need such a charter? The answer to this question is based on a common observation. People claim their own rights as
much as they can but they are less keen to realize that every right implies
a duty or responsibility to protect the rights of other people as well. We
prefer people defending their own legitimate rights instead of being cared
for by paternalistic do-good practices. Although responsibilities are recognized as the other side of the coin of rights, they are not our prime concern.
Many social workers call attention to this imbalance between claiming our
rights and being committed to our responsibilities. In order to restore the
distorted balance, they want a charter of universal responsibilities.

However, a charter of universal responsibilities runs the risk of remaining a cosmetic operation if we don't succeed in changing our basic attitude
towards rights and responsibilities. If we don't succeed in substituting the
symmetry thesis by a claim that responsibilities are *prior* to rights, we will
not overcome the imbalance between rights and responsibilities. But the

problem is that the priority claim of responsibilities over rights doesn't mesh with the dominant paradigm in political philosophy. It cannot be defended within the framework of liberal political philosophy that supports the symmetry thesis. Hence, the priority claim in the context of today can only be articulated as a spiritual commitment that generates important political consequences but without being a political claim.

The *political* claim for universal responsibilities looks at responsibilities as derivative principles reflecting the rights of people. Rights are not 'physical things' that are just there as a kind of real objects, they are 'moral things', i.e. things that exist as ideal objects and must be realized through free human commitment. If we claim rights as *universal* moral principles, we assume a commitment to apply them to everyone and everywhere. We are accountable for their realization and application. Universal rights and universal responsibilities are two sides of the same coin. They are symmetrical in their reciprocity. It sounds theoretically perfect, but in practice this view results in the already mentioned imbalance of claiming my rights first and implementing my responsibilities as a secondary, derivative duty.

The philosophical foundation for the *political* claim of symmetry between rights and responsibilities is the liberal and egalitarian concept of the human person ('all persons are equally free') extended by the idea that equal freedom requires a minimum of social and cultural conditions to be implemented. These minimum conditions are defined as social rights enabling people to fulfil their basic needs. The liberal-egalitarian foundation of rights and responsibilities can be strengthened by the utilitarian and rational argument that the implementation of universal rights/duties is also beneficial to every person. Being unable to foresee and control my future, I will be better protected if I accept minimum standards for everyone. This is the well-known Rawlsian argument to promote universal rights/duties 'under the veil of ignorance'.

In contrast to this political view, the spiritual approach views the foundation of rights and responsibilities as non-symmetrical, non-egalitarian and non-rational. *Non-symmetrical*: duties have priority over rights; *non-egalitarian*: the rights of the other take precedence over my rights; and *non-rational*: gift has precedence over utility maximization. We find one of the most powerful expressions of this approach in the works of the

French-Jewish philosopher Emmanuel Levinas (1971; 1996). In contrast
to the ego-centric approach to freedom and responsibility, he develops an
other-centric notion of freedom and responsibility. More generally we can
refer to the tradition of spiritual humanism or in terms of Levinas to the
Humanism of the Other (1972) as the philosophical base for claiming the
priority of responsibilities over rights.

The basic assumption of the other-centric humanism is the idea that
the ego/self is always preceded by the presence of the other (eventually perceived as an absence which is a particular modus of being present). My life,
my education, my freedom, my capabilities and my rights are always given
before I can appropriate them as part of myself. Gift is prior to ownership.
Before being a legal right autonomy exists as a gift from others eliciting me
to give in return real freedom to other people. Being respected as a free
and creative person, I am invited to respond to this gift by respecting other
people's freedom and creativity.

But the experience of gift and its appeal to reciprocity is not the only
way to become aware of the priority of the other over the self. In Levinas'
view, the presence of the other as a gift is too soft and too noncommittal.
A more radical and traumatic infusion of the presence of the other in the
self coincides with the experience of being claimed by the other before I can
claim my own rights. Being claimed by the other is not based on a physical,
emotional or other external superiority of the other. It is an ethical claim
expressed through the vulnerability of the human face. Only a powerless,
naked human face calling for understanding and respect can infuse in my
consciousness an immediate, deep and concrete sense of responsibility
that takes precedence over my own goodwill or free choice. Becoming
aware of this non-chosen responsibility makes it possible to transform
my freedom into a mission at the service of the other. It liberates my freedom from egocentrism and opens a space for servant leadership or servant
entrepreneurship. It makes me capable of doing things *for* the other without paternalism because the ethical priority of the other implies that I am
first of all accountable *to* the other before being responsible *for* the other.

The difference between being responsible *to* and *for* the other looks
subtle but is crucial for a non-paternalistic reading of the charter of universal responsibilities. A paternalist will appeal to feelings of goodwill and

compassion to support the rights of other people, while a non-paternalistic reading will appeal to the ethical claims of other people. A paternalist will focus on my responsibility *for* the other while a democrat will prioritize the idea of being responsible *to* the other. Caring for the other without being accountable *to* him runs the risk of reducing the other to an object of my caring instead of respecting him as the subject of caring activities.

A third experience revealing the priority of responsibilities over rights is our relation to future generations (Jonas 1984). We often speak about the rights of future generations. Actually non-existing beings cannot claim rights. Of course, we can imagine them as virtual beings and give them virtual rights. But this is only possible because there is already an intuition of our responsibility to the non-existing future generations. Our gift of rights to them is founded on a primary intuition of responsibility *for* future life and *to* the other as the future subject of life. The example of caring for the future generations illustrates very well that on the one hand a spiritual commitment is prior to every declaration of rights (and makes such a declaration possible) but, on the other hand, this commitment must be implemented by the political discourse of rights and by giving people instruments to realize their rights.

To conclude this section let me give an example of how different readings of human responsibilities are possible and assume a different value commitment. Take e. g. art. 3 of the Universal Declaration of Rights explaining that 'everyone has the right to life, liberty and security'. Reading this article in the political-liberal modus means 'I have a right to life, liberty and security and nobody can deny me this right'. Reading the article in the spiritual-ethical mode sounds different: 'I have to respect and protect everybody's right to life, liberty and security especially of those who cannot defend their rights'. Both readings are meaningful and complementary. From a logical point of view both claims can be deduced from the general statement that everyone has the right to life, liberty and security. The point however is that it makes a lot of ethical and practical difference to which of both readings we give priority and commit ourselves.

But where is Schumacher's position in all these interpretations of rights and responsibilities? As said, Schumacher did not articulate in his *Guide* these differences in self-awareness and responsibility. However, it is clear

from his practical philosophy in *Small is Beautiful* that he fully embraced
the values and attitudes of the other-centric idea of responsibility. To illustrate this I will focus in my last part on Schumacher's organizational ethics
which illustrates very well his commitment to the other-centric approach
prioritizing responsibilities over rights.

4   Schumacher's Ethic of Democratic Entrepreneurship

Schumacher's ethic of democratic entrepreneurship coincides with his plea
for *smallness*. It would be completely wrong to reduce Schumacher's concept
of 'smallness' to a descriptive, statistical instrument for measuring the scale
of organizations in terms of quantity. We have to realize that 'smallness' is
first of all a qualitative concept for assessing the capability of organizations
to sustain co-creativity and co-responsibility in their structures. Of course
the most natural expression of smallness is one where quantity and quality
measures coincide. But we find in *Small is Beautiful* an interesting theory
of smallness in large-scale organizations (Part IV, ch.2) based on the idea
that a productive organization needs to balance order and creative freedom
in the determination of its scale and size. 'The specific danger inherent in
large-scale organization is that its natural bias and tendency favor order,
at the expense of creative freedom [...] The man of order is typically the
accountant, and generally, the administrator; while the man of creative
freedom is the entrepreneur' (Schumacher 2010: 259–60).

   To define smallness as a dimension of entrepreneurship in large-scale
organizations, Schumacher introduces five principles: (1) the principle of
subsidiarity which states that the burden of proof in justifying centralization always lies on those who want to deprive a lower level of organization
of its freedom and responsibility; (2) the principle of *vindication* enabling
subsidiary units to defend themselves against reproach or accusation. This
implies that the subsidiary units are able to justify their activities on the
basis of one or a few transparent criteria (e.g. profitability for a commercial organization); (3) the principle of *identification* which requires each

subsidiary unit to have both a profit and loss account and a balance sheet; (4) the principle of *motivation* warning us that without a positive work ethic that transcends the pay-packet at the end of the week, no sense of co-creativity and co-responsibility can be expected; (5) the principle of the *middle axiom* which introduces intermediate structures that support people in realizing the objectives of top management without denying their responsibility and creativity (e.g. giving people the relevant information and statistics for a good self-assessment).

For Schumacher these principles were not the outcome of academic research. They resulted from his work and experience as chief economist of the National Coal Board in the UK where he was deeply involved in the process of decentralization of the nationalized Coal Mine Industry. He was convinced that public institutions and activities must be infused by a philosophy of smallness in order to realize a more democratic and efficient use of human skills and talents. 'If they can do that, they have the future in their hands. If they cannot, they have nothing to offer that is worthy of the sweat of free-born men' (Schumacher 2010: 278).

But the most unambiguous case for relating smallness to a culture of responsibility is expressed in Schumacher's view on private ownership which was based on his involvement in experiments in social ownership as practiced e.g. in the Scott Bader Company. I will not elaborate here on these particular experiments of 'cooperative ownership', but I would like to stress here the relevance of Schumacher's organizational ethic in the context of some debates about corporate social responsibility in business.

The idea of CSR (corporate social responsibility) emerged as a key notion in business ethics during the late 1970s and the beginning of the 1980s. In contrast to Schumacher the new business ethics movement was not related to small-sized enterprises or to co-operative firms. CSR was developed as a strategy for big and globalized companies to gain trust in consumer markets and to respond to the growing pressure of NGOs such as Greenpeace, Amnesty International, Human Rights Watch and other organizations promoting ecological and social values in global markets. CSR was mainly concretized in ethical codes guiding stakeholder management and in an effort to enlarge the concept of value creation from a narrow profit and shareholder perspective into a 'profit-people-planet' perspective that balances the interests of all stakeholders.

I suspect that Schumacher would enjoy very much the emerging idea of social responsibility in business but that he would remain very critical about its implementation. The reason for Schumacher's virtual criticism can be easily connected to his insight that introducing responsibility claims without changing the deeper motivational and institutional structure of the capitalist system is an illusion. Here is a somewhat longer quote from Schumacher to illustrate this point:

> The *modern* private enterprise system ingeniously employs the human urges of greed and envy as its motive power, but manages to overcome the most blatant deficiencies of *laissez-faire* by means of Keynesian economic management, a bit of redistributive taxation and the 'countervailing power' of the trade unions. Can such a system conceivably deal with the problems we are now having to face? The answer is self-evident: greed and envy demand continuous and limitless economic growth of a material kind, without proper regard for conservation, and this type of growth cannot possibly fit into a finite environment. We must therefore study the essential nature of the private enterprise system and the possibilities of evolving an alternative system. (Schumacher 2010: 280)

In retrospect, we have to admit that CSR as an ethical and social corrective to the neoliberal globalization of markets did not anticipate, nor prevent the ecological or financial crises we are confronted with. The cause of this failure of business ethics is its inability to question the underlying assumption of 'always more and always bigger' in capitalism. The move from business ethics to business spirituality is an effort to overcome the business ethics failure (Bouckaert 2010a). I believe that Schumacher could be very helpful in guiding the perplexed business ethicist.

In Schumacher's view changing the conditions of ownership in the service of the size of the company is the key to creating conditions for responsible and democratic entrepreneurship. In this regard, he makes a very useful distinction, inspired by Tawney, between a) property that is an aid to creative work and b) property that is an alternative to it (Schumacher 2010: 281). In the case of small-scale enterprises, private property is natural, fruitful, and just. It motivates and supports entrepreneurship by giving the worker the produce of his toil. But in the case of large-scale enterprises, the rights of property are divorced from work and personal responsibility. Shareholders of large-scale companies are owners who live parasitically on the labour of others. Hence in the case of medium and large-scale companies, co-operative forms of ownership are necessary preconditions for building relations of reciprocal responsibility.

Schumacher makes very clear what I have elsewhere called the difference between stakeholder management and stakeholder democracy (Bouckaert: 2010b). While stakeholder management instrumentally uses stakeholder creativity and responsibility in order to realize the aims of profit-seeking shareholders, stakeholder democracy is a practice that enables stakeholders to co-define themselves as the aims of the company. Participative structures of ownership transforms stakeholders into co-responsible partners of a company. Most of the criticism against stakeholder democracy is related to the problem of finding a consensus or of taking adequate and quick decisions. But the banking crisis revealed the contrary. Shareholder-driven companies looked like the playthings of financial markets unable to take real decisions while those companies rooted in a culture of participation and democratic entrepreneurship displayed more resistance to the financial tsunami (e.g. Triodos bank). The reason for this is that in the case of genuine stakeholder democracy, there is an investment in spiritual capital – relations of trust, co-creativity and co-responsibility – that enables a company to overcome the overdrive of market fluctuations and the greed pressure of 'always more'.

5   Conclusion

Although the notion of responsibility is not fully articulated in Schumacher's *Guide for the Perplexed*, it remains the cornerstone and the inner drive of his work. In the *Guide* wisdom is searched as a precondition for acting in a right and responsible way. Disrespecting the different layers of reality leads to exploitation and violence. If there is no *inner* sense of limitation, there will be no sufficient motivation to respect and to implement *outer* limitation.

Claiming more responsibility in politics and business can have different sources and lead to different ways of implementation. We can stress the theoretical symmetry between rights and responsibilities which corresponds with the dominant liberal egalitarian view of social life. Or we can claim the priority of responsibilities over rights as is done by spiritual humanists. Inspired by Levinas and in line with Schumacher's legacy we believe that the idea of responsibility requires a spiritual and other-centric foundation to overcome the ego-preference in the interpretation and implementation of human rights.

Parallel to the different readings of rights and responsibilities in the political sphere, we find a similar ambiguity in business. Corporate social responsibility can be viewed within a neoliberal shareholder perspective and practiced as stakeholder management. The alternative is a practice of stakeholder democracy based on new patterns of ownership and participation. Schumacher's concept of *smallness* presents us with a blueprint for stakeholder democracy, not only in small and medium-sized companies but in big organizations as well. I believe it is fair to consider Schumacher's business ethics paradigmatic for what we need in business as a response to the ecological and financial crises. Schumacher's idea of democracy presupposes a spiritual-based model of leadership which is still lacking in mainstream political and managerial philosophy.

References

Bouckaert, L. (2010a). 'From Business Ethics to Business Spirituality: The Socratic Model of Leadership'. In S. Nandram & E. Borden (eds), *Spirituality and Business. Exploring Possibilities for a New Management Paradigm*, pp. 73–87. Heidelberg: Springer.

Bouckaert, L. (2010b). 'Economic Democracy as a Social and Spiritual Utopia'. In L. Bouckaert & P. Arena (eds), *Respect and Economic Democracy*, pp. 13–29. Antwerp: Garant.

Bouckaert, L. & Zsolnai, L. (eds) (2011). *The Palgrave Handbook of Spirituality and Business*. Hampshire: Palgrave Macmillan.

Jonas, H. (1984). *The Imperative of Responsibility: In Search of an Ethics for the Technological Age*. Chicago University Press: Chicago.

Levinas, E. (1972). *Humanisme de l'autre homme*. Montpellier: Fata Morgana.

Levinas, E. (1974). *Totalité et Infini*. The Hague: Martinus Nijhoff.

Levinas, E. (1996). *Basic Philosophical Writings*. Ed. by A.T. Peperzak, S. Critchley and R. Bernasconi. Indianapolis: Indiana University Press.

Opdebeeck, H. & Zsolnai, L. (eds) (2011). *Spiritual Humanism and Economic Wisdom*. Antwerp: Garant.

Schumacher, E.F. (1979). *Good Work*. New York: Harper & Row.

Schumacher, E.F. (2004, first edn 1977). *A Guide for the Perplexed*. London: Harper Perennial.

Schumacher, E.F. (2010, first edn 1973). *Small is Beautiful. Economics as if People Mattered*. London: Harper Perennial.

PAUL JORION
UNIVERSITÉ LIBRE DE BRUXELLES

15   Profit as One of the Questions of Schumacher

1   Introduction

Fritz Schumacher moved so swiftly from a Buddhist to a Roman Catholic approach to the economy that one has to wonder what was the motivation behind these commitments. The answer is I believe simple: in both his beliefs, the idea of changing institutions through personal commitment was foremost. Moss however, in his remarkable biographical account of Schumacher (Moss 2010), draws our attention to Schumacher's difficulty with making personal life decisions meet the aims he set himself out of principle. There is certainly a lesson to be drawn from the danger of such a gap: the longing for personal virtue is an exacting task when a framework buttressing it is lacking.

2   The Apparently Arbitrary Level of Profit

The question of profit and of the meaning of profit is prominent in Schumacher's work. A search for the word 'profit' in *Small is Beautiful* (Schumacher 1973) retrieves seventy-one instances; 103 if one includes 'profitability'. Here are a very few samples:

> [...] something is uneconomic when it fails to earn an adequate profit in terms of money. The method of economics does not, and cannot, produce any other meaning. Numerous attempts have been made to obscure this fact, and they have caused a very great deal of confusion: but the fact remains (28).

That is to say, the capitalist today wishes to deny that the one final aim of all his activities is profit. He says: 'Oh no, we do a lot for our employees which we do not really have to do, we try to preserve the beauty of the countryside; we engage in research that may not pay off', etc. etc. All these claims are very familiar; sometimes they are justified, sometimes not (216).

[...] if all this is rather a sham and private enterprise works for profit and (practically) nothing else; if its pursuit of other objectives is in fact solely dependent on profit-making and constitutes merely its own choice of what to do with some of the profits, then the sooner this is made clear the better (217).

One of the things that struck Schumacher was the arbitrary nature and therefore arbitrary level of profit from the seller's point of view. When the early anarchist Pierre-Joseph Proudhon (1809–65) once wished to draw attention to what a good man his father had been he told an anecdote about him being unable to find any justification for profit and therefore always selling at cost price. Here is what Proudhon says on the subject in his correspondence with Mme d'Agoult:

Madam, do you happen to know who my father was? An honest brewer who never reconciled himself with the thought that in order to make money one needs to sell above costs. He forever maintained that such would be ill-gotten gains. 'My beer, he would say, costs me so much, my wages included, I can not sell for more'. What happened? My good man of a father lived as a pauper, died as a pauper and left after him poor children. (Letter to Mme d'Agoult [Proudhon, *Correspondance* t. II, 289] quoted in Gide and Rist 1909: 334)

Where does profit settle indeed? For the seller, the lower boundary is set, as Proudhon's father knew, by costs. A price lower than costs threatens the seller's business. It can therefore only be set below costs on very few occasions. Assuming that the price obtained is higher than costs, any margin emerging thus will be deemed profit. But how high can profit be? In the same way as there is a lower boundary for price, determined by costs, there is an upper boundary defined by the buyer's own pursuit. And here also, the buyer cannot afford – unless very occasionally – to buy at a price which threatens his or her very subsistence.

So there are two boundaries for price and therefore two boundaries for profit: the lower one is that set by the seller's costs while the upper one is set by the buyer's subsistence level, profit being the difference between price and costs.

Where does profit settle between its upper and lower boundaries? This is where supply and demand kick in. Supply may be larger or smaller than demand. Let's call the first occurrence, when supply is larger than demand: 'abundance', and the second, when supply is smaller than demand: 'scarcity'.

When abundance prevails, the buyer has a choice from which seller to buy. When there is scarcity, the seller can choose to whom he will sell. Thus in the case of abundance, competition exists between sellers as their aggregate supply is larger than demand. Conversely, in the case of scarcity, a competition arises between buyers as the aggregate supply is time smaller than demand.

Competition between sellers when abundance prevails is bound to lead some of them to lower the price required to a level below its virtual upper bound, in order for them to sell their merchandise. The fiercer the competition, the stronger the pressure in their lowering their price. Conversely, in case of scarcity, buyers may try to outbid each other in order to ensure access to the merchandise.

Thus in the case of scarcity, the price will be set by competition between buyers and the seller will reap as profit the difference between the price and his costs, wherever that price ends up settling. But in times of abundance, competition between sellers will offer each seller a choice of where he wants the price to be set. There is room here of course for individual strategizing and tactics.

In the case of abundance, the seller has to think about what to do and there is some optimization to be achieved here in selling a smaller quantity for a higher price and a larger quantity for a lower price. As different approaches in that respect may very well end up producing the same overall profit, there is a certain arbitrariness and undecidedness inherent to the set-up.

And as is the case with choosing lanes in a traffic jam, there is always room for the suspicion that one has made the worst possible choice.

Such is the seller's dilemma in the case of abundance. What this suggests is that the seller's quandary about profit and profit level will in most circumstances be illusory as the overall set-up will actually determine at what level within the existing range between the virtual lower and upper price limits, the price will settle.

3   Profit as the Root of All Evil

The Welsh reformist and philanthropist Robert Owen (1771–1858), founder of the cooperative movement, also of socialism and according to Gide and Rist, a communist properly so-called, regarded profit as the root of all evil. Profit is the reason says Owen preventing a worker from buying back the product of his or her own work and therefore of being a consumer of the same number of goods which he or she has produced. Could fair competition possibly reduce profit to nothing? Not so claims Owen: 'competition' is but the name for the type of war and 'profit' for the type of loot.

About this, Gide and Rist (from whom I must confess I borrow most of my information about Robert Owen) make the well-grounded observation:

> It seems that the following could be objected to Owen. The alternative is such: – Either profit is part of production costs and it is indistinguishable from interest in that respect. In this case it is true that competition, even perfect, will not make it vanish as it cannot do more than bringing the selling price down to the costs of production, but should this be the case, profit is in no way unfair or parasitic since the product then sells at costs, nothing more nothing less, – Or profit does not belong to production costs and is not to be confused with interest: it is nothing but the excess of sale price over cost price, and in this case, indeed, can be considered abusive, but if so will necessarily vanish under a regime of perfect competition, since such income can only be due to a more or less characterized monopoly situation. (Gide and Rist 1909: 275)

4   Is Profit Undeserved?

There is indeed an essential question to be solved and thinkers of the nineteenth century spent a lot of their mental energy and efforts trying to solve it. The question is this: among the rent earned by the owner of land and ore, the interest earned by the owner of capital, the profit made by the entrepreneur and the wages earned by the worker, is any of them arbitrary and therefore undeserved?

The only agreement among all of these I believe lies in this: the beneficiary of wages definitely deserves his reward, at least unquestionably for the part amounting to his subsistence level. Workers work, and as it goes without saying that they'd better show up for work tomorrow morning again, that part of their wages allowing them to survive until the following day is undeniably deserved. As far as the other rewards go, things are discouragingly muddled.

Building on David Ricardo's (1772–1823) approach, Karl Marx (1818–83) simplified the issue drastically by claiming that wages only are justified: value is created by work and nothing else and any benefit assigned to other stakeholders such as owners of land, 'capitalists' as owners of capital or industrialists as entrepreneurs, is undeserved. Any payment made to other parties than workers is deemed spoliation by Marx.

Other nineteenth-century authors, socialists and anarchists essentially, following in the footsteps of eighteenth-century economists such as Richard Cantillon (168?-1734), François Quesnay (1694–1774) or Adam Smith (1723–90), held a different view: several separate components get combined in the process of production and each of them deserves some reward in terms of a share in the newly created wealth. Thus rent deriving from property rights rewards work previously invested – even if sometimes in earlier centuries by some ancestor of the contemporary beneficiary, the profit of the entrepreneur rewards his orchestrating and supervising of the productive process, while the interest or dividends of the capitalist compensate him for getting back later the advances he's making right now.

The way out of this quandary is far from obvious: clearly the newly created wealth results from the combination of a variety of elements, but how do we assess the *true* contribution of any of them? One thing is for sure: in the absence of any straightforward answer to this, only the power balance between the parties involved has determined over the ages and until now who is getting how much.

5   Aristotle's Views on Price Formation

Relying on a rediscovery, I've personally tried over the years to come up with a satisfactory theory of price formation. While doing fieldwork in a Breton fishing community in the early 1970s I had the opportunity to collect extensive data pertaining to prices local fishermen were obtaining for their catch. I then attempted to account for these data with the help of the model most commonly used, that of supply and demand. My attempt ended however in total failure. It is only when my attention turned to Aristotle's price theory that I found the model which was actually required. Back in the 1950s, Karl Polanyi, one of the founding fathers of my own field of economic anthropology, had shown interest in the ancient philosopher's approach. Polanyi had however failed to understand the very mechanism which Aristotle was describing, stating erroneously that 'the method is obscure, the result incorrect' (Polanyi 1957: 107), while he was also under the mistaken impression that the philosopher was offering a prescriptive model of how price should get established while there was no doubt in my mind that Aristotle was in truth proposing a mere description of the facts as he saw them.

What Aristotle's model of price formation assumes is that when two parties are free to set the price of some good they wish to exchange, this price will be defined by their reciprocal status, meaning that it will be established in such way that their status within society after the transaction has been concluded remains identical to what it was before it took place. That is to say that if the parties are not of equal status, each will continue to be exactly as he was, the richer one remaining as rich as he was before while the poorer one will remain just as poor as he was before. Another manner to express the same is to say that for similar goods, the rich will pay less and the poor will pay more, a fact that sociologists have had no difficulty confirming empirically (Jorion 1998).

6   Conclusion

Starting from the question of profit and refusing to believe, as Schumacher did, that changing institutions is limited to personal commitment, I discovered the importance of the principle of price formation.

The principle of price formation is that of an unadulterated power balance between seller and buyer of which the terms are determined by the social order emerging from the reciprocal status of all social groups in relationship to each other. With every new transaction taking place, the price agreed upon confirms and rebuilds at the same time the existing social order. A career of eighteen year in the financial world has only brought me additional evidence supporting this view.[1]

This means that unlike what is sometimes believed that Schumacher assumed, reform as a solitary pursuit may never succeed. As for instance Schumacher's substantial contribution to Keynes' proposal for Bretton Woods proves (Moss 2010), our efforts may be more efficiently allocated if instead of only being devoted to improving ourselves they are devoted to making institutions arise which would favour our virtuous behaviour.

---

[1]   I've collected all evidence and analyses in a book called simply 'price': *Le prix*, published in 2010, and which the French economist Philippe Herlin has been kind enough in his textbook on the new economics to enthusiastically hail as revolutionary (Herlin 2012: 171–203).

References

Gide, Charles and Rist, Charles (1909). *Histoire des Doctrines Economiques depuis les Physiocrates jusqu'à nos Jours*. Paris: Sirey.

Herlin, P. (2012). *Repenser l'économie*. Paris: Eyrolles.

Jorion, P. (1998). 'Aristotle's Theory of Price Revisited', *Dialectical Anthropology*, 23 (3), 247–80.

Jorion, P. (2010). *Le prix*. Broissieux: Le Croquant.

Moss, W.G. (2010). *The Wisdom of E.F. Schumacher*, <http://www.wisdompage.com/SchumacherEssay.pdf> accessed 15 May 2013.

Polanyi, K. (1968). 'Aristotle Discovers the Economy' (1957). In G. Dalton (ed.), *Primitive, Archaic and Modern Economies*, pp. 78–115. Boston: Beacon Press.

Schumacher, E.F. (1993, first edn 1973). *Small is Beautiful. A Study of Economics as if People Mattered*. London: Vintage.

KNUT IMS AND OVE JAKOBSEN
NORWEGIAN SCHOOL OF ECONOMICS, BERGEN/
BODØ GRADUATE SCHOOL OF BUSINESS, NORDLAND

16 Initiating an Open Research System Based on Creativity

1 Introduction

In the Norwegian White Paper 'An Open Research System' (NOU 2011: 6) a call is made for initiatives to facilitate the experimentation with new types of knowledge and research methods. The reality of the ecological and societal challenges assaults us from many directions. The belief that scientific research could answer most of the challenges that arise in the interaction between man, nature and society has increased considerably in recent years. In this article we discuss critically to what extent specialized knowledge based on 'objective' research methods are able to live up to these expectations. The NOU 2011: 6 White Paper draws attention to the fact that the world around us is constantly changing, which leads to new challenges we must face and the need for new types of knowledge and skills. A key task for a well-functioning research system is that it has incentives to contribute to such renewal. This means that 'the individual researchers' ability for critical thinking, creativity, commitment, interest and exploratory behavior, must be stimulated' (NOU 2011: 6, 18). This means that scientists with other ideas or new initiatives across the established paradigms must get the chance to develop within the Norwegian universities and research institutions. The conclusion is that the research system in Norway must be able to contribute to 'the renewal of the specialized disciplines, renewal across established disciplines and to produce knowledge that covers the new needs of society and industry' (NOU 2011: 6, 133).

In the following paragraphs we discuss how such a renewal of the research system could be initiated from the need of a more open and creative attitude towards the world. Our point of departure is that our world is described too narrowly and in a biased way by the maps of life and knowledge – given to us through school and university. We are in particular inspired by Schumacher's *A Guide for the Perplexed* (Schumacher 1977). One of Schumacher's statements is that the maps are only showing things that can be proved to exist, based upon the principle 'if in doubt, leave it out'. It means that I may 'limit myself to knowledge that I consider true beyond doubt' and thus minimize the risk of error. But at the same time I maximize the risk of missing out on what may be 'the subtlest, most important, and most rewarding things in life' (1977: 3).

We argue that a more balanced approach between convergent and divergent thinking should be a central means to approach the problems in our time. We also argue that we need wisdom that may transcend the linear logic of either/or and that more is always better than less. Simple logic cannot help us to solve the most important divergent problems, which may be called divergent because they have no definitive answer. While convergent problems are solvable in principle, divergent problems cannot be solved by finding a correct formula. A divergent problem will not converge even when a number of highly competent experts try to study the problem and come up with answers. On the other hand, 'the more intelligently you study a convergent problem, the more the answers converge. And if they are not solved after a certain amount of time, they will be solved later with more time, and more money for research and development'. (Schumacher 1977: 121–2).

Schumacher does not use the concept of divergent and convergent thinking. His contribution is to make the distinction between convergent and divergent problems. To illustrate some of the importance of including divergent problems in the maps of the world, Schumacher refers to Aquinas who asserted that 'The slenderest knowledge that may be obtained of the highest things is more desirable than the most certain knowledge obtained of lesser things' (cited in Schumacher 1977: 3). Specialized research comes up with exact knowledge focusing on increasingly smaller parts of the reality. Holistic knowledge and understanding could never be exact in the same way, but holistic knowledge is of great importance in many real-life situations, e.g. as a context for understanding how more specialized phenomena are interconnected. We believe that a distinction between divergent and convergent thinking may extend, deepen and complement Schumacher's contribution.

We describe divergent thinking as a method used to generate creative ideas by being open to a variety of possible solutions. One important part of divergent thinking is to ask new questions. To stress this point we refer to Einstein who stated that; 'Any intelligent fool can make things bigger, more complex, and more violent. It takes a touch of genius – and a lot of courage to move in the opposite direction'. In other words new answers to old questions are within the frame of convergent thinking while asking new groundbreaking questions presupposes divergent abilities.

The counterpart to divergent thinking is convergent thinking, which follows a defined set of rules to come up with one correct solution. We see divergent and convergent thinking as dimensions along a continuum. The difference is manifested in the extent of input variation and the transformation of new information. A wide breadth of categorization characterizes divergent thinking, while analytical–logical thinking characterizes the convergent thinker. Convergent thinking will provide 'the prevailing functions when the input information is sufficient to determine a unique answer' (Guilford 1967, 171).[1] Concerning divergent thinking we will emphasize two fluency-factors and two flexibilities factors, plus one redefinition factor. Divergent thinking consists of 1) *ideational fluency*, the speed of beliefs, an ability within a limited timeframe to produce ideas that satisfy certain criteria. 2) *Expressional fluency*, ability to produce new arrangements of words rapidly so that they satisfy certain structural criteria. Guilford emphasizes 1) because in a problem solving process usually a search for alternative answers and alternative solutions will be a key variable. Guilford argues that ideational fluency plays an important role in

---

[1] We use Guilford's definitions because he was one of the first modern psychologists that made an important distinction between divergent and convergent thinking, and thus he opened a more nuanced way to look upon intelligence (see Grimsø 1976).

problem solving because many problems will need new and creative solutions. In addition, more creative thinkers are often flexible, stepping out of old thought paths, and dare to think in new directions. 3) *Spontaneous flexibility*, defined as an ability or disposition to produce a large variety of ideas, in particular across different categories. And 4) *Adaptive flexibility*, defined as an ability to vary ideas in accordance with the characteristics of the task. This ability will be manifested when it is impossible to come up with a good solution within the established frame of reference. Originality may be seen as part of adaptive flexibility because it involves the capability of leaving what is obvious, ordinary or conventional. In addition one more factor in our interpretation of divergent thinking may be added: 5) *Redefinition*, an ability to let go of old interpretations of known objects in order to use them in new ways. In general 'improvisation' will mirror the ability of redefinition (Grimsø 1976: 17–22).

A concrete example of divergent thinking may be found in some personal reflections by Martin Seligman, one of the fathers of 'positive psychology'. In a biographical note Seligman tells how he arrived at the conviction that a movement toward positive psychology was needed.

> The moment took place in my garden while I was weeding with my five-year-old daughter, Nikki [...] I am goal oriented and time urgent, and when I'm weeding in the garden, I'm actually trying to get the weeding done. Nikki, however, was throwing weeds into the air, singing, and dancing around. I yelled at her. She walked away, then came back and said. 'Daddy, I want to talk to you'.
> 'Yes, Nikki?'
> 'Daddy, do you remember before my fifth birthday? From the time I was three to the time I was five, I was a whiner, I whined every day. When I turned five, I decided not to whine anymore. That was the hardest thing I've ever done. And if I can stop whining, you can stop being such a grouch'. This was for me an epiphany, nothing less. I learned something about Nikki, about raising kids, about myself, and a great deal about my profession. First I realized that raising Nikki was not about correcting whining. [...] I realized that raising Nikki is about taking this marvelous strength she has [...] amplifying it, nurturing it, helping her to lead her life around it to buffer against her weaknesses and the storms of life. Raising children I realized is vastly more than fixing what is wrong with them [...] The broadest implication of Nikki's teaching was about the science and profession of psychology. (Seligman and Csikszentmihalyi 2000: 5–6)

In short, the turn towards positive psychology was a radical change from a disease framework by repairing damage to a new field based upon a human flourishing framework by studying strength and virtue. Psychology should not only be the study of pathology, weakness and damage, but also work, education, insight, love, growth and play. And for Seligman his little girl was the inspirational source for breaking out of the old paradigm and enter a new one.

Referring to the requests in NOU 2011: 6 asking for renewal in the research system we argue that the complexity of today's challenges force us not only to find new answers – it is even more required to ask new questions that pave the way for divergent thinking. Divergent thinking is styles of thought that are employed both in problem understanding and in solutions at the edge of or even outside the established scientific paradigms. The tradition of posing questions is not new. One tradition can be traced back to Socrates who posed a series of questions to help a person to discover his beliefs about some topic. However, Socrates' dialogues cannot simply be characterized as divergent, because seemingly the process had a known outcome defined a priori by Socrates himself. If so we might rather call his questioning a convergent process. The Socratic method, arriving at the one correct conclusion via logic and induction, was considered by Aristotle to be the essence of scientific inquiry.

To deal with the requirements of a renewed research system focusing on the connection between specialized science, holistic understanding and real life challenges, it is necessary to go deeper into the concept of divergent thinking. As already mentioned, we argue that it is necessary not only to use divergent thinking to find new solutions to the most important environmental and societal questions of our time, rather it is even more urgent to use divergent thinking to define new interdisciplinary questions. The reason is that the most threatening problems of our time are part of the living universe, while the existing 'materialistic science', to use Schumacher's terminology, is first and foremost concentrated on solving problems that are adequate for studying the dead parts of the universe – the most shallow part of it which may be called the mineral domain.

2   The Context of the Arguments – Levels of Being and Adaequatio

To grasp the importance of the distinction between convergent thinking related to the dead aspects of the universe, and divergent thinking involving life, it is necessary to determine what characterizes life. Schumacher introduced four Great Levels of Being (or Chain of Being); on the first level he defined characteristics of the mineral world (m), on the second level, characteristics of the plant world (p), on the third level, a description of the animal world (a) and on the fourth level Schumacher described characteristics of the human world (h) (Schumacher 1977: 15–38). According to Schumacher self-awareness which leads to freedom and inner experiences are features especially of the fourth level in the life pyramid. The idea is that physics and chemistry deal with the lowest level, the mineral world which consists of inanimate matter. Botanists work with the plants – the next level which consists of living beings, then zoologists investigate the animal world – the third level, which is characterized by living beings with consciousness. Finally, a number of professions deal with the human world – the top of the pyramid. Because human beings differ from all other beings by having self-awareness, professions like sociologists, economists, philosophers, psychologists are active on the 'top level' in the life pyramid.

An important aspect of the life pyramid is that human beings are on all the different levels. Man = m + p + a + h. Each higher level comprises everything lower and is open to influences from everything higher. According to Schumacher the 'most important insight that follows from the contemplation of the four great Levels of Being 'is that [...] at the level of man there is no discernible limit [...] Self-awareness, which constitutes the difference between animal and man is a power of unlimited potential [...] to become superhuman' (Schumacher 1977: 37–8). As an example, this understanding leads to a need for a revision of the rational instrumental definition of the economic man in economics.

Given the different levels of being – Schumacher introduces the concept of 'adaequatio' or adequateness in order to evaluate the fitness of different methods to the different levels of being. The point is that nothing can be known without an appropriate method or instrument 'fitted to the object', i.e. the understanding of the knower must be adequate to the thing to be known. What Schumacher calls 'materialistic scientism' denies the reality of 'the invisibles' and focuses instead on what can be counted, measured, and weighed. This way of looking upon the world drastically reduces the richness of what exists in the world. The problem may be seen as a mismatch between the level of the knower – the scientist – and the level of the object of knowledge. Schumacher stresses that the result of materialistic scientism is not only factual errors, but something much more serious: 'An inadequate and impoverished view of reality' (Schumacher 1977: 42). The reason behind this statement is that perception is not determined simply by the stimulus pattern, rather it is a dynamic searching for the best interpretation of the available data.

This means that data do not speak for themselves. There are no innocent data. Data have to be seen, identified and interpreted by the scientist. And the essential question is then what is the scientist's context of interpretation? Or more precisely, what are the scientists' accepted theories? One consequence of this argumentation is that at the highest levels of being, science needs different methods and scientists that have developed their higher faculties in order to understand the depth of different kinds of lives.

A renewal of a research system inspired by Schumacher's life pyramid could contribute to creative interdisciplinary perspectives. In other words, research inspired by the life pyramid stimulates divergent thinking.

3   Convergent and Divergent Thinking

To understand the deeper difference between convergent and divergent thinking we must elaborate on the connection between text and context of interpretation. From the discussion so far, we can conclude that convergent thinking is based on a mechanical worldview while divergent thinking is based on an organic worldview. According to Schumacher convergent thinking is the predominant style of thinking in our modern technological society.

This connection is also of great importance to understand the need for renewal of the research system in Norway. According to the distinguished Norwegian economist and humanist, Holbæk-Hanssen (2009), the mechanical worldview has been dominant in Norwegian institutions for higher education and science for a long period of time. He was particularly critical of the reductionist thinking that prevail in economics and other social sciences.

In convergent thinking, we locate the problem at the 'center' of our focus and then we gather resources to solve the problem. In fact there is an anxiety not to find problems that are 'solvable'. One consequence is that resources 'converge' on the isolated problems. The idea is that there is a single best solution to all kinds of questions. An example of convergent thinking might be the demand to grant constantly increasing amounts of money to fund research focused on technical solutions to problems connected to the growth in the global emissions of CO_2.

We will also see linear thinking as one aspect of convergent thinking. In linear thinking more is better than less, and still more is even better. The current energy and material intensive growth model which defines the global economy is an illuminating example of linear thinking prevalent in economics. Exponential growth in GNP is defined as a common measure of welfare and progress in society. The result is that the more growth there is in GNP, the more welfare and 'well-being' there are in a society. According to the Norwegian White Paper, 'An Open Research System' (NOU 2011: 6), we have to encourage researchers to ask critical questions to the well-established truths, to come up with new solutions of society's complex environmental and societal problems.

Linear thinking also means that faster is better than slower, i.e. it is always good to speed up, without noticing that the vehicle might be on the wrong track – leading to an abyss. According to Holbæk-Hanssen (2009), one of the most important problems connected to convergent thinking is not the thinking per se, but that convergent thinking has displaced other possible ways of thinking. Examples of established truths within economics that could be questioned:

- To be healthy the economy must grow continually, i.e. increase the consumption of matter and energy
- In order to be happy people must consume more and more
- Economic growth is the presupposition for increasing the well-being for all people in the world
- To increase the level of well-fare amongst poor people, the rich must get richer.

An interesting path to follow, if we take the ideas in 'An Open Research System' seriously, is to put more focus on divergent thinking. We can summarize the previous discussion by saying that divergent thinking generates a much richer context of stimuli, which initiates new and creative modes of interpretation. A characteristic of divergent thinking is that the process of both problem identification and problem solving are located in integrated networks of occasions. This means that both the questions and the answers often are defined outside the original scientific paradigm. This understanding could be exemplified by a citation from the American economist Kenneth Boulding who discovered that 'the pursuit of any problem in economics always draws me into some other science before I can catch it' (Kerman 1974: 6).

Instead of doing research focusing on quantitative growth, more attention could be paid to stimulating qualitative growth in human well-being and environmental sustainability. Quantity, like matter and energy, tells us about the property of the parts. Within the mechanical worldview the sum total of the parts is equal to the whole. According to Capra and Henderson, qualities 'like stress or health [...], cannot be expressed as the sum of properties of the parts [...] Qualities arise from processes and patterns of relationships among the parts' (Capra and Henderson 2009: 7).

Today when we experience that most problems within economics and business administration are interconnected with an ecological and societal context, it becomes clear that the answers to economical challenges require understanding on a deeper holistic level (Ims and Jakobsen 2011). According to Boulding 'knowledge is a many-storied hotel with poor elevator service. Each floor or "discipline" has many alcoves and balconies peculiar to itself. Nevertheless there is some sort of common ground plan, which is worth investigating. Furthermore the plans of one floor may give leads as to the dark corners of others' (Kerman 1974: 40).

In order to solve complex interdisciplinary problems we have to use different procedures than are applied to convergent thinking. Rather than gathering information and converge it on the central problem, we may change perspectives and interpret the problem in a different context, opening new perspectives, novel ideas, and creativity. Instead of searching for the one correct answer, we must open a whole lot of different possibilities. An example of using divergent thinking might involve asking for new ways of organizing society in order to reduce the consumption of fossil fuels.

Schumacher views divergent problems as problems beyond problem solving in a narrow sense. Divergent problems characterize our moral life. They are not to be solved, but grappled with. They are challenging the logical mind to the extent that 'the pragmatic scientist' tries to avoid them. Simple logic cannot help to solve divergent problems because it implies that if a thing is true its opposite cannot be true at the same time. However, divergent problems have often a paradoxical nature – when one attempts to clarify them, the more they diverge, and finally they may appear as opposites of each other, as for example growth vs. de-growth. These problems cannot be solved within a solely economic paradigm; they must be transcended by interdisciplinary paradigms where values are included. The question cannot be solved by an algorithm or a formula, we have to develop a holistic perspective where growth and de-growth are parts of a bigger organism.

The difference between green economics and ecological economics gives an illustrative example of convergent and divergent thinking respectively. Both branches of economics try to solve the environmental and social problems embedded in mainstream economics. Green economics by introducing minor changes based on the same toolkit as in mainstream economics, ecological economics by questioning the frame of reference. In green economics environmental and social costs connected to business activities are increasingly internalized. The principle is that damage caused by business activity is paid by the polluter. The idea is that by making the environment into a costly commodity, business will be given an economic incentive to design environmental friendly products, procedures and uses of resources. Business managers will recognize that ecologically responsible activities represent a potential competitive advantage. Ecological economics accepts that our limited, linear way of thinking and problem solving often brings about unintended and undesirable affects. Management could not be studied in isolation since it forms part of a much larger network. Central in ecological economics is the concept of holistic thinking, including adaptability, flexibility, learning, self-organization and cooperation. The mechanical tool kit is replaced by the wisdom of organic life science in ecological economics.

Today it is more or less obvious that we can neither increase the total extraction of resources nor the total amounts of waste without disturbing Gaia's ecosystems seriously. This means that within a reduction to a scale appropriate for Gaia's source and sink capacity there will be continually changes. According to Capra and Henderson quantitative economic growth on a finite planet cannot be sustainable. Qualitative economic growth can be sustainable if 'it involves a dynamic balance between growth, decline, and recycling, and if it also includes development in terms of learning and maturing' (Capra and Henderson 2009: 8). This means that some industries may increase while others decrease. Economic growth may be pathological when we quantitatively use more resources than we have, on the other hand growth in quality of life could increase without damaging nature or society. Quality of life is connected to a fair distribution of resources within a sustainable nature.

4 Discussion

Based on 'An Open Research System' (NOU 2011: 6), which points out that research systems of great diversity are the most vigorous, 'diversity in methods and tolerance for alternative perspectives give a greater chance to obtain new knowledge' (NOU 2011: 6, 18). In the report we find arguments claiming that in more complex environments, greater diversity is necessary. According to Boulding the 'reality is always a great multidimentional splodge' (Kerman 1974: 20). In the following paragraph we will discuss how these goals could be actualized.

According to Schumacher (1977), Capra (1982), and Holbæk-Hanssen (2009) most challenges and problems have to be grappled with through a practice in which convergent and divergent thinking are to be combined. In many situations it is relevant to encourage divergent thinking as a first step, in order to stimulate creativity and generate many novel ideas. Then the second step could be to transform the ideas into practical problem solving procedures.

Therefore, in practical problem solving it is wise to diversify our thinking patterns to include both divergent and convergent thinking. The problem is that the educational system to a large extent focuses on convergent thinking. As a consequence most scientists are trained to practise convergent thinking. In addition to intellectual pursuits and training the tendency to use either convergent or divergent thinking can also be explained as a result of personal characteristics and personal relationships. In our opinion it could be a good idea to combine people and networks with opposite characteristics because a predominantly convergent thinker may be inspired by collaborating with a divergent thinker.

Holbæk-Hanssen (2009) argues that creative people are characterized by openness to new ideas and perspectives in addition to having special individual skills or traits. He declared that the most creative ones often give test results similar to those you get from schizophrenia. But because they seem to have a stronger ego, they can manage to live with some unrealistic ideas, thoughts and images. Holbæk-Hanssen stresses that the features that characterize the creative individual do not solely consist in specific abilities, but he adds that creativity is associated with certain attitudes, certain forms of orientation towards life. These phenomena could not be explained as a specific set of skills, it is more a question of connectedness to the living world. The researchers rely heavily on personal experience of relationships. To understand creativity we have to focus more on relations than on objects. Key concepts in this research tradition are imagination, inspiration and intuition.

Imagination refers to the capability to suddenly 'see the whole context', as if in a picture (cf. Holbæk-Hanssen) In other words, a creative process that consists in finding or creating a pattern where the individual elements are joined together, synthesized into a whole. The whole represents more than the sum of the elements and the patterns of the connections are essential. *Inspiration* refers to an experience where the researcher understands how the part is connected to the whole. The researcher experiences the interconnectedness in the living reality. This experience is essential in the process of finding new solutions to divergent problems. In this perspective creativity is interconnected to a process where ideas are confronted with reality. Holbæk-Hanssen defines *intuition* as the capability to translate ideas into practice. Intuition is of great importance to finding solutions on how practical tasks should be solved or handled.

Holbæk-Hanssen states that an important measure to foster creativity is to create the conditions to abolish the old thought forms and paths by expanding the understanding of the interpretative context. Creativity is defined as the ability to develop, understand and implement new and better solutions. An important instrument to achieve this deeper understanding is to develop the ability to question the established paradigms. To succeed, the research training should not only pave the way for loyal paradigm carriers, as is the case today in many academic colleges and PhD programs at the universities. We must allow researchers to break out of the paradigm limitations and ask questions that promote creative thinking.

Our contention is that higher academic institutions for a very long time have put too much emphasis on educating specialists who have little training in looking at reality from different perspectives and seeing connections between different subjects. The consequence is that more and more researchers are working within distinct paradigms in which new and challenging perspectives have little space. According to Schumacher researchers are mainly working with convergent problems based on the idea that knowledge can progress cumulatively and that there are no hierarchical levels of knowledge. The price is 'Dealing exclusively with convergent problems does not lead into life but away from it' (Schumacher 1993: 76). Schumacher cites Viktor Frankel who formulated the problem connected to specialism 'not so much the fact that *scientists are specializing*, but rather the fact that *specialists are generalizing*' (Schumacher 1977: 5).

To explore these questions further we will argue that the problem with specialization is not over-specialization, but the lack of depth of knowledge. With reference to the preceding paragraphs we argue that the complex problems in the real world must be analyzed holistically, i.e. as components of the whole of which they are component parts. The main assumption is the recognition that today's science to a limited extent is able to capture the systemic nature of complex relationships that exist in the real world. Therefore, the sum of discipline-based expertise is inadequate to deal with the challenges which are perceived as complex and global in character.

The inadequacy consists both in the absence of interdisciplinary knowledge and understanding, and in the limited collaboration between science, practice and art. Both Schumacher (1977), and Holbæk-Hanssen (2009) argue that Western civilization is in a state of permanent crisis. According to Schumacher 'we are suffering from a metaphysical disease, and the cure must therefore be metaphysical' (Schumacher 1993: 80). Holbæk-Hanssen used the concept of 'spiritual cleaning' (åndelig storengjøring) to illustrate the same phenomenon.

Schumacher argues that we must have deeper knowledge, i.e. we must go deeper into the topics we are studying. In our opinion this means that it is necessary to disambiguate ontology and epistemology. To grasp the unity of the real world we have to develop knowledge on more basic levels. On this deeper level we may well think in terms of intradisciplinarity (on the ontological level) instead of interdisciplinarity (on the epistemological level).

5   Conclusion

We argue that a fair interpretation of the ideas and intentions articulated in 'An Open Research System' (NOU 2011: 6) is, firstly, to give students the opportunity to see their own discipline in relation to other traditions and to reflect on values from other paradigmatic points of view. Secondly, according to Schumacher the divergent problems cannot be solved by logical reasoning only, they have to be experienced and transcended. These kinds of problems 'force man to strain himself to a level above himself; they demand, and thus provoke the supply of forces from a higher level, thus bringing love, beauty, goodness, and truth into our lives (Schumacher 1999: 75). We agree with Schumacher arguing that the higher things cannot be known with the same degree of certainty as can the lesser things. Therefore it would be a dangerous loss if knowledge were limited to things beyond the possibility of doubt. Thirdly, to develop an open research system in Norway, we need a radical change in education to focus more on development of the students 'higher faculties', such as self-awareness, creativity and judgment. For economists it may, e.g. mean that 'the economic man' must be questioned. Maybe 'the ecological man', a person deeply embedded and integrated in society and nature would open up for new perspectives in economics (Ingebrigtsen and Jakobsen 2009)? It might e.g. have important impact concerning man's sensitivity for other living beings. A misplaced use of binary logic may, according to Schumacher, have negative influence on people's sensitivity. The danger is that the mind becomes rigid and lifeless, fixing itself on only one side of the pair of opposites. We think, in accordance with both Schumacher and Boulding that by stimulating to more 'tension into the world', we can sharpen man's sensitivity and increase his self-awareness (Schumacher 1977: 127). Fourthly, in accordance with Boulding's organic theory of knowledge we argue that higher education and research must stimulate initiatives leading to creativity. Research should no longer be like a mechanical process, but processes which depend to some extent on the unreliable processes of inspiration. To sum up, it is of great importance to inspire researchers and students to look for connections between fields of knowledge, to see '[...] the treads of theory that would tie together economic man, biological man, perhaps even the religious man, and bring the fragmented back together again' (Kerman 1974: 7).

References

Capra, F. (1982). *The Turning Point. Science, Society and the Rising Culture.* London: Fontana Paperbacks (Flamingo).

Capra, F. and Henderson, H. (2009). *Qualitative Growth.* London: The Institute of Chartered Accountants in England and Wales.

Grimsø, R.E. (1976). *Divergent Tenkning og Problemløsning. – en Teoretisk Diskusjon og en Empirisk Undersøkelse av Problemløsende Adferd hos Personer i Forskjellige Utdannelseskategorier.* Universitetet i Bergen: Magistergradsavhandling.

Guilford, J.P. (1967). *The Nature of Human Intelligence.* New York: McGraw Hill.

Holbæk-Hanssen, L. (2009). *Økonomi og Samfunn – Når Mennesket blir Virktigst.* Oslo: Antropos.

Ims, K., and Jakobsen, O. (2011). 'Deep Authenticity – an Essential Phenomenon in the Web of Life'. In A. Tencati and F. Perrini (eds), *Business Ethics and Corporate Sustainability*, pp. 213–23. Cheltenham: Edward Elgar.

Ingebrigtsen, S. and Jakobsen, O. (2009). 'Moral development of the economic actor', *Ecological Economics*, 68, 2777–84.

Kerman, C.E. (1974). *Creative tension – The life and thought of Kenneth Boulding.* Ann Arbor: The University of Michigan Press.

NOU 2011: 6, *Et åpnere Forskningssystem (A More Open Research System).* Ministry of Knowledge, Oslo.

Schumacher, E.F. (1977). *A Guide for the Perplexed.* New York: Perennial Library.

Schumacher, E.F. (1993). *Small is Beautiful. A Study of Economics as if People Mattered.* London: Vintage.

Schumacher, E.F. (1999). *Small is Beautiful. Economics as if People Mattered. 25 Years Later... with Commentaries.* Vancouver, BC: Hartley and Marks Publishers.

Seligman, M. and Csikszentmihalyi, M. (2000). 'An Introduction in Positive Psychology', *American Psychologist*, 55 (1), 5–14.

ALEXIS VERSELE, BARBARA WAUMAN AND HILDE BREESCH
UNIVERSITY COLLEGE GENT

17 Achieving Sustainable Housing

1 Introduction

Sustainable and energy-saving building is confined nowadays to the exclusive domain where it is only accessible to those who can afford it. Domus Mundi is a social-profit organization that opens sustainable building up to vulnerable groups in Belgium and in developing countries. Technical and financial support for social building projects is the main objective of the organization. In particular, three aspects are crucial within the method of working: (1) to pay extra attention to the use of natural, reusable or inexhaustible mineral materials, preferably from the local region, (2) to strive for an optimum comfort with a minimum energy use and (3) to take care of the supply and the saving of water: everyone should have access to drinking water. In the process Domus Mundi focuses on the poorest and most vulnerable groups of our society. Domus Mundi entered into a partnership agreement with the city of Ghent to help renovate houses in order to improve energy performance and living conditions in Ledeberg. Domus Mundi was asked moreover to take part in the start of Ghent Social Housing Co-operative, which is a Community Land Trust. Community Land Trusts are organizations (similar to non-profit organizations, co-owner societies) that create affordable housing for low-income people, on building plots owned by the trust.

The initiatives are in agreement with the Ecopolis project, in which Tjallingii (1995) pleads in defence of the flows (of energy, water, raw materials, traffic) and the urban development quality of urban places and regions. Both aspects are only possible if the people involved – inhabitants, designers and policy officers – are willing to join in. Therefore, we have to strive for a city that is at the same time 'responsible', 'living' and 'participating'. The initiatives also fit in with one of the key ideas of The Economy of Communion (EOC) (Linard 2003): the idea of being 'vulnerable with the most vulnerable', applied already by the AMU (Action for a United World: www.azionemondounito.org). Making ourselves poor with the poor is a way proposed by the 'Economy of Communion'. It contrasts sharply with the *homo economicus* who is just indifferent, not even supposed to be selfish or altruistic, not interested in the welfare of the other person. Indeed the predominant thought in economics today has been dictated by the fact that the individual is motivated by personal interests. The logic of the 'Economy of Communion' is an attempt to go beyond empathy and to find a place for the concept of love in economics, understood as a deep concern for the other as a person. The governance of the economy in that sense cannot be based on the market alone, but takes into account also the needs of the poor (Bruni and Zamagni 2004).

Even E.F. Schumacher, one of the first economists who integrated the principles of Corporate Social Responsibility and Sustainability, gives an answer to the question: 'How can we understand the bearings and real implications of problems and pains of real poverty?' In his *A Guide for the Perplexed* he makes the following observation: 'A person who had never consciously experienced bodily pain could not possibly know anything about pain suffered by others'. The example of bodily pain, in his book, is instructive. The same applies to poverty. Further, in his quest for the fields of knowledge, Schumacher asks the embarrassing question: 'If all these forces or movements inside me are not real, they need not be taken seriously, and if I do not take them seriously in myself, how can I consider them real and take them seriously in another being?' (Schumacher 1977: 83).

Providing decent housing to poor and low-income groups has been a big challenge for governments in countries all around the world. Most governments, even the Flemish one, cannot afford to heavily subsidize the capital-intensive housing sector in the hope of solving the housing short-age (Demyttenaere 2006). The performance, therefore, of many subsidy programs is not optimal. Ironically, the poor may not be eligible for hous-ing subsidies that will benefit middle-income households, because they operate through the mortgage market or require the recipient to build a house before obtaining the funding. Low-income households are often excluded from traditional mortgage markets.

In developing countries new actors, working together in a concept of 'Hybrid Value Chains', defined as business models for commercial partnerships between businesses and social profit organizations, are emerging to support efforts made by the poor themselves (Schmidt and Budinich 2008).

The Council of Europe Development Bank (CEB) adds to the business approach a multi-sector and integrated approach that combines housing components with broader social perspectives (CEB 2010). The objective of the CEB is the establishment of sustainable communities in urban areas that would represent areas of solidarity and a balance between economic development, social equity and urban setting. It has dedicated an important part of its lending to housing and associated infrastructure within an integrated approach towards building sustainable communities in urban areas. It links economic, social and environmental issues and solutions, involving projects in housing for low-income persons as a principal activity.

2 Solutions for Problems of Dilapidation

In Belgium housing is one of the major reasons for poverty. Since the middle of the nineteenth century policymakers have become aware of the problems of slums as an issue in their fight against social disorder. From that time on initiatives are taken to offer solutions. Proposals made before World War II seem not to be effective. The De Taeye law of 7 December 1953 aimed at eliminating insalubrious dwellings (Avramov 2003). The order implementing the new law of 1953 made it possible to re-accommodate people from the slums to social housing estates. The legendary neighbourhood Marollen (Dutch) or Marolles (French) situated between the Law Courts of Brussels (Palace of Justice) and the Brussels-South railway station became the experimental place for the fight against dilapidation. In a first stage solutions consisted in delocalizing people in apartment buildings. Afterwards, partly spurred on by social organizations, the physical and social qualities of the old urban fabric were discovered. In 1969 its residents staged the 'Battle of the Marolles' to oppose wholesale demolition and to demand renovation of existing buildings instead. Although the traditional city neighbourhoods originally were considered problematic, from that moment on neighbourhoods were considered an essential basis for a qualitative social network and for the social welfare of its dwellers (Van Herck and Avermaete 2006: 147–61).

Inspired by the Brussels example, from the beginning of the 1970s, Ghent started to stimulate renovation projects too on a systematic and planned basis, by defining 'urban renovation districts' which received special financial facilities and subsidizing.[1] The city of Ghent started urban renovation projects in three town districts: Sas- en Bassijnwijk, de Brugse poort and Dampoort district, all part of the nineteenth-century belt around Ghent. Currently, a fourth district, Ledeberg, is involved in a process of urban renewal, initiated by the Administrative Body for Territorial Development of the city of Ghent. Ledeberg, Ghent's most densely populated sub municipality, has a number of problems, such as the ageing housing stock, traffic chaos, a major outflow of residents, the socio-economic situation and the lack of green areas and meeting spaces. The urban renewal has six objectives: more beautiful green areas, higher living quality, more fluent and safer traffic, renewed entrances, more active service and more meeting space. The old part of Sint-Amandsberg will be the next to be tackled by the city of Ghent in its 'neighbourhood after neighbourhood' approach.

1   A special word of thanks to the city of Ghent, 'Cel Woonbeleid – Dienst Huisvesting', and to the Community Development Service ('Samenlevingsopbouw').

3   Housing Stock in Ghent Ledeberg

Ledeberg has a total population of 8,214 inhabitants and a high population density of 56.41 inhabitants/ha (Ghent 14.65 inhabitants/ha). Almost 12 per cent (985 inhabitants) have no Belgian citizenship (Ghent per cent). Among underprivileged families, in 2005 there was an increase in the birth rate of 40 per cent (Ghent 11 per cent) compared to 2000. Ledeberg has a building density of 31.2 per cent (Ghent 11.6 per cent) (Stad Gent 2005).

3.1   Private Ownership

From the creation of Belgium in 1830 on, real estate and private ownership have always been considered an important index for wealth and social success. As a reaction to the very poor housing and living conditions of the labourers after World War II, the government decided to promote private property by adopting the 'De Taeye' law of 29 May 1948. With this law, named after its Catholic sponsor, individual house building was stimulated, even for very young families, through grants and cheap mortgage loans. This has resulted in a very high property range of about 68 per cent. Although poverty and homeownership may seem to be unrelated (De Decker, Kesteloot and Newton 2008: 10–13), quite a lot of underprivileged people in Ledeberg still have private ownership of their houses. Most of them have Belgian citizenship. In Ghent 68 per cent of native Belgians have a privately-owned house compared to only 28.5 per cent of people of Moroccan and 49.9 per cent of people of Turkish origin (Termont 2009).

The De Taeye law of 1948 was later extended to renovation works on existing houses and is still valid. Many initiatives were taken to promote housing renovation, such as the VAT reduction to 6 per cent instead of 21 per cent or the special 'revitalization subsidies' in some old and decayed city districts.

3.2 Social Housing

In Flanders only 6 per cent of the total building stock consists of social housing estates. Although Ghent, with about 11 per cent, scores remarkably better than the Flanders average (Termont 2009), compared to Holland and France (30 per cent and 65 per cent) (Demyttenaere 2006: 175), the number of social housing estates is still too small. Even if poverty and social housing is an inconvenient relationship (De Decker 2001: 14–21), there still is a lack of new social housing projects. In Ghent there were 848 new units compared to a demand for 6,162 units in 2004. Anyhow, 27 per cent of the private tenants in Ghent belong to the group of so-called 'social tenants'. 60 per cent of this group pay more than 30 per cent of their income as a rental price despite the low social rental amount. Rent amounts increase furthermore faster than income. Expelling tenants for non-payment or forcing them to move by legal means increased in Ghent from 5.8/1000 in 2006 to 6.5/1000 in 2008 (Termont 2009: 52–3).

3.3 Private Tenancy

As in other parts of Flanders, most of the vulnerable people in Ledeberg are confined to the private rental sector, where nearly all dimensions of housing rights are violated: affordability and housing quality are problematic and security of tenure is not guaranteed (De Decker 2001: 21).

Private tenancy regulations strongly protect tenants from excessive rent increases to the extent that freely negotiated rent amounts cannot be raised more than once a year, nor may they exceed the official index of increases in living costs.

In order to increase access of low-income groups to private rentals, 'social rental agencies' have been established (<http://www.vob-vzw.be/SVK/tabid/64/Default.aspx>). Furthermore, low-income private tenants who are aged or living in an objectionable dwelling may receive assistance to cover the costs of moving into more appropriate housing or to finance rent down-payments. No system of rent subsidies is in place.

3.4 Housing Quality

To assess housing quality we consider five criteria as described by Winters and De Decker (2009: 212):

1. The physical quality; structure, moisture, humidity, quality of the foundations and roof.
2. Comfort; technical equipments for domestic cold and hot water, bath and shower, central heating.
3. Living environment: maintenance of the public domain, proximity of playgrounds, schools and supply facilities, safety.
4. Occupancy rate: the relationship between dwelling size and household size.
5. Sustainability: thermal insulation, way of heating, the use of renewable energy sources.

This paper focuses on the improvement of physical quality, comfort and sustainability. Even though physical quality and comfort of Flemish dwellings have improved over the last decades (Winters and De Decker 2009: 212–15), there is a considerable quantity of very bad houses, for instance in Ledeberg. Over 50 per cent have no or a very low level of comfort. The houses are not adapted to their inhabitants, are unhealthy and dangerous to live in, moreover they generate a huge energy waste. As Ledeberg used to be an industrial village near to the Schelde from the early nineteenth century on, with flourishing economic activities in cotton factories, flax mills, a brickyard and a shipbuilding company, a lot of low-quality small terraced houses were built very fast for working-class people. In the twentieth century, industries started to leave the area, causing many people to lose their jobs and move out of Ledeberg, thereby creating much space for immigrants, today originating from forty-four different nationalities.

Most of the houses are still in use today and occupied by people who cannot afford to buy a house, such as low-income working families, young people and immigrants. Moreover a lot of house owners are too old or alone and impecunious to take initiatives to renovate, even basically; these houses have often a very low occupancy rate.

Energy performance of buildings has the most prominent place if we consider sustainability as intended by Winters and De Decker (2009: 218). Energy consumption for heating and domestic hot water represents 14 per cent of the total electricity and fuels consumption in Flanders. In 25 per cent of the houses windows have single pane glass, 33 per cent of the roofs have no thermal insulation, 74 per cent no floor insulation and 55 per cent no wall insulation. (<http://www.energiesparen.be>) Energy poverty has become an increasing problem as in 57 per cent of Flemish dossiers about debt mediation energy debts appear as the most important debts (Vrancken 2009: 93). Reducing energy poverty is one of the UN's Millennium Development goals by 2015.

Since 2006 a lot of owners can benefit from a substantial Flemish renovation grant (30 per cent of the renovation costs – maximum of 10,000 euro) (see <http://www.energiesparen.be>). In order to stimulate the inhabitants to renovate their houses, the city of Ghent even launched a grant for low-income people to recover 50 per cent of their investments. An important contribution though is supposed to be paid by the owners, which means that underprivileged people without financial resources cannot claim the grants. Another problem of the important differences between underprivileged and privileged is the lack of social and technical skills. Poor people have learned to survive, not to handle the mechanisms that are essential to function in society. They have not learned to handle money, to run a household. They do not even manage to fulfil their minimal administrative commitments, not to mention the possibilities of taking advantage of assistance and grants (Demyttenaere 2006).

4 Developing Sustainable Housing

4.1 Co-operative Housing

Different sustainable and especially co-operative housing initiatives are taken nowadays all over the world. In a number of developed countries, especially in northern Europe and the USA, from the second half of the last century housing co-operatives have played an important role. Conversions of public housing into co-operatives have been achieved, bringing new investments, both in renewal of physical infrastructure and housing, and also in the social capital that is needed to make high-density, low-income housing estates work. Social inclusion, even here, has to be considered in all its dimensions, also considering home ownership. It is likely however that permanent co-operative models will have little impact in housing the very low-income people if members have only limited individual equity. Solutions like house-building co-operatives using collective actions to lower the cost of building homes for individual households who then become individual owners are suggested by Birchall (2003). He pleads in favour of community land trusts as they are a good way to secure collective tenure of land by its residents, while the same residents continue to own and improve their own homes (Birchall 2003: 34). Community provision of infrastructure such as clean water, roads and sanitation to informal settlements allows people to keep individual ownership and control of the dwelling, while collectively providing a decent environment.

Over the last few years resident/tenant-owned co-operatives have become popular. In Britain for example, tenant-owned co-operatives work together with conventional social housing landlords to involve more tenants in the governance over social housing (Rodgers 2001).

4.2 Community Land Trust

Involvement of very low-income groups can take place only if the government is involved too. The Community Land Trust is a way to take both
financial and social/collective challenges. The annual World Habitat Award
competition (<http://www.worldhabitatawards.org>), established to identify innovative and sustainable housing solutions worldwide, awarded in
2008 the Champlain Housing Trust (CHT) that pioneered the community land trust (CLT) approach of guaranteeing long-term affordability
and providing a successful means of community engagement and decision
taking (Diacon 2008).

In order to consider a number of proposed measures, reference is made,
also here, to the ideas of E.F. Schumacher. They were widespread and various but closely interrelated (Schmidt and Budinich 2008). Besides his
thoughts about economics, work, technology, development, education,
traditional wisdom and religions, in this paper, particular attention goes
to his concepts about energy, ownership and size.

There is an astonishing topicality about Schumacher's quote on energy
taken from his book *Small is Beautiful* first published in 1973: 'It might be
said that energy is for the mechanical world what consciousness is for the
human world. If energy fails, everything fails' (Schumacher 1973: 99). It
seems to be, even today, very prophetic. Schumacher considers that energy
supply must be at tolerable prices, as 'There is no substitute for energy. The
whole edifice of modern life is built upon it [...] as it is the precondition of
all commodities, a basic factor equally with air, water and earth' (Kirk 1983).
These basic assumptions are particularly appropriate to the case of Ledeberg.

In *Small is Beautiful* Schumacher also pleads for private ownership as a
way to personal independence as far as it may lead to a healthy willingness
to work. He writes: 'As regards private property, the first and most basic
distinction is between (a) property that is an aid to creative work and (b)
property that is an alternative to it. There is something natural and healthy
about the former – the private property of the working proprietor; and
there is something unnatural and unhealthy about the latter – the private
property of the passive owner who lives parasitically on the work of others'
(Schumacher 1973: 222). Schumacher's ideas on ownership are the basis

for the E.F. Schumacher Society's initiatives on Community Land Trust founded in 1980. '[D]espite the increase in private homeownership, ever more land is being held in relatively fewer hands [...] and the poor, as always, are almost totally excluded' (Swann and King 1972).

The Ghent Social Housing Co-operative, which is a consortium of corporate organisations (including the city of Ghent), is trying to translate the basic ideas of a Community Land Trust (affordable housing / grant retention / community development) and to apply them to the traditions and objectives of the Flemish housing policy. It wants to give a new impetus in Flanders that again unites 'housing' with 'well-being'. A similar initiative in Brussels had the ambition to investigate the applicability of Community Land Trust in Belgium (De Pauw 2009: 16) (Nicolas and De Pauw 2010). The initiative ran into the project 'l'Espoir' at rue Fin near Brussels in Molenbeek. Through the radical choice of passive energy building, the Molenbeek administration has set the bar high in terms of energy management and sustainable development (De Pauw 2009: 27). The Ghent initiative is different because, for the first time, instead of acquiring building plots, it aims to take in co-operative management the dwellings owned and occupied by vulnerable groups and to renovate them. Based on the everyday experience many players have determined how difficult it is for these vulnerable residents to keep their acquired property or maintain it in a qualitative way. The Ghent Social Housing Co-operative will offer people a tailored guidance and support them for the refurbishment of their house and allow a community dimension and multiplier effect.

4.3 Quality Assurance Process

The city of Ghent has put aside a sum of 25 million euros until 2013 for the urban renovation project 'Ledeberg Lives'. In order to reach the target group, the 'Woonzorgzone' was founded. This is a workgroup with different partners, located in Ledeberg. This workgroup is part of the 'quality assurance system' in which every partner has its own goal within the renovation process. The quality assurance system integrates the measuring system for sustainability (Stad Gent 2008). The instrument tries to achieve a transformation of the houses towards low environmental impact buildings, with comfortable and healthy living conditions in an economic context of added value and affordable living.

The used methodologies take into account the different needs of knowledge by the different building partners involved in each project. Even if each project deals with new building partners a univocal work system could be finalized. The first partner is the city of Ghent. All houses have to comply with the Flemish housing code (Wooncode) in which the basic housing needs are defined. The housing law 'Vlaamse Wooncode' (Vlaamse Regering 1997) is the legislative basis of the housing policy in Flanders introduced to facilitate access to housing and to combat insalubrious housing conditions affordable for everyone. The city is responsible for guidance, advice and co-ordination of the renovations for owners who need this help. The second partner is the Social Welfare Centre (OCMW). It focuses on adapting to lifelong living for older people. The third partner is the non-profit organization ReGent (<http://www.vzwregent.be>) which is concerned with energy saving measures. ReGent monitors the energy losses and gives habitants simple tips for saving energy. All residents willing to invest in energy saving measures, such as roof insulation, can be helped with the coordination of these works. ReGent can give cheap loan rates for energy saving measures. The fourth partner is the Community Development Service (Samenlevingsopbouw). The organization focuses on the renovation for private tenancies. It tries to reach the tenants and to assist them in their rehabilitation and their contact with the owner.

In order to be easily accessible, a low threshold office is set up in the centre of Ledeberg, staffed alternately by the different partners. Some of the partners also go door-to-door, to reach the 'hard to reach' people. The first contact with the residents takes place with a random partner. After the initial contact the inhabitants are referred to the appropriate partner, who coordinates the entire renovation process. All projects are discussed within a working group to make sure no aspects are overlooked during the renovation.

Any owner or tenant, eligible for the renovation grant 'Ledeberg Lives', who wishes to renovate his home in a sustainable way can call upon the services of Domus Mundi. Domus Mundi assists the client throughout the construction process, providing technical assistance and advice. It helps also to find the right professionals and coordinates the services and works.

5   Conclusion

We can conclude that Schumacher's ideas concerning poverty, energy, ownership and size find a very concrete articulation in what is developed in this chapter on sustainable housing. The quality assurance system that has been developed in Ghent Ledeberg, a working-class neighbourhood in Ghent, is a concrete application of sustainable housing. The quality assurance system integrates instruments in order to evaluate sustainability and to achieve a transformation of the houses towards low environmental impact buildings, with comfortable and healthy living conditions in an economic context. The used methodologies take into account the differences in needs of knowledge by the different building partners involved in the project. The idea to start a Community Land Trust is a way to encourage affordable low energy and comfortable private ownership for very low-income people.

References

Avramov, D. (2003). *Housing Conditions and Housing Policy in Belgium*, Research Project 'Impact': The Housing Dimension of Welfare Reform. Vienna: The Interdisciplinary Centre for Comparative Research in the Social Sciences (ICCR).

Birchall, J. (2003). *Rediscovering the Co-operative Advantage: Poverty Reduction through Self-Help*. Geneva: International Labour Organisation.

Bruni, L., and Zamagni, S. (2004). 'The 'Economy of Communion': Inspirations and Achievements', *Finance & Common Good*, 20, 91–7.

CEB (2010). *Sustainable housing and urban development: Synthesis*. Paris: Council of Europe Development Bank.

De Decker, P. (2001). 'Jammed between Housing and Property Rights. Belgian Private Renting in Perspective', *European Journal of Housing Policy*, 1 (1), 17–39.

De Decker, P., Kesteloot, Ch., and Newton, C. (2008). *In my Caravan, I feel like Superman: Essays in Honour of Henk Meert 1963–2006*. St Andrews: Joe Doherty & Bill Edgar.

Demyttenaere, B. (2006). *In Vrije Val, Armoede in België*. Antwerpen: Manteau.

De Pauw, G. (2009). 'Les Community Land Trusts: un Modèle qui Rend la Propriété à Nouveau Accessible?', *Dossier Trimestriel du RBDH, Rassemblement Bruxellois pour le Droit à l'Habitat*, 37, 16–27.

Diacon, D. et al. (2008). *Presentation of the World Habitat Awards, Building and Social Housing Foundation*. Mexico: Aguascalientes.

Kirk, G. (1983). *Schumacher on Energy*. London: Sphere Books.

Linard, K.T. (2003). 'Economy of Communion: Systemic Factors in the Rise of a New Entrepreneurship', *Systems Research and Behavioral Science*, 20 (2), 163–75.

Nicolas, B., De Pauw, G. and Géronnez, L. (2010). 'Coopératives de Logement et Community Land Trusts', *Courrier hebdomadaire CRISP*, 2073, 5–52.

Rodgers, D. (2001). *Co-operative Housing, The New Mutualism in Public Policy*. London and New York: Routledge.

Schmidt, S., and Budinich, V. (2008). 'Housing the Poor by Engaging the Private and Citizen Sectors: Social Innovations and "Hybrid Value Chains"', *Global Urban Development Magazine*, 4 (2), 205–28.

Schumacher, E.F. (1973). *Small is Beautiful: A Study of Economics as if People Mattered*. New York: Harper and Row.

Schumacher, E.F. (1977, reprint 2004). *A Guide for the Perplexed*. New York: Harper Perennial.

Stad Gent (2005). *Startnota: samen werken aan Ledeberg, Dienst Stedenbeleid en Internationale Betrekkingen*. Gent: Cel Gebiedsgerichte Werking.

Stad Gent (2008). *Duurzaamheidsmeter; objectief meetinstrument voor duurzaamheid en kwaliteit in stadsontwikkelingsprojecten, toelichting*, <http://www.gent.be/ docs/Departement%20Milieu,%20Groen%20en%20Gezondheid/Milieudienst/ duurzaamheidsmetertoelichting.pdf> accessed 20 May 2013.

Swann, R., King R. et al. (1972). *The Community Land Trust: A Guide to a New Model of Land Tenure in America*. Cambridge, MA: Center for Community Economic Development.

Termont, D. (2009). *Het Indicatorenrapport. Met Meer Cijfers Bouwen aan een Beleid tegen Armoede*. Gent: Stad Gent Cel Armoedebestrijding en OCMW.

Tjallingii, S.P. (1995). *Ecopolis: Strategies for Ecologically Sound Urban Development*. Leiden: Backhuys Publishers.

Van Herck, K., and Avermaete, T. (2006). *Wonen in Welvaart. Woningbouw en Woon-cultuur in Vlaanderen, 1948–1973*. Rotterdam: Vlaams Architectuurinstituut and Centrum Vlaamse Architectuurarchieven, Uitgeverij 010.

Vlaamse Regering (1997). *Vlaamse Wooncode; Geconsolideerde versie oktober 2009*. Brussels: Departement Ruimtelijke Ordening, Woonbeleid en Onroerend Erfgoed.

Vrancken, J. (ed.) (2009). *Armoede en Sociale Uitsluiting, Jaarboek 2009*. Leuven: Acco.

Winters, S., and De Decker, P. (2009). *Wonen in Vlaanderen: over Kwaliteit, Betaalbaarheid en Woonzekerheid, De Sociale Staat van Vlaanderen.* Brussels: Studiedienst van de Vlaamse regering.

Wood, B. (1984). *E.F. Schumacher: his Life and Thought.* New York: Harper and Row.

JOEL THOMPSON
AFRICURRENCY LTD. LONDON

18 Recreating 'Economics of Permanence' in Africa

1 Introduction

In *Small is Beautiful* Schumacher made several damning indictments of the manner in which development is conceptualized and practised. Unfortunately, these practices continue to the present day – to the increasing detriment of hundreds of millions of poor people worldwide. After all, as Schumacher pointed out: 'We do not have thousands of poverty-stricken villages in our country; so what do we know about effective methods of self-help in such circumstances?' (Schumacher 1999: 166).

The billion dollar development business entrenched in the so-called 'developing world' has yet to come to terms with its gross failings over the decades. Despite (and to a considerable extent because of) increasing aid to African countries over the past forty years, aid has been commensurate with a rise in poverty and instability in the sub-Saharan region. Many African states are teetering on the brink of collapse or sinking into a humanitarian and ecological abyss in lands that once exhibited what Schumacher would have described as 'economics of permanence'. Sustainable development efforts will continue to be ineffectual until the current economic development model pursued is radically altered.

To alter the model, systemic interventions must target that which 'makes the world go round': *money*. By changing the way money functions, the way it is issued and how it circulates, the required alteration can take place through incentivising economic behaviours which promote the common good. Ultimately, a highly desirable attitudinal and cultural change can take place concerning the way development is conceptualized and implemented.

To this end, it is important that serious research and development of alternative monetary systems for Africa takes place. The process could benefit from being informed by the traditional values and wisdom which once formed the basis of the 'economy of permanence' in African societies.

2   The Economy of Permanence

Schumacher understands permanence to be wedded to peace (Schumacher 1999: 11ff). Rather than a continuation of the economic thought that has lead humanity and the planet towards the means and practice of 'self obliteration' (Schumacher 1999: 10), economic security for the world's billions can only be ensured through a global economy protected by the ecological economy. Only the ecological economy provides the means to sustain life in peace. But to provide this sustenance it must be prudently managed by man who 'experience[s] himself as a part of nature' and not 'an outside force destined to dominate and conquer it' (Schumacher 1999: 4). While heterodox economics does tend to recognize man as part of nature and the ecological economy at large, what remains economic to 'modern man' is that which makes 'adequate profit' (Schumacher 1999: 28). Heterodox economic thought and praxis has yet to counter the orthodox economic culture of GDP growth fever, and to mainstream the idea that there comes a point when economic growth becomes 'uneconomic' (Daly 2008: 210–11).

3   Permanence and Civilization

Civilized society began when early nomadic peoples began to settle and benefit from trade through economies of scale and division of labour. But the archetype of civilization soon became the rise of an aristocratic and later royal class to separate the haves from the have-nots (Bauer 2007: 51).

By enshrining socioeconomic inequality in blood, the working classes were separated from the ruling class, and '[t]he egalitarian structure of earlier hunter gatherer groups had shattered. A hierarchy now existed: the city first, the countryside second' (Bauer 2007: 20).

While civilization has since enveloped the world, indigenous economic structures rooted in egalitarianism continue to remain in pockets of the world untouched by modernity (although the numbers and traditional practices of native peoples are dwindling fast). Examples of the terrorization of indigenous populations stretch over thousands of years, but today the biggest threat is the encroachment of the state and its acquiescence in the swallowing up of native and untouched lands for industrial economic gain. This encroachment is a necessary feature of a monetary-economic system which forces the economy to grow. Yet while the system may benefit a few individuals or groups, in the long run 'the modern industrial system, with all its intellectual sophistication, consumes the very basis on which it has been erected' (Schumacher 1999: 9), namely the biocapacity of the Earth, and therefore it is ultimately a zero sum game for all involved.

To be indigenous or 'non-civilized', on the other hand, is to participate in traditional ways of being, doing and relating learned over countless generations in order to sustain the population indefinitely. Central to indigenous wisdom is the recognition of the rights of nature and the wisdom of living in cooperation with all living things. Therefore, to be non-civilized bears no relation to primitiveness or backwardness, but instead bears witness to an ancient body of wisdom which modern civilization ignores at its peril. As Hartmann points out: 'What has evolved as the most highly functional, stable, and sustainable form of human organization is the decentralized, small-tribe, egalitarian, and democratic community structure as practiced by the Shoshone and other native peoples worldwide' (Hartmann 2004: 306).

Non-civilized and indigenous economics of permanence are similar in philosophical nature to the Buddhist economic ways Schumacher makes references to in *Small is Beautiful*. The commonality is the spiritual centre and metaphysical grounding of the broader meta-economic narrative in the human person, which affirms the rights of living things as ends in themselves and not mere factors of production (Schumacher 1999: 73, 84). In redesigning and rebuilding our economic system to save the world from

the myriad catastrophes the current system creates, Schumacher enunciates one particular piece of wisdom in *Small is Beautiful* known for many
years to native peoples: '[N]o system or machinery or economic doctrine
or theory stands on its own feet: it is invariably built on a metaphysical
foundation, that is to say, upon man's basic outlook on life, its meaning
and its purpose' (Schumacher 1999: 221).

When examining the metaphysical foundation adopted by today's economic system, Schumacher describes it as one of 'the crudest materialism,
for which money costs and money incomes are the ultimate criteria and
determinants of human action, and the living world has no significance
beyond that of a quarry for exploitation' (Schumacher 1999: 89).

Schumacher turned to Buddhist economics for insight into metaphysical foundations more dignifying in work and more spiritually rewarding
in life.

4   African Economics of Permanence

Whether Buddhist economics or traditional African economics, it must
be recognized *a priori* that economics with a metaphysical grounding can
never be a distinct discipline in its own right. Traditional African economics
were an *integrated* framework of philosophy, religion, education, politics,
and societal and environmental well-being built upon reciprocal human
relationships that promote prudent and frugal use of collectivized resources.

The word 'economics' therefore can be misleading and does not do
justice to traditional economic conventionalism in Africa, which was an
essential guide to becoming fully human. Instead, the word *ubuntu* is a
more suitable word for the traditional economics in the indigenous sub-
Saharan African context. Although the etymology of *ubuntu* belongs to the
Xhosa ethnic group of South Africa, the term may be used to summarily
refer to similarities of philosophy which governed pre-colonial (and to an
increasingly limited extent, post-colonial) economic and societal structur-
ing across the sub-continent.

Ubuntu can be loosely defined as 'I am because you are, and you are because I am'. That is, to be human is to exist in relationships with others; since our humanity is inextricably bound up in one another's. Therefore, to succeed in life is never to succeed in isolation from others. To act selfishly is, according to *ubuntu*, to act as a madman or a stranger. Instead, the success of one is measured by how his or her success improves the survival and well-being of all. Consequently, *ubuntu* politics, economics and social interaction were rooted in virtues of service to others and to the common good. The *ubuntu* notion of the common good can be simply defined as the stability, harmony and well-being of all, by all and for all. This is the essence of the African proverb 'the only tree that grows is a forest', which likens the individual's place in the socioeconomic reality of the community to that of a single tree participating in the 'forest of permanence'. African economics of permanence exhibits an economic paradigm which explicitly integrates economic behaviour within a rigid metaphysical framework of general concern for the community and achieving the common good.

One example can be given for the Kikuyu people of Kenya. Mount Kenya is cherished in the tradition of the Kikuyu tribe as the resting place of their god, *Ngai*. The mountain slopes and surrounding soils provided the Kikuyu with plentiful land, food and water and therefore social, economic and environmental well-being were integrated and revered as a god. To offend nature would be to offend a greater power. This is an important lesson to take from African economics of permanence.

Riches are found in cultivating together (Kikuyu proverb)

5   Destruction of African Economics of Permanence

Traditional ways of being, doing and relating characterized by *ubuntu* are sidelined by globalized economic theory and practice. Social, economic, political and cultural implants across the sub-continent since the political independence era in Africa recognize one economic voice as correct and the others as wrong. The 'wrong' includes the indigenous wisdom and practices of African peoples that pre-date colonialism. Modern African economics have been thoroughly moulded in the image of economic orthodoxy; a tremendous amount of development aid is dedicated to 'capacity building' towards this end.

Capacity building works towards building African capacity in submission to an 'all growth is good growth' GDP-oriented economic development model which is contextually inappropriate, socially exclusive, unsustainable, the antithesis of *ubuntu* – and unachievable in any case. Development under this model is a fraudulent promise that will never take place as long as the paradigm remains unaltered. Moreover, it is spiritless and metaphysically groundless, trampling on social capital and systematically transferring the money and wealth of the majority poor to a minority rich. The privatization of land, wealth, the natural world and human life itself for economic gain reigns supreme to support this system. In *Small is Beautiful*, Schumacher warned against this, recognising that 'private ownership of the means of production is severely limited in its freedom of choice of objectives, because it is compelled to be profit-seeking, and tends to take a narrow and selfish view of things. Public ownership gives complete freedom in the choice of objectives and can therefore be used for any purpose that may be chosen' (Schumacher 1999: 218).

When Schumacher wrote *Small is Beautiful* nearly four decades ago he described the modern economy as 'propelled by a frenzy of greed [which] indulges in an orgy of envy, and these are not accidental features but the very causes of its expansionist success' (Schumacher 1999: 18). Today, the empirical evidence for this takes the form of a disastrous post-colonial economic, political, social and environmental record owned by African countries genuflecting to the 'idolatry of economism' (Schumacher 1999: 91). It is a testament to the relevance of Schumacher's thought today. The idolatry of economism infests the modern economic system and dissolves ancient African economics of permanence, instead favouring the socially exclusive well-being of a minority rich.

6   The Money Problem in Africa

> If human vices, such as greed and envy are systemically cultivated, the inevitable result is nothing less than a collapse of intelligence. A man driven by greed or envy loses the power of seeing things as they really are, of seeing things in their roundness and wholeness, and his very successes become failures. If whole societies become infected by these vices, they may indeed achieve astonishing things but they become increasingly incapable of solving the most elementary problems of everyday existence.
> — SCHUMACHER 1999: 18

According to Schumacher, the human vices are derived from the modern economic system. It is certainly true in the African context that vices are systemically cultivated by the modern economic system. But what then drives the economic system which creates this culture of greed and anti-permanence? The monetary-economic system is arguably the principal culprit.

The monetary-economic system in Africa (or 'the money problem' as it is addressed in this section) can be simplified down to a set of rules governing how money is created, issued and circulated. Few are aware of these rules, and this is part of the reason why, although granted political independence, African countries have been denied economic independence. Historically instituted and driven by former colonial powers, today an increasingly diverse array of elitist interests maintain economic hegemony over the continent's resources through instruments of debt, high finance, usury, flawed development paradigms and perpetual poverty.

The outcome is the accumulation of money among a minority rich who increasingly gain the means to buy up the means of production and wealth of the majority poor in an ever quickening cycle of compounding inequality. The socially and environmentally destructive nature of the money problem not only counters sustainable development efforts but further plunges the sub-continent into worsening humanitarian and environmental crises. The continent-wide fallout from the money problem has rendered many modern African states either failed or failing.

In sensing this force overwhelming the continent, one common question arises among students, academics, development practitioners and others: *How can it be that a continent with so much wealth can be so poor?* Ordinary answers to this question can be misleading, pinning the blame on 'bad leadership' or 'bad governance' or a whole host of other things, instead of upon the monetary-economic system and development paradigm upon which all governmental and most non-governmental institutions are built.

Asking the question is nevertheless a step in the right direction, for it recognizes a distinction between *wealth* and *money*. The distinction is made below.

6.1 Money

Money is a claim made on the economic output of society. Whoever controls, earns or has access to the largest amounts of money lays strongest claim to economic output in society. However, money can be possessed, earned or generated without contributing a single thing of value to society, the common good, or the economy. Hence, despite the fact that money allows an individual to lay claim to the creative wealth of productive individuals in society, it does not require the spender to have produced anything at all, and certainly not anything of social value – it only requires that one party offers something of value and the other party has money. Rather than a meritocratic system of earning money, African countries exemplify the opposite: the hardest working in society, such as farmers, who do no less than feed the nation, are some of the poorest and most downtrodden members of society. Circumventing the toil of labour while still making or otherwise obtaining 'easy money' is a feasible and attractive option. The system allows for it, so why not live off of the work of others, especially if one has plausible deniability of how the system works?

Of course not everyone can make money in this way. If everyone could make money by doing nothing the economy would have a big problem. The system relies upon the vast majority to remain poor and produce the country's wealth while a minority few 'sit on their backs' (Schumacher 1999: 173) and are allowed to claim the economic output of the working classes 'for free', without adding value to the economy, society or social capital.

Money further allows the extraction of wealth from its rightful owners and producers through purchasing power and hence the richest members of society also tend to be, or become, the wealthiest.

6.2 Wealth

Wealth, unlike money, is tangible or intangible capital or assets not necessarily represented (or 'monetized') by currency. There are many examples of wealth among the majority poor of Africa, including young and educated populations, land, cattle, social and communal welfare systems, social capital, entrepreneurial spirit and vast natural resources. While wealth may have a monetary or market value, it is not necessarily 'monetized' and indeed there is currently no mechanism which allows for the direct monetization of wealth as and when such monetization is needed.

Once the difference between wealth and money is understood, it becomes clear that it is indeed true that Africa's wealth among the majority poor and that of the commons greatly exceeds the amount of money representing this wealth. Without monetization – and therefore the ability to earn money from this wealth – the majority poor are destined to poverty, regardless of individual, familial or collective wealth or potential. What wealth exists must be continually sold off in the desperate bid for medium of exchange kept permanently scarce by the debt-based monetary system.

Africa arguably has greater amounts of human and natural capital than any other continent, yet no where else in the world is the disparity between the amount of wealth and the amount of money which represents this wealth greatest than in Africa. There is a huge amount of work and needs proliferating across the sub-continent, and indeed there exists a young and upcoming generation of educated Africans that can do this enlivening work and fulfil their economic aspirations. Yet unemployment is rife and young people are idle – a waste and a burden on the state, rather than the demographic boon that they should be. As Schumacher avers: 'If a man has no chance of obtaining work he is in a desperate position, not simply because he lacks an income but because he lacks this nourishing and enlivening factor of disciplined work which nothing can replace' (Schumacher 1999: 39–40).

The paradox, then, is that despite the existence of both the work and the people to do the work to build utopian African societies based on permanence, there are no jobs. Why should this be the case?

One reason is that jobs go where the money flows, which usually means the capital city or economic capital of the African country in question. These cities concentrate the nation's money supply and vacuum it up from the rural areas, aggravating the poverty cycle. Even in the cities, the money does little if any social good. Hoarded by a minority rich, it resides in the coffers of foreign banks, or travels abroad in payment for imported goods. Slums, urban decay, crime, destruction of social capital and other symptoms typical of rural-urban migration are some of the consequences, as the rural masses move to the cities in a desperate bid to obtain the national currency for use as a medium of exchange.

Obtaining satisfying and socially rewarding work is debilitated by scarcity of money which excludes the majority poor from an abundant medium of exchange. The majority poor of Africa cannot purchase goods and services they need or desire not because they do not have wealth, but because they lack the necessary instrument to exchange for it: money. In the desperate bid to obtain medium of exchange, wealth is either sold at undervalued prices or abandoned all together as a rural producer migrates to the cities in search of money. Under this regime, the potential economic output and societal contribution of the majority poor may be great, but the financial reward will always be poor.

If African governments at independence had the power, knowledge and will to create and prudently manage their own money, nationally created to meet the economic needs of their populations, Africa could not only be the wealthiest continent today, but the richest one too; and far more powerful politically, economically and culturally than it is at present. This scenario has never been in the interest of those countries desiring a geopolitically unipolar world and the fulfilment of the post-World War Two 'project of global dominance' (Chomsky 2011). For this and other reasons, when the colonial powers ceded political independence to African countries, and in the fifty odd years since, economic independence has never been ceded. Instead, African governments and their citizens were put in a position in which to obtain money they must:

1. Borrow money into existence from foreign institutions (at interest)
2. Receive money in the form of foreign aid (creating a culture of dependency, and with plenty of conditions attached to the aid)
3. Open up to foreign privatization of natural and common resources and/or
4. Depend upon remittances and tourism

As a result, today, African states rely chiefly upon their enormous natural resource wealth to earn the foreign currency needed to service the debt on borrowed money and keep the state's head above water for a little while longer. This is akin to a Ponzi scheme in which African states must give up increasing amounts of natural and human resources to service their debts; including clean air, aquifers, land, fisheries and forests. The masses are increasingly faced with two options: submit to serf labour (if one is fortunate enough to find a job) or become socioeconomically destitute.

The Ponzi scheme forces a growth imperative upon the economy in order to service the debt. It then becomes a race to the bottom to obtain foreign exchange as quickly as possible, and with the cheapest production methods possible, ignoring social and environmental costs. This, then, is what drives the modern economic system and its culture of anti-permanence described by Schumacher. Short term profiteering replaces long term thinking and social concern.

Besides countless avoidable humanitarian and ecological catastrophes since political independence, the fallout from the money problem continues to deny even short-term viability to African states. African children today, rich and poor alike, have little future to look forward to if dramatic, systemic change does not take place.

7   Recreating Economics of Permanence

The money problem opens up opportunities for innovative alternative monetary systems to step in and create an enabling environment for African economics of permanence to thrive. Complementary currencies, in particular, can tackle the current monetary-economic hegemony by designing new media of exchange which empower the majority poor and systematize a cultural shift away from the anti-permanence and greed of economism towards an economic culture founded upon the wisdom of *ubuntu* and permanence.

By introducing complementary currencies to Africa, groups of individuals, farmers, producers, NGOs, public sector services, local businesses and others can create, issue, circulate and democratize their own money supply and thereby begin to decouple from some of the speculative whims of monetary policy, international trade, high finance and investment banking. By partially or wholly circumventing the current monetary-economic regime, the majority poor can be supported in their bid to take greater control of their economic destiny. This type of intervention bolsters self-sufficiency, agency, economic stability and empowerment by, for example, encouraging the localization of the means of production through a locally circulating currency.

Design features of complementary currencies open up the door for a myriad of socioeconomic opportunities. For example, complementary currencies can be designed to prevent withdrawal from circulation to major cities by only having validity in a certain geographic area. Mechanisms can be implemented to prevent hoarding too, such as negative interest for holding onto money (also known as demurrage). In instances where complementary currencies are backed by national currency fully or partially, exchange out of the currency can be permitted under the predetermined terms which are agreed to by the complementary currency participants. Essentially, participants can directly control the terms and conditions for members who wish to benefit from the new money. By collectivising money in this way, alternative currencies can be designed to serve the interests of these groups. Some currencies can be designed interest and inflation free and others, such as mutual credit systems, can guarantee that as long as a member has something of value to offer the group or community, s/he will never be short of money for exchange.

Particularly in the African context, there is large untapped potential for complementary currencies utilising mobile payment technology. This renders the currency media electronic, although it could possibly have a physical form too. One advantage of digital over physical complementary currency is the immense liquidity advantages that instant money transfers provide for Africa's unbanked millions. Another advantage of a digital currency is the ability to monitor and decide what the money can be spent on by the currency administrators and, hence, what it will monetize for trade and what it will not. For example, ecological goods and services could be 'taxed' when they are used in an unsustainable manner by participants, but fully monetized generating the greatest financial gain when used in a socially responsible way. Tweaking the design of complementary currencies to internalize social and environmental externalities can be a straightforward process, and defectors from the rules can simply be suspended or excluded from using the currency.

Importantly, the economic sovereignty of a non debt-based currency can avoid the growth and scarcity imperatives built into the current monetary system. Instead, money can be issued and circulated interest-free to support a steady state economy that does not need to grow continuously in order to pay off compounding interest on debt. Within this flat line economy, complementary currencies can incentivize attitudinal and behavioural changes which improve social relations, social capital and community among members or participants through the trust of participants and joint effort towards common interests and goals. These are bedrock incentives to recreate African economics of permanence in the spirit of *ubuntu*.

Conventional donor money can continue to serve a purpose, but the monoculture of donor money leaves the NGO sector and its beneficiaries vulnerable to fluctuations in funding. 'Aid dollars' tend to leak out of the country whereas complementary currencies can avoid leakage and bolster community development through careful design and limited geographic or institutional validity. While donor money will have a role to play in the future, diversification of income through alternative means and mediums of exchange can play a complementary role in financial and economic stability for communities and institutions.

8 Conclusion

The desire for recreation of economics of permanence in Africa is not an idyllic or nostalgic pining for days gone by. It is a desire to meet human needs not currently met by the current system and it is borne of a desire to halt a monetary-economic system which continues the cultural, humanitarian and ecological descent of Africa at an accelerating pace. Sustainable development in Africa is absolutely impossible under the present monetary-economic regime.

Experimenting with new monetary systems in African societies and communities is a way to test and gather empirical evidence for the systematization of positive cultural and economic change through new currency media. This work has yet to begin in earnest in Africa; only several, mostly short-lived, complementary currency projects have been piloted on the sub-continent to date, despite the great potential for their introduction to Africa. Nevertheless, a grand opportunity presents itself to innovate a new model of development based on abundance, rather than scarcity.

References

Bauer, S. (2007). *The History of the Ancient World*. New York: W.W. Norton & Company.

Chomsky, N. (April 2011). 'Is the World Too Big to Fail?: The Contours of Global Order'. <http://www.guernicamag.com/blog/2607/noam_chomsky_is_the_world_too> accessed April 2011.

Daly, H. (2008). 'Frugality First'. In L. Bouckaert, H. Opdebeeck and L. Zsolnai (eds), *Frugality*, pp. 207–26. Oxford: Peter Lang.

Hartmann, T. (2004). *The Last Hours of Ancient Sunlight*. New York: Three Rivers Press.

Schumacher, E.F. (1999, first edition 1973). *Small is Beautiful*. Vancouver: Hartley & Marks.

BENNIE CALLEBAUT AND LUIGINO BRUNI
SOPHIA UNIVERSITY FIRENZE/UNIVERSITY OF MILAN-BICOCCA

19 The Economy of Communion as a Charismatic Practice

1 Introduction

Ernst Friedrich Schumacher is among the great figures of social science that have anticipated, prophetically, most of the problems that characterize the present age of crisis. He published his most well-known book, *Small is Beautiful*, during a very creative period of heterodox economic science, the 1970s. In that period most of the papers and books that were then considered classics of the non-mainstream economics of their time, however, are rediscovered today as classics of a new paradigm.

In 1970 A.O. Hirschman published his *Exit Voice and Loyalty*, a little book, and mostly misunderstood by his fellow economists, that opened a new season of dialogue (at least in his wishes) between the tools of politics (voice) and those of market (voice). Hirschman claimed the importance of bringing more 'voice' into market and economy, and more 'exit' into organizations and politics.

In 1971 N. Georgescu Roegen published his book *The Entropy Law and the Economic Process*, where he brought to the attention of the economic discipline (that nevertheless remained very inattentive) the innovative issue of the natural limits of natural resources and of the planet, by applying the laws of thermodynamics to economics, a methodological step that could have changed radically the economic paradigm and that, instead, remained totally ignored.

In 1974 the American economist and demographer Dick Easterlin published the seminal paper on the so-called 'paradox of affluent happiness', showing that US and western society had reached a sort of a steady state in subjective well-being or happiness. Three years later Tibor Scitovsky published a book on the same topic, *The Joyless Economy*, denouncing the American way of life as no longer producing the happiness of its people, who substitute the lack of authentic happiness with the consumption of comfort goods. Today we know, with the present crisis, how true this prophecy was, because the deepest root of our economic and financial crisis is the poverty trap of American society which, facing a great decrease in social and civil life, replaces the lack of sociality and relational goods with commodities: this search for commodity has brought the Western society and family (and the US in particular) to increase their debts in order to foster the increasing rate of consumption, up to the explosion of the subprime in 2008. This was, however, the end of a relationship between happiness-sociality-consumption which went wrong.

Fred Hirsh in his book *Social Limits to Growth* in 1976 introduced into the social sciences the issue of 'positional goods'. He also launched the central issue of positional competition as one of the key elements of modern economy and society that brings people to compete with each other in a sort of zero sum game. New forms of 'prisoner dilemma' games came to the fore where the social scarcity of most of the contemporary goods (i.e. the 'positional ones') does not allow market competition to achieve its traditional benefit in terms of efficiency and welfare, but it only leads to mutual destruction of natural, economic and relational resources. A topic that has old roots in the works of T. Veblen and later on in the works of K. Galbraith, and that has been developed at a later stage by economists such as Robert Frank or Richard Layard.

In 1977 the Indian economist Amartya Sen wrote his paper 'Rational fools', showing that the king of the assumption of economics, i.e. the 'rationality of the economic man' is naked, opening in this way a season of deep reflection on the nature of rationality in economics, following something similar to what happened in psychology thanks to the works of H. Simon a few years before.

It is in these 1970s that E.F. Schumacher published his book *Small is Beautiful*, and we are convinced that this book is one of those classics that was too innovative to be understood by his contemporaries. However, today it is a book that deserves to be rediscovered and listed among the new books about the forthcoming paradigm of post-crisis economics. In fact, in *Small is Beautiful* Schumacher was dealing with all the issues that we find in the classic books and papers we just mentioned. The well-being and happiness of people, the environmental challenge, the rationality of the standard economic man, the importance of the dialogue with politics for a true 'political' economy, are topics that are at the core of *Small is Beautiful*. In this book we find even other very original issues such as the attention paid to the economics of religions (Buddhism in particular), the attention paid to land and the propriety of firms, for social and economic justice, for the social responsibility of businesses, for the use of technology in order to foster the common good, for the critical role of nuclear energy, and so on. These issues were too new for Schumacher's time, but they were prophetic, because they anticipated, thirty years ahead of time, the new tendency of the more alive and humanizing streams of contemporary economics. For these reasons Schumacher deserves the gratitude of all economists and social scientists that are trying today to humanize economy and economics, convinced, as Schumacher was, that people matter. In particular, Schumacher's thought is very relevant for those who work in social civil economy.

We consider Schumacher in particular as a spiritual ally for the 'Economy of communion' project that will be presented in this chapter. Most, if not all, the issues dear to Schumacher (well-being, social justice, new governance of firms, destination of profits, involvement of workers in the propriety of a company, corporate social responsibility, relational goods, the importance of the creation of social capital within and outside the business) represent the very core of the 'Economy of communion' project. He died before the birth of the Economy of communion, but we are convinced that the entrepreneur and the scholars committed today in this project are 'handing in the baton', continuing the same 'race' toward a more just and fraternal economic and social world.

When faced with an author like Schumacher and initiatives such as the 'Economy of communion' that surprise and attain a certain social dimension, social scientists refer spontaneously to Max Weber's ideal-typical approach regarding exceptional, charismatic figures. It is in the same way that we will treat this subject in the following analysis. We want to find out what sort of insights can be gained from E.F. Schumacher. Can for instance E.F. Schumacher's view on adequateness teach us something about the 'Economy of Communion' (from now on abbreviated as EoC)? Schumacher in his little book *A Guide for the Perplexed* (1978) explains that the bodily senses are adequate for perceiving inanimate matter; but he argues that we need 'intellectual' senses for other levels of perception. And some people have more accurate intellectual senses than others. And was Chiara Lubich who founded the EoC (Gold 2007) also seeing something others did not perceive? We believe that the dialogue with Schumacher helps us to study in a more accurate way the genesis of Chiara Lubich's initiative. Firstly, we will present some important elements from Schumacher's writings that relate to this topic. Then we will examine elements of Chiara Lubich's life, the Focolare Movement and EoC from the point of view of both Schumacher and Weber.

2   The Schumacherian Approach and EoC

Schumacher observes that science has shown that we perceive not only with the senses, but also with the mind. He illustrates this with the example of a complex scientific book; it has very different meanings to an animal, an illiterate man, an educated man and a scientist. Each person possesses different internal 'senses' which means they 'understand' the book in quite different ways.

He argues that the common view that 'the facts should speak for them-selves' is problematic because it is not a simple matter to distinguish fact and theory or perception and interpretation. He quotes R.L. Gregory in

Eye and Brain (1966), 'Perception is not determined simply by the stimulus pattern, rather it is a dynamic searching for the best interpretation of data'. He argues that we 'see' not just with our eyes but with our mental equipment and 'since this mental equipment varies greatly from person to person, there are inevitably many things which some people can "see" while others cannot, or, to put it differently, for which some people are *adequate* while others are not'. (Schumacher 1978: 53). This remark by the German born economist who was also keenly interested in philosophy became very relevant for me when we began to study the very first foundational moments of the initiative of the EoC. We remembered a trip we made in 1988 to Brazil. On 15 September 1988 two theologians, friends of ours, and we met for a conversation that lasted for four hours with the well-known Liberation theologian, Leonardo Boff. During the conversation Boff expressed his disappointment as to the actual situation of social injustice in Brazil and commented on the incapacity of the leaders of Liberation Theology and Base Ecclesial Communities to mobilize the energy and creativity of the middle class in favour of the poor. If we agree with Schumacher that perception is a dynamic search for the best interpretation of data, Chiara Lubich saw the same drama of social injustice and in her dynamic search for a solution launched by the EoC as a way of involving the creativity of the middle class in a common project. How come she had a better view than other people as to Brazilian society?

In Schumacher terms it could be said that 'The lower abilities, such as seeing and also counting, belong to every normal person, while the higher abilities, such as those needed for the perceiving and grasping of the more subtle aspects of reality, are less and less widely available as we move up the scale' (1978: 54). But we cannot think about the Brazilian elite of the Liberation Theology in these terms. What was it that made Chiara Lubich capable of proposing a solution that others did not think of?

Schumacher reasons on the basis of his own philosophy of science. He notes that after Descartes science became 'science for manipulation'. Descartes promised that we would become 'masters and possessors of nature', a point of view first popularized by Francis Bacon. For Schumacher this was something of a wrong turn, because it meant the devaluation of wisdom, that is, the devaluation of the 'science for understanding'. One of Schumacher's criticisms is that 'science for manipulation' almost inevitably leads from the manipulation of nature to a manipulation of people. Schumacher argues that 'science for manipulation' is a valuable tool as long as it is subordinated to 'science for understanding' or wisdom; but otherwise 'science for manipulation' becomes a danger to humanity (1978: 67).

Schumacher argues that if materialistic scientism grows to dominate science even further then there will be three negative consequences: the Quality of life will decrease, because quantitative solutions are incapable of solving problems of quality. 'Science for understanding' will not develop, because the dominant paradigm will prevent it from being treated as a serious subject. Problems will become insoluble, because our higher abilities will atrophy through lack of use.

Did Chiara Lubich carry out a particular 'science for understanding' or wisdom? Schumacher argues that the ideal science would have a proper hierarchy of knowledge ranging from pure knowledge for understanding at the top level of the hierarchy to knowledge for manipulation at the bottom level. At the level of knowledge for manipulation, the aims of prediction and control are appropriate. But as we move to higher levels they become increasingly absurd. As he says 'Human beings are highly predictable as physico-chemical systems, less predictable as living bodies, much less so as conscious beings and hardly at all as self-aware persons'.

The result of materialistic scientism, in Schumacher's view, is that we become rich in means and poor in ends/goals/purpose. Lacking a sense of higher values Western societies are left with pluralism, moral relativism and utilitarianism, and for Schumacher the inevitable result is chaos. Chiara Lubich's initiative is clearly aimed at very ambitious goals: to solve the problem of poverty and social inequality. We now want to analyze with the help of Max Weber's thought how she reached this point of linking an 'ideal formulated in evangelical terms' with a practical proposal of an economic kind. Keeping Schumacher's approach in mind, we want to conclude in quite a synthetic way by reflecting on the consequences of the EoC for the issues of quality of life.

3 The Weberian Approach and Chiara Lubich

'The charismatic economy is often left in the shadows as if the institutional dimensions were the only relevant way for understanding economic and social life'. This formulation brings me back to an observation offered by the Oxford sociologist Bryan Wilson who asked the question if charismatic experiences were still possible in our contemporary society. His conclusion was that only feeble charisms were available and they were to be found only in the interstices of society, and not in the very heart of the dynamic of society nor in the sectors that matter most (Wilson 1975). Studying the so-called Economy of Communion or Sharing (EoC or EoS) as a sociologist it seemed to me to be an example of an economic initiative with charismatic influence. It seemed to me that here was an action by a contemporary religious leader aimed not at the margins, but rather at the very heart of the economy.

Chiara Lubich's initiative of the EoC was about asking people, competent in economics, to start new business enterprises in order to make profits and then to share these profits with the poor. It seemed to me that this proposal was not directed towards people in the margins but rather towards a very central actor in the entire economic process: the entrepreneur. And in doing so, Chiara Lubich proposed that the economic world should establish a more direct relationship with the social aspect of life in society.

The EoC project (Lubich 2001) was directed at the heart of two major areas of human activity, two fundamental functions of our society, the economic function and the social one, and aimed to mediate in a new way between two symbolic figures: the entrepreneur and the poor, to intensify the link between them, taking them into a new alliance, a new relationship of specific solidarity. Was this not a proposal of a charismatic type? We wanted to engage such a question following the logic of sociological research, but how?

I followed the sociological approach practised by M. Weber, particularly in his studies on charismatic leadership (Weber, 140–2; 654–87). Normally, centring the whole matter on his core concept of charismatic leadership supposes the presence of concrete needs and innovative proposals. Therefore the question is: does the EoC project respond to those needs and is it doing so in an innovative way?

The very idea of charismatic economy presumes at least from the Weberian point of view a person who acts as a charismatic leader! Are we here in the presence of a charismatic actor? The person who launched the 'Economy of Communion', Chiara Lubich (1920–2008), during her visit to the local Focolare community in Brazil in May 1991, had in her biography clear elements that correspond to the requisites of the Weberian ideal type. Today in the (Catholic) Church and also elsewhere, few doubt that she was an eminent religious figure of the twentieth century (De Lorenzo 2009). A charismatic leader has followers, people who feel the leader possesses an exceptional idea or gift and who become 'disciples' of the message he or she brings. The Movement Chiara Lubich is today one of the most widespread in the Catholic world, and counts on the support of millions of people; the group of people who are strongly committed to her spirituality and lifestyle amounts to more than 100,000 members, young and old, rich and poor, white and coloured (Callebaut 2010).

The founding idea, too, is an original one. The spirituality she brings is called 'the spirituality of unity' (Lubich 2001). The idea *per se* is not absolutely original, while pertaining to the central texts of the Gospel, even if we must say that none of the other initiatives which call for unity in our times, awoke such a following at grass root levels. But we are not simply here in the presence of a pure type of charismatic prophet nor are we in the presence of a mere reproduction of current Catholic discourse. Chiara Lubich demonstrated in various moments of her life a particular capacity for creative re-interpretation (Shotter 1984) of Christian spirituality.

She is known most of all for the original perspective she developed, based on her comprehension of Jesus' cry of abandonment on the cross (Rossé 1984, Gillet 2010, Tobler 2002) that represents for her the secret for the renewal of the relationships among people and humankind and God. Her development of the comprehension of what she called 'Jesus forsaken', offers without doubt in the history of Christian spirituality a truly original point of view. It permits people to think of the possibility of creating links that overcome barriers that exist between people and that impede universal brotherhood! And notwithstanding the normal difficulties inherent to every implementation of an ideal concept, the fact is that the ideal of unity as it is incarnated in the lifestyle of the Focolare, born in the Catholic Church, not only inspires Catholics and Christians, but has also demonstrated in recent decades that it is capable of breaking through the barriers among various religions. It even inspires people without religious preferences to become actively engaged in the Focolare Movement. In Schumacherian terms, Chiara Lubich seemed capable of a kind of science of understanding the world from the point of view of universal brotherhood,[1] and to act according to these insights as few others did in the same circumstances.

But the question that remains here is: is the launching of the EoC in Weberian terms a charismatic moment as well?

4 The Context, Brazil, Social Injustice and the Preferential Option in Favour of the Poor

Before coping with this theme, it is important to describe in general the context of 29 May 1991, the day that Chiara Lubich launched the EoC project. In the Focolare Movement, the reality of Brazil matters. The Movement

---

1	Many people speak about Chiara Lubich as a prophet of unity because of the numerous dialogues she had with many religious personalities and currents, but the main reason would be because she was also able to promote bonds of brotherhood and build bridges between parts of society in conflict with one another outside of the religious sphere. A sociological inquiry covering several years oof her story and the Focolare Movement brought me to the conviction, in the Weberian way of speaking, that we are in the presence of a religious leader with clear elements in certain moments and in certain aspects very near to the type of a prophetic charism. And as the Movement develops, this will bring forth a myriad of projects that aim to create bridges between different worlds, increasingly expressing key concepts configuring a kind of culture of brotherhood.

had been present in the country for decades (starting in 1958) and developed very quickly, all over this immense country. It was the first time in twenty-five years that Chiara Lubich was visiting the country and there was a sense of eager expectation, also because it might be her last visit and it might therefore be decisive for the future development of the Focolare in the country. There was a wish, in particular, that the founder would address the problem of social inequality in the context of an economy potentially among the most important in the whole world. This illustrates how Focolare people in Brazil expected that Chiara Lubich was able to see some solution, was adequate, to say it with Schumacher, to formulate a breakthrough in the blocked situation of the poor in the country.

When the Focolare arrived in Brazil in 1958, its members were clearly convinced that the Gospel-based way of doing things needed to be offered as a priority to address the situation of social injustice.

The Focolare supported 'the preferential option for the poor' that the Brazilian Church made in the 1960s, but the issue as to which of the numerous ways to implement this option remained open for them. It was hoped the founder would say a decisive word, an indication consistent with her own message and lifestyle. With the presence of a large number of poor people within the ranks of the Focolare and in spite of a large and generous communion of goods between haves and have-nots, this communion was not enough to provide sufficiently for all the poor within the Focolare community in that country. In the early 1960s the Focolare in Brazil seemed to represent a culmination in the experience of the Catholic Church, while Liberation Theology and the birth of base ecclesial communities (BECs) presented another culmination point a few years later, developing its own pattern pushing the whole Brazilian Church forward on its way to a more Gospel-based presence in society. This situation, however, gave birth to a kind of dialectic that expressed itself in sectors of Brazilian Church reprimanding the various ecclesial movements of European origin that had come to flourish at that time all over Brazil, privileging the middle class and not succeeding in implementing a preferential option for the poor (Comblin 1983, Motta 1998).

In her travel diary describing 15 May 1991, Chiara Lubich reaffirmed that poverty constituted one of the biggest problems on earth, and asked in a prayer to God the Father for new insights on how to act. A few days later, an idea emerged. Her reflection was nurtured by the fact that she saw with her own eyes the economic dynamics of the city of Sao Paulo where she stayed. The city is still the economic heart of Brazil, but Chiara Lubich noticed at the same time the existence of an enormous periphery of slums ('baraccopoli' or 'favelas') as a kind of crown of thorns around the city. Other elements which played a part in her thinking about the whole problem were the fall of the Berlin Wall, and the conclusions of a papal encyclical that had just been published, 'Centesimus annus' celebrating that the first papal social encyclical ('Rerum Novarum') had been published a hundred years ago. The pope made clear that any evolution whatsoever in the economic field had to take into account the very idea of freedom for the entrepreneur because economic creativity demands freedom. These elements further a Schumacherian conviction that some people are better capable than others at developing a kind of knowledge of the object as a whole, a kind of 'science for understanding' or wisdom as Schumacher called it. The kind of wisdom Chiara Lubich possessed demonstrates the contrary of what Schumacher describes about materialistic scientism where we become rich in means and poor in ends. Chiara Lubich indicated a rich purpose or goal and from there starts the process of change even with poor means.

5 Was the Proposal for an 'Economy of Communion in Freedom' Really Innovative?

Weber had a conviction about prophets: an authentic prophet generally creates, preaches or demands new obligations (Weber 1980: 141).[2] No authority asked Chiara Lubich to say what she said. We are in the presence

2   The original German text says: 'der genuine Prophet [...] überhaupt verkündet, schafft, fordert neue Gebote' (Weber 1980: 141). The English translation says:

of a certain amount of 'charismaticism'. In her speech on the subject that precedes the formal proposal to share the benefits of companies she said: 'Here, now (...), is born an idea: that God asks our Movement in Brazil, that amounts to some two hundred thousand people with all the sympathizers, to make possible a communion of goods that engages the Movement as a whole' (Quartana 1988, pp. 15–16)![3] Weber continues his analysis affirming in the very phrase already quoted that in the primitive definition of the charism, this would take place by way of revelation, oracle, inspiration or a specific will to change, and all this recognized as something original by the community of believers, of the military, of the party or of something else.[4] Chiara never referred to more than this: 'an idea' and that it seems to her 'a call coming from God himself'. She never used the term 'inspiration'; she used the more neutral term of 'idea', but clearly considered it as a thing to accomplish because it was welcomed as God's will. But afterwards she insisted on neither of the two legitimations. That is what it was, and this sobriety was consistent with the style of Chiara Lubich on similar occasions. She never 'played' the prophet, even if she was conscious of the gravity of the occasion. But for Weber it's not only important who gave the order or put forth the original idea. What matters also is that the disciples believe it and that it is in line with the charism, with the message already given!

What was then the precise proposal launched by Chiara Lubich? Her reasoning was that it was not enough to exercise a bit of charity, a work of

---

'The genuine prophet, like the genuine military leader and every true leader in this sense, preaches, creates, or demands new obligations' (Weber 1968: 51).

3　In *Essential Writings* the choice was made to present the Economy of Communion by an extract of the lesson professed on 29 January 1999, in the Siege of Piacenza of the Università Cattolica del 'Sacro Cuore', on the occasion of the attribution of a Doctorate honoris causa in Economics (Lubich 2007).

4　'[...] im ursprünglichen Sinn des Charisma: kraft Offenbarung, Orakel, Eingebung oder: Kraft konkretem Gestaltungswillen, der von der Glaubens-, Wehr-, Partei- oder anderer Gemeinschaft um seiner Herkunft willen anerkannt wird' (Weber 1980: 141), in English: 'In the pure type of charisma, these are imposed on the authority of revelation, oracles, or of the leader's own will, and are recognized by the members of the religious, military, or party group, because they come from such a source' (Weber 1968: 51).

mercy, a small amount of communion of goods between single persons. The key concept in her speech was that she wanted entrepreneurs, capable of efficiency in the way they direct their firms so as to make them be profitable. And the innovation consists of this very point, the profits should be shared (Quartana 1988, p. 16). Chiara Lubich also immediately had a scheme for the division of the profits. One part for the company itself, one part to distribute to the poor, and one part to invest in programs that promote education in the key concepts of a culture of communion.

What is new about all this? The fact of calling on the business world to solve problems of justice and brotherhood. Chiara Lubich does not appeal to a traditional way of doing things, ways the managers were used to; she did not pronounce a traditional speech where she transmits an inherited knowledge about charity. At the same time she is in the very heart of the Christian tradition. The idea of sharing things is as old as the first Christian community of Jerusalem according to the Acts of the Apostles. Although the first communion of good was essentially for consumers (and in fact it does not' seem that it became a model for the early churches – see Paul asking Antioch to help the community of Jerusalem) Chiara Lubich invites a communion to involve the production process, and not the consumption cycle. The reflection on 'innovation' in sociology is connected to the idea of relative innovation, socially situated. The explanation which is given is that 'the original text is necessarily always reinterpreted by the mediation of the socio-cultural coordinates of the times, place and tradition lived by the group, which is itself particularized, differentiated, conditioned, and by this very fact innovative' (Séguy 1999: 129, own translation). As a way of legitimizing the practice of the communion of goods in the Movement, Chiara Lubich always recalls the experience of the first Christians. But now, she applies it to a new field, even if the very idea is not original. Nobody has ever put it in such a systematic articulated way before – applying the idea of a communion of goods to the level of companies and enterprises. The real innovation is here. The cooperative firm was a formula that surely realized in a certain way the same ideals for more than a century. Here the form of the companies does not matter and Chiara Lubich addresses herself to the most common figure in the world of enterprise: the entrepreneur who possesses his own company. We will find cooperative firms among the companies engaged in the EoC years later, but they are not the majority. Ordinary companies are the ones best represented in the whole group of firms adhering to EoC.

It seems important to me to stress the point that this proposal not only takes into account a social aspect (the marginalization of the poor out of the normal labour circuit) but also an economic aspect (because of the very fact that the economy excludes them), and gives an answer which is not made up of religious terms (prayer, communion of personal goods as was done by the first Christians). It gives an answer in economic terms and goes straight to the heart of the economy. The answer for Chiara Lubich is that we need to form new companies which should decide from the very beginning to share the profits they will make. That the answer is an economic one, we can also deduce from the reasoning about the distribution of the profits where the first part has to go to the companies themselves in order to help their own business grow. Second, they are used to help people, who are in need, giving them the possibility of living a dignified life while looking for work or by offering them work in the business itself. Finally, there is the attention to the cultural aspect of the initiative. If one is a charismatic leader, he or she is so because of people who believe in his or her message and that is so for all social movements: without a group that supports the initiative, nothing is possible.

But once the group exists, and here the group supporting the EoC is the whole Focolare Movement, you must ensure that the lifestyle of this group also 'becomes' a culture, a common conviction also on the part of the group supporting the initiative. In order to realize this goal people need to be educated to such a lifestyle. A cultural mediation needs to be elaborated that considers sharing as vital. 'I give, therefore I exist' should become one of the popular slogans of this cultural program, clearly as an alternative to the reigning slogan in the world of mass consumption: 'I buy, therefore I exist'.

But at this point, you have to stress first of all that as a religious leader Chiara Lubich formulates an economic proposal in view of a problem, a foreseen need: to found companies that produce more profits. In doing so entrepreneurs are promoted to the dignity of actors in a new economic culture. In the mentality of many actors in the social field,[5] entrepreneurs are more easily viewed with suspicion than with respect. They were seen as being part of the group of exploiters rather than as part of the actors in favour of the poor! We see a proposal here that in this sense breaks with a certain tradition.

6 The Economic Theory as a Problem (an Achilles' Heel)

How can we situate this proposal in the context of the relationship of modern Catholicism with economics? E. Poulat (1988), a well-known French specialist of contemporary Catholicism, saw three ways of building relationships between modern Catholicism and the economy: an unending struggle (traditionalism), a way of upgrading [Catholicism] and fight [modern society] (progressivism) and accommodation (modernism).

As a matter of fact, none of the three approaches succeeds in catching the very point of the EoC project because the EoC integrates a respect for economic logic but opens it from within to a more solidarity-based evolution. With the economy going beyond the economy, it would be possible to summarize the slogan from a book published only a few years ago along the same lines: with Marx going beyond Marx. The link to Schumacher's plea that a 'science for manipulation' should be subordinated to 'science for understanding' seems evident. Chiara Lubich using economic mechanisms wants to integrate them in a humanitarian horizon, the relief of the poor, the disappearance of social injustice.

---

5   When the sociologist speaks of the *social*, one needs to see more precisely what he means by this. The normal ambition of a sociologist is to analyze and try to understand society as a big whole. But here the term social is used in a more restricted way, when one talks about economy and social politics. The term 'social' then has a more restricted field of application, being linked with the questions of distribution of riches as the economy is intended to produce riches.

A fundamental question is raised here: how was the Church itself doing during throughout the centuries with economics? E. Poulat summarizes his own research into the cultural reaction of the Church regarding economic thinking by expressing the conviction that it 'was always the Achilles heel of the Catholic Church. She was given to social thinking, but never possessed a true economic thought. [...] [Catholics active in the economy] have lived in an unorganized way, without worrying about gathering their experience in view of a specific doctrinal elaboration'.. There is another quote of the Parisian sociologist that is relevant here: 'Everything started with the long conflict between holy poverty [the Catholic approach, symbolized by Saint-Francis] and holy enrichment [Calvin and the bourgeois of Geneva], where pastors and theologians thought they moved on their own territory. When holiness disappeared, there remained two naked forces face to face. The question for Catholic thought remains then to know what it is that she really can do on her own terms for this topic' (1988: 55).

The Church in the very last decades has begun to reflect in a more systematic way on the economy, with the famous letter of the Bishops of the United States on the economy in 1983 as the best example. This cannot hide the fact that the Catholic world has serious and enduring problems to think about in terms of integrating the economy in its own perspective. In this sense the initiative of the EoC stimulates the Catholic world to foster new ways of interpreting the economy taking this vital initiative from within the economic world.

The proposal of Chiara Lubich comes from a non-economist, a non-professional who has nothing to do with the sector, and who is obviously also a non-entrepreneur (at least not in the economic context of the term)! It is much more surprising also because an economic type of approach is not really the core business in the social thinking of the 'Catholic house', as we mentioned above! Certainly her proposal is nothing more than an intuition, not an articulated reflection that is scientifically validated. But it uses the economy as her principal leverage. This can be one's very objection: it is an intuition, an inspiration of a mystical type rather than of an economic one. But one can also reply that with the audacity of a prophet, she defines what constitutes the very heart of economic acting which should ultimately be love, a love articulated as successful specific reciprocity: in other words communion, or to paraphrase Poulat's 'holy sharing', a value you can translate in lay-terms as solidarity. This is the very reason that it deals with the most symbolic collective figure of the modern economic world, the company, and its major actor, the entrepreneur. Chiara Lubich wants to push the companies to function in their own logic: the logic of entrepreneurship, so as to produce more goods and services, with the firm conviction that this effort can be put at the service of the social cause *par excellence*: 'and there was nobody poor among them'!

It is not surprising then that this approach has awoken the interest of the academic world in the field of economics and that Chiara Lubich herself was awarded a doctorate honoris causa in economics (Piacenza 1999). From the very beginning of the project (1991) Chiara Lubich stimulated young students in economics to study the project, and from 1998 on she called on Focolari scholars in economics to organize their studies in order to give 'scientific dignity' to the efforts of those who in daily life demonstrated with facts that the economy of communion is working (Lubich 2001: 75),[6] a very Schumacherian way of thinking. The answer to this call has been generous and it has generated a series of studies and given rise to numerous scientific and academic initiatives and publications which have earned a certain success.[7]

---

6   The speech Chiara Lubich pronounced on 7 May 1998 in the little town of the Focolari near Sao-Paulo, addressed at especially the Focolari scholars, goes as this: 'The Economy of Communion cannot limit itself at the only exemplifications of new firms inspired by it, with some comment of people more or less expert in the matter, now it has become necessary to give birth to a science born out of the collaboration well prepared economists who are able to formulate theory and practice, confronting them with other scientific traditions in economics, and this not only stimulating thesis on master level but authentic schools where many can come and attain new insights. A real science that gives a real dignity to the ones who demonstrate with the facts the reality of the EoC and illustrate that we're here in front of a real vocation for the ones who engage themselves in whatever way they do it for the EoC' (Lubich 2001: 75).

7   One can follow the evolution in the review *Economia di comunione*, available also on the website: <www.edc-online.org>, and on the site of the Worldwide Archives of the theses of EdC: <www.ecodicom.net.>

7   The Economy of Communion and the
Charismatic Practice of Economics

There is another way to illustrate the novelty of the proposal of May 1991.
Weber's approach also touches upon the aspect of the charismatic fulfilment of needs. J. Séguy, in an article he wrote on religious institutes (1992:
35–51), answers in the affirmative the question whether there will remain
certain elements of the charismatic economy also in our most contemporary
modernity.[8] In the way Séguy sees it, Weber distinguishes two possible
regimes in his notion of charismatic economy:

> The one who corresponds to the pure type – the ones who consider the fulfilment of
> needs with only an answer in the charismatic way, out of all rational economy – and
> the one less conformed to it but at certain moments very near to the charismatic
> economy. This is the case of those who have a minimal routinization or a relatively
> administered charismatic economy, even if it introduces a certain degree of daily
> economic rationalization, but that does not impede the rationality in value to domi-
> nate the whole process. He stresses the fact that many religious institutes don't have
> anything more urgent than to produce – in part following an ascetic rationality –
> some surplus in order to let this surplus escape for a relatively important part from
> the logic of accumulation and of the logic of investment, in other words to escape
> from the very logic of the capitalistic market. (1992: 47)

With the EoC, these enterprises that also started to adopt the way of con-
ducting their companies according to the distribution of profits as envisaged
by Chiara Lubich, remain businesses which obey rational economics and
thus submit themselves to the logic of capitalistic markets. But at the same
time they are starting to leave part of their profits out of this logic. So here
we are not in the logic of charismatic experiences which become routinized,
but rather in the case of a rational economy which is becoming partially
charismatic. It is difficult to deny the presence of an innovative aspect here.

---

8   J. Séguy defined rational economic practice in the sense of the capitalist economy
     as a rationality of 'accumulation, from the investment on the market of capitals,
     the return on the investment and the profit, of modern daily life'. The charismatic
     economy functions for him with 'the gift, the sharing, the ascetic motivations, gratu-
     ity, the non-daily exceptional' (1992: 48).

And as we know we are not in the presence of religious people who administer the undertakings of an abbey or of their proper religious institute, we are in the presence of laypeople who act as entrepreneurs.[9] Of the three terms of the expression 'Economy of Communion in freedom' which represents the entire title of the project, the company integrates two terms spontaneously: 'freedom' and 'economy', but it adds from the Focolare inspiration the impulsion towards communion, and thus a way of managing the enterprise that integrates also the logic of gift, gratuity, ascetic motivations, a more acute sense of the exceptional out of the daily routine.

8 Revaluing also the Middle Class in order to Reach Social Justice

A few years ago, a book with the title: *The working class doesn't exist anymore* had some success in France. Many times, specialists have difficulties in their studies on social movements, and most of all in theoretically reflecting on the condition of the poor, to figure out a positive role for the middle class. With respect to this very point, another element emerges which is still not often highlighted when studying the EoC. We remembered at the start of this contribution the quote from the well-known theologian L. Boff, that the cause for the relative lack of real impact of Liberation Theology and the BECs on Brazilian society as such consisted from his point of view in the fact that they did not succeed in engaging the middle class in this process of 'liberating' the poor.

---

9   J. Séguy observes that in the case of religious institutes the function of internal cohesion is a consequence of the practice of sharing the profits. In the firms which practise the EoC one very rapidly could observe an analogous evolution, the operation of distribution of the profits is perceived as an element that is ethically and religiously valorising. Séguy concludes: 'It permits the interested people to be free of the feeling of guilt eventually contracted by the obligation to produce capital following the rules and for scopes that are beyond their will, and to risk so the rupture or the weakening of the solidarity ad intra' (1992: 47).

As sociologists, we could accept this reasoning without difficulty. At that time we were already aware that a society is more socially balanced when it has a developed middle class, because it safeguards the possibility of social mobilization and a good rate of turn-over for the elites. It is also the middle class which manages the dynamic of the small and medium-sized enterprises whose presence is very often the sign of a country's good economic health, and also because of their capacity to have an elastic reaction to the most variable conjunctures.

I remembered this element of my bibliography when EoC emerged. Without being a specialist at economic and labour sociology, Chiara Lubich with her basic 'philosophy' and following her evangelical 'instinct' in linking between them very distinct realities, counted for the realization of the EoC precisely on the middle class as important actors, and in our case she made this very specific appeal to the symbolic figure of the entrepreneur. Not that she stopped there, but she wished them to be of service for the cause of better social justice. If one carefully reads the speeches of Chiara Lubich at the time, the core question for her remained the situation of the poor, as they are the centre of her attention. In order to realize the dream of Gospel equality for all the children of God, the EoC was born. We a're clearly at the very heart of the preferential choice for the poor made by the Latin-American Church.

But Chiara Lubich, giving a central place to the entrepreneur in this project as well – and thus not only or not exclusively to the poor – puts the entrepreneur's dynamism at the service of this major 'cause' which gives him a new dignity and a supplementary motivational structure.[10] N.M. Hansen already drew attention to this point: 'ideological and religious values – in other times underestimated as irrational or suspect and of uniquely negative significance for economic growth – could in numer-

---

10   It helps him to acquire a capital of social prestige. J. Séguy, talking about the religious institutes, made this statement about this theme of the social capital: 'The religious acquire prestige (in religion as well as in modernity) practicing a poverty that is partially adapted to the modern daily economy; transferring with an ascetic conduct the products of the ordinary capitalist market rationality into another market, having his own logic, the one of the social economy, based on humanitarian and religious motivations' (1992: 47).

ous cases be utilized as fundamental motivations for a rational economic action' (Hansen 1963: 462–74).

One must know that as early as 1964 Chiara Lubich had said in Recife to the Focolare directors that the way for the Movement in Brazil was the poor, but for that they first had to focus on building up the Focolare. The Focolare has developed from then on in all social classes, among the poor, the rich and in the perception of some observers primarily in the middle class. In 1964, Brazilian society seemed incapable of closing the gap between the rich and the poor.

The EoC was not only to free the poor, but also the rich and the creative middle class, to put the dynamics of the rich and the middle class at the service of another cause than only their own private enrichment. With charismatic intuition, the founder of the Focolare bypassed in her proposal for an Economy of Communion in 1991, the difficulty formulated by L. Boff three years earlier on the missing responsibility of the middle class. We could not explore in this chapter how EoC developed the relationship with the poor and how it stimulated a series of practices of self-development of the poor in the sense of the best practices today in this field. As we know, Schumacher had in mind the cooperative firm as the model of developing the poor as an actor, and paid attention to the risk of paternalism. So did Chiara Lubich from her point of view.

9   Conclusions

Does the EoC project innovate in the Weberian ideal sense a charismatic economy? With this in mind we searched for a need and an innovative way of solving this problem.

The need: more social justice, the opportunity for the poor to find a job and an insertion in social life in the Brazilian society (or elsewhere). The innovative way: help the firms complete their usual scope of economic acting: to produce, transformed now in: producing, in order to be able to distribute more.

We saw in various ways that we face a novelty here: by engaging the middle class in an active role, recuperating for the area of production a distributive role as well (giving it a more social role) and leaving this not only to the state agencies; by recuperating a charismatic aspect or role for the world of enterprises as well, by redirecting theoretical reflection, integrating themes as gratuity, gift, ascetic motivations, a more fine-tuned sense of the non-daily exceptional things present in the economic process.

It puts the holy enrichment at the service of the poor with the help of 'holy poverty' that renders the entrepreneur more detached. The EoC project is also innovative in this sense that it stimulates an ecclesial reflection on economics and not only on some social aspects of economic life, studying a practical project that recuperates the economy as a dimension worthy of Christian engagement but also worthy to be subject to Christian reflection. In a sentence, a simple intuition, Chiara Lubich innovates within the framework of the Focolare Movement completing her conception of labour, communion of goods and Providence, with a fourth pillar for building a Gospel-based relationship to economics: the EoC project (Gold 2007).

In this way, she puts 'holy enrichment' at the service of the poor by practising a 'holy poverty' that renders the entrepreneur detached from his own profits but stimulates him in being dynamic as an entrepreneur. In other words, the undertaking of Chiara Lubich consisted ultimately in joining 'holy enrichment' and 'holy poverty' at the service of the real poor! Would that not have been the very dream of Francis and Calvin?

And Schumacher? The whole analysis of the efforts to produce elements for another, a richer, wiser economic science starting from the experience of the entrepreneurs of the EoC, illustrates Schumacher's insight that 'science for manipulation' (the reigning economics) is a valuable tool when subordinated to the 'science for understanding' or wisdom. The wisdom in the slogan: 'I give therefore I exist', which Chiara Lubich asked scholars to prove is wiser and in the end also economically more efficient than 'I buy, therefore I exist', and provide in this way scientific dignity to those who on the grassroots level do live and realize the EoC. The scholars studying and transforming the intuitive insights of the EoC and bringing them to the level of scientific debate realize the importance of Schumacher's plea for wisdom and quality in our reasoning about life (Schumacher 1978: 19).

References

Callebaut, B. (1988). *Notes de Voyage au Brésil*, inédit (en archives personnelles, 1420).

Callebaut, B. (2010). *Tradition, Charisme et Prophétie dans le Mouvement International des Focolari. Analyse Sociologique.* Paris: Nouvelle Cité, Bruyères-le-Châtel.

Cambón, E. (2009). *Trinità, Modello Sociale.* Rome: Città Nuova.

Comblin, J. (1983). 'Os "Movimentos" e Pastorale Latino-Americana', *Revista Eclesiastica Brasileira*, 170, 239–67.

De Lorenzo, M.-C. (2009). 'Hanno detto di Chiara e dei Focolari'. In M. Zanzucchi (ed.), *Focolari. La fraternità in movimento*, pp. 136–9. Rome: Città Nuova.

Gillet, F. (2009). *La Scelta di Gesù Abbandonato, Nella Prospettiva Teologica di Chiara Lubich.* Rome: Città Nuova.

Gold, L. (2007). 'The Economy of Communion'. In L. Bouckaert and L. Zsolnai (eds), *Spirituality as a Public Good*, pp. 53–66. Antwerpen-Apeldoorn: Garant.

Gold, L. (2010). *New Financial Horizons: The Emergence of Economic Communion.* New York: New City Press.

Gregory, R.L. (1966). *Eye and Brain: The Psychology of Seeing.* London: Weidenfeld and Nicolson.

Hansen, M.N. (1963). 'The Protestant Ethic as a General Precondition for Economic Development', *Canadian Journal of Economics and Political Science*, 29, 462–74.

Lubich, C. (1999). 'L'esperienza "Economia di Comunione": Dalla Spiritualità dell'Unità una Proposta di Agire Economico', *Nuova Umanità*, XXI, 126, 613–19.

Lubich, C. (2001). *L'Economia di Comunione. Storia e Profezia.* Rome: Città Nuova.

Lubich, C. (2007). *Essential Writings. Spirituality, Dialogue, Culture.* London: New City.

Motta, J. (1998). 'Una Sfida Permanente', *Città Nuova*, 12, 30–1.

Poulat, É. (1983). *Le Catholicisme sous Observation. Du Modernisme à Aujourd'hui.* Paris: Centurion.

Poulat, É. (1988). 'Pensée Chrétienne et Vie Economique', *Les Cahiers de l'Unité*, 16, 37–58.

Quartana, P. (1992). 'L'Economia di Comunione nel Pensiero di Chiara Lubich', *Nuova Umanità*, XIV, 80–1, 9–20.

Rossé, G. (1984). *Il Grido di Gesù in Croce. Una Panoramica Esegetica e Teologica.* Rome: Città Nuova.

Schumacher, E.F. (1978, first edn 1977). *A Guide for the Perplexed.* London: Abacus.

Séguy, J. (1992). 'Instituts Religieux et Economie Charismatique', *Social Compass*, 39, 35–51.

Shotter, J. (1984). *Social Accountability and Selfhood*. Oxford: Blackwell.

Tobler, S. (2002). *Jesu Gottverlassenheit als Heilsereignis in der Spiritualität Chiara Lubichs. Ein Beitrag zur Überwindung der Sprachnot in der Soteriologie*. Berlin-New York: Walter de Gruyter.

United States Conference of Catholic Bishops (1986). *Economic Justice for All. Pastoral Letter on Catholic Social Teaching and the US Economy*. Washington D.C.

Weber, M. (1980, 1922). *Wirtschaft und Gesellschaft*. Tübingen: Mohr (Siebeck); English version 1968: *On Charisma and Institution Building. Edited and with an introduction of S.N. Eisenstadt*. Chicago: The University of Chicago Press.

Wilson, B.R. (1975). *The Noble Savages. The Primitive Origins of Charisma and its Contemporary Survival*. Berkeley-London: The University of Berkeley Press.

STEWART WALLIS
NEW ECONOMICS FOUNDATION

20 The Urgent Need to Transform Economics

1 Introduction

Schumacher was unequivocal about the evils of modern industrial society.
He thought it guilty of 'four great and grievous evils'

1. Its vastly complicated nature
2. Its continuous stimulation of, and reliance on, the deadly sins of greed, envy and avarice
3. Its destruction of the content and dignity of most forms of work
4. Its authoritarian character, owing to organisation in excessively large units.

He went on to say that modern industrial society should fail because, inter alia, it was depleting and polluting the earth's resources, degrading human moral and intellectual qualities and breeding violence – a violence against nature which, at any time, could turn into violence against fellow humans.

I want to show today how true his insights were and why we are now in a situation where we face a number of systemic and interlinked crises of unimaginable proportions.

I will argue that there are ways through these crises, but only if we take responsibility ourselves for leading a transformation of our current economic system – a system which is morally and intellectually bankrupt. Fritz Schumacher's brilliant insights and moral courage can help show us the way.

2   Four Systemic Interlinked Crises

I believe that there are four systemic, interlinked problems with the current global economy – I call them the four U's. Our economy is unsustainable, unfair, unstable and is making us unhappy.

Unsustainable: We are running out of planet. We face a serious risk of at least a 4 degree Celsius temperature rise compared to pre-industrial levels, with all the extinction of species and other problems that go with it. We are well on track for that. We are running out of much else as well, which is not widely known. The Millennium Ecosystem Assessment of a couple of years ago, which looked at the various life-support systems of the planet and the ecosystem services that flow from them, showed that fifteen out of the twenty-five major ecosystems, the life support systems the whole planet depends on, are in decline or even serious decline. This includes fresh water, topsoil, pollination systems, fish, etc. So the problem is much wider than climate change alone.

The fundamental problem is not population – although the growing population is not helping – but rather overconsumption. The pervasive social modelling of 'I want more' provides incentives to acquire more stuff. Let's be clear what the issues are and how fast the situation is worsening. There is a measure called the global footprint, which basically assesses whether we are living within the planet's resources or not. Back in 1980 the population of the planet was living within just about one planet's worth of resources, a sustainable state. In the space of thirty years we have moved to consuming 1.3 planets' worth of resources every year. If you consider how long human beings have been on the planet, this statistic shows that in the space of just thirty years we have moved to overshooting the planet's carrying capacity by 30 per cent. The trend will become worse if we continue on the path we're on now. If everybody in the world lived at the level we do in my country, the United Kingdom, we would need three planets. If everybody lived at the US level, we would need five planets. Because we have only one, it doesn't work for everybody to aspire to our lifestyle. We have got to change. We are also running out of scarce materials, not just ecosystems. Aside from oil, look at the mineral shortages we face. The discovery and extraction rates can't keep up with the consumption rate, which inevitably leads to wider scarcities or ballooning prices.

Unfair: The second major problem is illustrated by growing inequality, and the two are systemic and linked. Here I think people tend not to be aware of how fast this has changed. At the beginning of the twentieth century the richest 20 per cent on the planet were between five and seven times richer than the poorest 20 per cent. At the end of the twentieth century, the ratio had moved to seventy-five to one. A dramatic change. The biggest driver of the social ills we face isn't poverty per se, isn't necessarily even unemployment although that is a major factor. It is inequality. The degree of inequality in a country corresponds closely to all sorts of social ills within that country, from the prison population to the number of unwanted teenage pregnancies to drug use. In the USA, 80 per cent of the new wealth created between 1980 and 2005 went to not the top 50 per cent of the population, not to the top 25 per cent, not even the top 10 per cent, but unbelievably to the top 1 per cent. Economists used to talk about wealth 'trickling down' to the poorest as the economy grew. What we are seeing now is wealth being 'hoovered up' from all sections of society to the very rich.

Unstable: We need our economic systems to be both resilient and efficient, the way ecosystems are. Economics is terribly bad on resilience, which it does not have easy ways of measuring. Because we have designed our economic systems only for efficiency, we have minimized safety nets, buffers, and firewalls. As a result, we have systems that are neither efficient nor resilient because they keep on collapsing. For example, the subprime crisis in the US housing market spread throughout the world and nearly brought down the banking system. There is no resilience built into the system. You can see the same thing happening with currency crashes in Ireland and Greece. All across the world the frequency of unstable events is increasing.

Unhappiness: Well-being is declining in many of the so-called developed countries. What I think most of us don't realize is that mental health problems are increasing rapidly in many places. In 'advanced' English-speaking countries, it is now reckoned that close to one out of four people is suffering from some kind of mental health problem or illness. We are not happy people.

Putting all four problems together, it is clear that we are running faster and faster in the direction of unsustainability. We are burning up the planet, we are causing huge instability and inequality (with all the associated social problems), and we are not making ourselves any happier – if anything, less happy. Moreover these problems are interconnected.

About five years ago we calculated how much the global economy would need to go up if those who are now living on one dollar a day were to have an additional dollar. You need to raise the GDP of the whole world by \$166 a day to in order to add one more dollar for each person now earning one dollar a day. It's ecologically impossible to keep doing that. If you want to have everybody on the planet earning \$1,000 a year, which is \$3 a day, and you keep global income distribution as it is and keep the resource intensity of output as it is, you need fifteen planets' worth of resources in order for everybody in the world to make \$1,000 a year. We haven't got fifteen planets. So the need for transition is overwhelmingly clear when you start looking at these simple facts that can be figured out on a slip of paper.

3   The Underlying Causes

Let's look at the underlying causes of our predicament. I believe that much of economics, as it is now taught and practised, is both intellectually and morally bankrupt. That's a strong statement for me to make, but I think this is much truer for economics than for many other disciplines. So much of what we base our thinking on are old myths and half-truths in addition to some new myths that have developed. The renowned economist Maynard Keynes said, 'Practical men who believe themselves exempt from any intellectual influences are usually the slaves of some defunct economist'. I think that statement applies to many politicians and leaders today.

There are three pervasive economic myths that have been around for a long time. The first is that markets are fair. Markets do *not* provide the right outcomes for the benefit of the most people. Sometimes this myth is linked to the idea of 'the invisible hand'. Well, Adam Smith did mention that invisible hand once in *The Wealth of Nations* when he was talking about a bakery. But the situation on which he predicated it was that there were large numbers of buyers and sellers, none of whom could influence the price and furthermore that those actors were behaving in a moral way. Now neither of these assumptions applies. We see huge concentrations of power in many markets. There are four or five companies that control 80 to 90 per cent of the world grain market; the same is true for numerous other markets. And look at the purchasing side: do people have equal purchasing rights? No, they don't. The richest 1 per cent of the people in the world earn as much as the poorest 57 per cent. That doesn't come close to resembling a level playing field.

What happens to markets where power balances aren't equal? It's fairly simple. If you go into a market with more power than the other players, you don't end up with the same amount of power but rather with even more power. The idea of self-levelling simply doesn't apply. We need to remember that Adam Smith also wrote *The Theory of Moral Sentiments* in which he argued that markets work only if the actors are moral – and of course they're not.

Now, let me be clear. I am pro-markets; I am pro-profits and pro-companies. I think they play a critical role. But markets and companies are social and political entities we have created, not some mysterious black box. They need to be managed by us. I certainly don't recommend a planned market like the Soviet Union's, but I do believe that we need to start managing markets for the wider good. Environmentalist and energy-efficiency expert Amory Lovins put it very well when he said, 'The markets make a good servant but a bad master, and a worse religion'.[1] What we have now are markets as religion, and let's not be surprised that we are suffering the consequences.

1   *The Guardian*, 20 November 2008.

The second of the three myths is that prices tell the truth. Prices don't tell either the social or the environmental truth. In his book, *Eco-Economy*, Lester R. Brown quotes Øystein Dahle, retired vice-president of Esso for Norway and the North Sea who says, 'Socialism collapsed because it did not allow prices to tell the *economic* truth. Capitalism may collapse because it does not allow prices to tell the *ecological* truth'.[2] At the moment, prices don't tell the ecological truth at all, and in a whole range of cases they don't tell the social truth either.

The third myth is the one I've already touched on – that more income equals more happiness. For many people in the world it does not. It probably holds true only if you're poor.

The new myth is that we can continue growing forever. Economist and systems theorist Kenneth Boulding said, 'Anyone who believes exponential growth can go on forever in a finite world is either a madman or an economist'.[3] What he perhaps should have added was that there are quite a few who fall into both categories. Present company excepted of course. Much of economics is morally and intellectually bankrupt because so many people cling to the old myths. Clearly, it suits the most powerful people to keep perpetuating these myths. But it's important for us to know that they are not valid; otherwise we won't tackle the resulting problems effectively.

Most of the philosophical underpinnings throughout much of human history are based on two types of view. There are the utility theories of Jeremy Bentham and others that promote the maximum benefit for the maximum good, and don't worry about those who are left behind. This has been the prevalent attitude in economics. But many in this room, including me, identify much more strongly with the individual-rights-based view that we each have a whole series of rights. The trouble with the individual-rights-based approach – and there are many different variations from Kant to John Rawls – is that it doesn't fully apply anymore. We might *individually* be acting ethically and according to our rights, but if the *collective*

2   Lester R. Brown (2001). *Eco-Economy*. Earth Policy Institute, New York: W.W. Norton & Co, 23.

3   Attributed to Boulding in: United States. Congress. House (1973). *Energy reorganisation act of 1973: Hearings, Ninety-third Congress, on H.R. 11510*, 248.

outcome is that we consume more than our fair share of existing resources
at the expense of other people on the planet or we consume resources that
then are not available to the next generations, this is not moral behaviour.
Thus, we don't even have a common moral framework anymore, with the
result that our operating systems, philosophically and economically, are
broken. It's critical that we rebuild them, because without them we won't
get where we need to go.

I'll end this part on economic myths by telling you what President
Clinton should have said instead of 'It's the economy, stupid'. He should
have said, 'It's the economy that's stupid, stupid'.

4   A Great Transition

Let us be clear what type of economy we should be trying to build. We
need an economy which has, as its main goal, to improve human needs,
not wants. This economy needs to create and support sufficient good jobs
and good work, and to do so in a way that is much more equitable – both
between peoples alive now and between current and future generations. It
needs to be an economy that recognizes that it is but a subset of the ecosystem and which therefore works within planetary limits. Perhaps above
all though, it needs to be an economy constructed with a bio-centric view
of the world, not an anthropocentric one. We need to move from being
consumers to stewards. Such an economy must also factor in the spiritual,
the aesthetic and the symbolic.

Dream-on say most economists. Many economists believe that we will
solve the environmental limits and climate change problems by human inge-
nuity and technology – heroic technological advances and social changes
are needed for this to happen – neither facts nor human history back up
their thesis. Others see an unsolvable problem – carrying on as we are is
totally unsustainable, but putting the brakes on consumption will throw
millions out of work, and cause further great recessions!

The New Economics Foundation – NEF – believes that this latter problem is solvable. It is possible to live within planetary limits and create enough good jobs for all. We are building an economic model that demonstrates this. But to make it happen will require a transformation of our current economic thinking and practice. A Great Transition.

What does this mean? It means starting to measure, at the national level, the real goals of society. It means a shift in societal values – including from being consumers to stewards. It means radically changing incentive systems, regulation and taxation systems. It means governments starting to ensure that markets are our servants, not our masters. It means reforming the financial and banking systems to ones that are stable, fair and socially useful. It means stopping the creation of money by commercial banks for non-productive and speculative purposes. It means Governments ensuring much greater equity within societies and much fairer distribution of not just incomes, but wealth, land, natural resources and time. It means companies moving from a prime purpose to make money for shareholders to ones which have a wider social purpose benefiting a wider group of stakeholders and which need to make more money to achieve this. It means much greater devolution of economic power and activity to the local level and many of us becoming food growers and renewable energy producers, whether individually or communally.

It means radically rethinking economics. For example, the productivity function needs to move from 'maximizing returns to financial capital' to creating maximum well-being per scarce unit of national resource.

How will all this happen? It will happen if enough of us start to live differently; to buy differently, and above all, demand that our politicians change the 'rules of the game' and the incentive structures. At the minute the problem is that we are still playing our different instruments to different scores in different orchestras. We need to start playing our different instruments to one broad score in one orchestra. If we fail to get our voices heard and the necessary changes made then the world is heading for disaster of one kind or another. Perhaps those disasters will bring people to their senses, but they could equally do the opposite.

We at the New Economics Foundation can provide much of the 'what needs doing', but we cannot make it a reality on our own. There is a fearsome responsibility resting on all of us that have been inspired by Fritz Schumacher's work and life. We cannot say we did not understand. His insights, 100 years after his birth, are like a lighthouse illuminating the path forward. We need to draw on his wisdom and courage and together follow this path.

HENDRIK OPDEBEECK
UNIVERSITY OF ANTWERP

21 Conclusion: From a Utopian towards a Uglobian Economic Paradigm. Schumacher's Plea for Frugal Responsibility

> Prudence cannot be perfected except by an attitude of 'silent contemplation' of reality, during which the egocentric interests of man are at least temporarily silenced. Only on the basis of this magnanimous kind of prudence can we achieve justice, fortitude, and temperantia, which means knowing when enough is enough.
>
> — SCHUMACHER 1973: 279

1 Frugality and Responsibility

More than ever our economic system is confronted with its negative effects on man and environment. For Schumacher, when we want economics to be in equilibrium with our social and ecological environment, it is clear that a shift to frugality and responsibility assumptions will be necessary. Frugality means an ethics of a sustainable lifestyle with a prudent use of material and non-material goods. Schumacher emphasizes the consequences of the non-frugal ethics behind our economic system. In a special edition of *Time Magazine* (April/May 2000) on *How to save the Earth*, he was described as one of the heroes for the planet who brought frugality to the fore. For Schumacher reliance on individual self-restraint was crucial, but he also points out that the spreading of responsible conduct will only be realized if institutional changes (see chapter 15 in this volume) are introduced as well.

In general it is clear that from this frugal and responsible perspective, the core of the dominant economic paradigm, namely its basic assumptions like eliminating scarcity and utility maximization, can be called into question (chapter 3). These basic assumptions appear to be grounded on the nowadays untenable negation of frugality and responsibility. With a view to stimulating consumption, ever new varieties of scarcity are put forward to be tackled with as much utility maximization as possible. At the same time our world faces specific problems in the ecological and social environment. Schumacher's contribution to a less one-sided economic paradigm aims at finding a way out of these urgent problems.[1] A more inclusive paradigm based on frugality and responsibility puts in doubt whether eliminating scarcity or utility maximization are valid as relevant points of departure for our time.[2] Rather, the case can be made that today's major problems may well in essence be caused by the central position awarded to both scarcity and utility as fundamental categories.

In 1973 Schumacher publishes his bestseller *Small is Beautiful-Economics as if People Mattered*. It contains the core of his view on contemporary economic problems. In *Good Work*, he wonders how methods of labour and production that attach more value to man and his social and ecological environment really function both on the theoretical and the practical level. The essence of Schumacher's philosophical and spiritual foundation for his economic theories is elaborated in *A Guide for the Perplexed*.

---

1   W. Coolsaet's characterization of Schumacher is very revealing against the background of a less one-sided paradigm. Coolsaet writes: 'It is highly possible that a way out of the problems and not just those caused by unemployment can only be found in the direction of the alternatives proposed by Schumacher' (Coolsaet 1980: 434).

2   Cf. D. Colander who affirms that most academic economists are local utility maximizers that operate within a narrowly defined institutional structure, go about their daily business doing what they were taught to do and spend little time thinking about the broader meaning of their research, or broader ideological issues in general: 'They [...] only select problems to study that could be brought to the data, whereas many of the interesting problems could not be' (Colander 2005: 13 and 18).

2 Schumacher's Frugality- and Responsibility-based Economics

2.1 The Academic Looking for Practice

Ernst Friedrich Schumacher opted to follow in his father's academic footsteps when he went to Bonn University in 1929 where he visited the classes of Joseph Schumpeter. On a study trip to Cambridge, also in 1929, he sat in on the seminars of John Maynard Keynes with whom after the Second World War he prepared the UK plan for Bretton Woods. His academic career seemed to be taking off, but Schumacher preferred employment that would enable him to keep in closer touch with the practical world. As will be obvious, this was a necessary precondition for the author to be able to test his theories against reality. Being an economist, at that time he found employment as a financial adviser in the London City (chapter 2).

2.2 An Equilibrium between Freedom and Order

From the beginning Schumacher's economic theories concentrate on this middle way not only between theory and practice (see also 2.3) but also between an economic system that prioritizes freedom (like capitalism) and an economic system that posits order (like communism) as its central concept. In other words, Schumacher envisages an economic system that guarantees both enough freedom and enough order. He considers this tension between freedom and order to be one of the pivotal elements of his philosophical foundation (Schumacher 1973: 265), because it is so deeply incorporated in many economic problems that he considers to be *divergent* problems (chapters 14 and 16). In contrast to converging problems, in diverging problems one does not manage to arrive at one solution (either freedom or order). The reason for this is that in many economic problems lifeless nature is transcended (Schumacher 1977: 136-7). A higher degree of freedom is manifested and a lower degree of necessity or order. In such a diverging economic situation, the characteristic human element of self-consciousness is needed, with a high degree of freedom. Only when self-consciousness is included is one able to establish a balance between freedom and order. Without self-consciousness one easily slips back into the one-dimensionality of order without freedom, thus reducing all problems to converging problems.

In solving economic problems, one faces the choice between either allowing more freedom or postulating more order (norms and planning), or yet arriving at a sensible compromise. This applies to the macro-economy as well as to the micro-economy. In this way a government can either give enterprises free reign in deciding whether or not they will respect certain limits (e.g. for countering unemployment or environmental pollution) or it can impose stringent norms. In an enterprise the entrepreneur can feel free to treat his workers merely in the service of maximizing his profit, but he can also try to arrive at norms of human development and co-operation.

2.3 An Equilibrium between the Micro- and the Macro-level

Starting from this philosophical distinction between convergent and divergent problems, Schumacher stresses the importance of the basic human condition of constantly having to reconcile opposites.[3] We need both order and freedom. However, this is not a purely technical problem that can be solved by reason in only one way. It is possible, within an economic system, to either opt for more freedom or rather to impose order. The results of such choices will, obviously, diverge from each other. Schumacher therefore emphasizes that divergent problems are resolved in the optimal manner by tackling the macro-economic practice from the point of departure of the economic practice on the micro-level. The reason for this is that the distinguishing feature of a diverging problem, as explained, is that one has

3   A. Rich is of the same opinion as Schumacher when he underlines that if the system
     of the market economy has the advantage of being thoroughly reformable, it also
     requires regulations which are equitable and responsible: in this view, one better
     understands the inescapable failure of Marxism but also the ethical ramifications of
     savage deregulations (Rich 2006).

to rely on the human factor of self-consciousness in attempting to solve it. Consciousness of the self allows man to generate understanding, will, power and sympathy, which allow him to transcend the freedom/order opposition. The starting point of these typical characteristics of self-consciousness lies not primarily on the macro-level but on the individual level (chapters 10 and 11) where man is able to make the conscious choice of showing understanding and sympathy in practice with a view to realizing concrete changes. In the words of Schumacher: 'People are no longer angry when told that restoration must come from within; the belief that everything is "politics" and that radical rearrangements of "system" will suffice to save civilisation is no longer held' (Schumacher 1977: 152; Schumacher 1979: 36). We are therefore not exclusively dealing with the structural, large-scale, macro-level in this case, but first of all with the personal, small-scale, micro-level (chapter 17). Since in this approach of Schumacher practice is emphasized above all, at this stage one leaves, as it were, the theoretical macro-level for the practical micro-level.[4]

2.4 Frugality and Responsibility Rediscovered

Schumacher emphasizes that we need virtues like frugality and responsibility as the central viewpoint for this personal and structural dimension. The trap of slipping back into a narrow-minded, scarcity-based attitude towards the marketplace, in which only the utilitarian is considered, needs to be avoided. However, the economic system has reduced the virtues of frugality and responsibility to vices by focusing on scarcity and utility as the phenomena to be conquered in the service of economic growth. Environmental degradation and social exclusion are the externalization of this trend – the clear opposite of frugality and responsibility.

---

4   Cf. what R. Lekachman writes about *Good Work*: 'The message here, as in Schumacher's previous volumes is a call, not for class or economic warfare, but for the improvement of individual behavior and activity and the transformation of industrial society into a human residence [...]. He asks us to start where we are with ourselves and our immediate environment' (Lekachman 1979: 12).

A characteristic example of Schumacher's frugality- and responsibility-based economics is the way in which he sees labour can be performed (chapter 6). Labour can contribute to the satisfaction of three fundamental human needs. Man can express himself in labour both as a personal being and as a social and spiritual being. When man is left out in the cold when it comes to these needs, Schumacher argues, his happiness is nipped in the bud. Man is not satisfied with simply performing labour as an autonomous centre of power on the basis of his available talents.

Besides his specific views on labour, in Schumacher's theories one also discerns a strong emphasis on intermediate technology (chapter 13). Intermediate technology avoids the pitfalls of both modern and primitive technology. Intermediate technology is more oriented to smaller scales, less complexity, less capital-intensity and less violence towards man and nature. In co-operation with others, by means of intermediate technology individuals can lay the concrete foundations of an optimal economic system. According to Schumacher, the existing economic system is a product of modern technology and can only be moved in a better direction when technology is reoriented in a different way. However, the intermediate economic system Schumacher focuses on relies not only on intermediate technology, but also on changes in other aspects such as the labour conditions, different types of ownership and the reorganization of large-scale enterprises.[5]

2.5 The Micro-Meso-Macro Approach

Finally Schumacher insists on the fact that the emergence of this concrete economic alternative starting from the micro-level is essentially linked with the possibility of encouraging others to move towards a better practice by themselves. This practice then can reach the macro-level via the meso-level. The power of the example, the importance of exercising virtues and

5   For a more inclusive survey of Schumacher's intermediate economics see: Opdebeeck 1986.

of a broad humanistic education are vital here.[6] Schumacher therefore attaches the utmost importance to responsible experiments with intermediate technology, as well as to the elaboration of small-scale enterprises that exhibit the features of a more frugal optimal economic system in developed and less developed countries (chapter 18). By extension, and taking the necessary corrections into account, these features can also be introduced on the meso-level (large-scale enterprises with a more human face, for instance) and on the macro-level. Schumacher's personal practice in organizations like the Intermediate Technology Development Group and the Scott Bader Commonwealth, as described in the last chapters of the three parts of this book, can be viewed as a permanent realization and confirmation of this vision.

3   From a Utopian towards a Uglobian Economic Paradigm

Viewed from the dominant paradigm in economic science Schumacher's theories are very deviant. They rather point to another economic paradigm. However, considering the current interest in and need for more sustainability in business and economics, Schumacher's legacy may well become increasingly relevant. Normally an author like Schumacher is relatively quickly referred to as charismatic (chapter 19), or marginalized as naïve or utopian. Any reference to the real possibility of such an economics of responsible frugality is rapidly thought to be utopian. One argues that the ethics behind it would not agree with the essence of man as a covetous animal that always wants more. In this way Schumacher's project is a utopia, given man's limited possibilities and the political and social constellations one is faced with.

---

6   A recent articulation of this concern can be found in publications of Martha Nussbaum (Nussbaum 2010) and Peter Sloterdijk (Sloterdijk 2009).

As a matter of fact Schumacher's thinking is often described as utopian because at first sight he indeed belongs to a tradition of utopian authors like Saint-Simon, Fourier, Proudhon, Sismondi, Carlyle, Ruskin, Morris, Hobson, Tawney and Gandhi.[7] Among these authors Schumacher himself devotes most attention to Owen, Ruskin, Morris, Gandhi (chapter 5) and Tawney. These authors are among the great representatives, since the eighteenth century, of what could be called in Kuhnian terms the utopian economic paradigm. When economic science first established itself with Adam Smith's *The Wealth of Nations* (1767) at the end of the eighteenth century, alternative paradigms simultaneously began to develop. The utopian economic paradigm for example comprises theories that strive for a more humane economic system. These theories have not yet reached the stage of a full-fledged 'normal' science. The core of Schumacher's work, for instance, is to be found more in his concrete pre-paradigmatic pioneering work than in a detailed theoretical elaboration of a complete new paradigm as such.

However, an author like Schumacher now allows us to increasingly conceive what we would like to call a rising *u-globian* economic paradigm. We first had the utopian vision of a better place (*topos*) in the future: utopian. Now, confronted with the socio-ecological impact of globalization, we realize we have to put energy not only into our city, our country or our continent. We are also urgently confronted with the sustainability problems of the whole world (*globos*), not somewhere in the future but in the concrete present. The need for a u-globian economic paradigm also finds its ground in the fact that in contrast with a utopian economic paradigm nowadays socio-ecological empirical facts really force economics to change radically as fast as possible. In a uglobian economic paradigm the pure, idealistic motivation we discovered behind the utopian paradigm since Plato and Thomas More can be left behind.[8]

---

7   For a survey see, among others: Manuel 1979.
8   The notion of 'uglobian' instead of 'utopian' that I launch here is a topical application of what E. Bloch (1885–1977) meant by a *concrete* instead of an *abstract* utopia (*Das Prinzip Hoffnung*).

4 The Spirituality behind Schumacher's Uglobian Economic Paradigm

Yet the fundamental difference between Schumacher's approach and the features that the different currents within the utopian economic paradigm have in common lies in Schumacher's specific spiritual thinking. As explained, Schumacher advocates practical economic experiments on the micro-level with a view to improving the macro-economic system. He accepts that one has to create the possible space in the present for what one wants to achieve, so that it can be realized in the future. This spiritual approach was obviously not explicitly shared by most of the typical representatives of the utopian paradigm.[9] The fact that before the war Schumacher had obviously been a humanist who chose not to become involved in any kind of spirituality, helped him later to situate this philosophy of life within a pluralistic openness. The time he spent in the internment camp and his reading of Marx strengthened this attitude. His humanist stance was further developed in the work on full employment he did for Beveridge. The ruined Germany of 1945 convinced him even more of the dire consequences of a political and economic system that is not primarily concerned with the value of human beings. Yet little by little Schumacher's fundamental concern with man in the system of economics was to find a place in a different world view. In the beginning of the 1950s the author had distanced himself from his a-religious stance and he began to study and practise Buddhism (chapters 4 and 7). He read the work of experts like G. Gurdjieff. As early as 1953 Schumacher discovered the books of M. Nicoll in which the thinking of the Buddhist Gurdjieff is related to Christianity. Schumacher embarked on an intensive study of the work of

9   Even if one were to include authors belonging to the Christian solidaristic school like J. Buchez (1796–1865), F. Huet (1814–69), and Charles Kingsley (1819–75) in the utopian economic pre-paradigm, this Christian source of inspiration remains a marginal phenomenon within the context of the totality of utopian theories.

Thomas Aquinas and that of other Christian philosophers like R. Guénon, J. Maritain and E. Mounier.[10]

One can briefly describe the difference between Schumacher and the representatives of the utopian paradigm as the difference between an eschatological spirituality and a utopian spirituality. In terms of the philosopher Martin Buber eschatology, especially in its most basic prophetic form, awards man an important, active share in the advent of salvation. But the decisive act takes place on a higher than human level. In utopian thinking, on the other hand, everything is subject to man's conscious will. One might even describe utopia as an imaginary image of society constructed as if there were no other elements involved except for man's conscious will (Friedman 1996).

It is entirely understandable that not everybody is at ease with this spiritual background to Schumacher's legacy. The impact of Schumacher's work might even be limited by this, because one might be tempted to think that man's self-realization and his social being actively demand a spiritual (Christian) background. Yet an economic system geared more to man's social and ecological environment, as Schumacher's legacy proves, appeals to both Christians and non-Christians alike. One can even say that the uglobian paradigm to which Schumacher belongs at present offers the possibility of elaborating economic theories that solve the really urgent problems within a pluralistic context.[11] Schumacher indeed considers spirituality not so much as a (religious) target but rather, in the line of the philosopher H. Bergson (Bergson 1932), as a plural source of what is called here the frugality ethics behind responsible economics. Seeking satisfaction and self-expression in a sustainable world is indeed a source of concern across different (religious) faiths. As mentioned in chapter 12, of course many atheists too are troubled by the social and ecological repercussions of consumerism. An atheist 'spirituality' here coincides with that of religion.

---

10   Just like Schumacher, personalists such as E. Mounier and J. Maritain were strongly influenced by the above-sketched utopian pre-paradigm. See: Bouckaert 2004: 34.

11   In this sense, the economics profession risks being the opposite of pluralistic and often is dogmatically tied to a value-laden neoclassical orthodoxy. According to Fullbrook more and more universities are eliminating competing ideas and in this way facilitate students' indoctrination: Fullbrook 2003: 2.

5 Epilogue

Owing to their special position, Schumacher and many representatives of the utopian and uglobian economic paradigm might be considered humanists who wrote about economics and tested their theories against practice. They contributed to the elaboration of an economics that tackles problems in a frugal and responsible way. In his 'General Theory', for instance, John Maynard Keynes refered to Hobson's theory of under-consumption. In the obituary for Keynes that Schumacher wrote in *The Times*, he explained how Keynes built bridges between academic economists and such important figures as Mandeville, Malthus, Marx and Hobson.

Schumacher's first theories directly influenced both Keynes's Bretton Woods proposal and Beveridge's employment plan. Schumacher's later theories not only provided various organizations, such as the Scott Bader Company and the Intermediate Technology Development Group, with a certain direction in which to develop, but they were also elaborated more systematically (chapter 9). Schumacher not only developed theories that question the basic presuppositions of the dominant economic paradigm, such as eliminating scarcity and utility maximization. Within a pluralistic perspective,[12] he also elaborated a specific philosophical and spiritual foundation for an economic paradigm based on frugality and responsibility. To construct an economic system more worthy of man's social and ecological environment, he offered a prospect on the further elaboration of such a paradigm.

More than forty years after the publication of Schumacher's *Small is Beautiful* one can safely state that orientations like (neo-)institutional economics, social economics, co-operativist economics, environmental economics, radical political economics and green economics are some of today's most important economic paradigms, inspired by what we explained

---

12 'In the Christian tradition, as in all genuine traditions of mankind, the truth has been stated in religious terms, a language which has become well-nigh incomprehensible to the majority of modern man. The language can be revised, and there are contemporary writers who have done so, while leaving the truth inviolate' (Schumacher 1973: 278).

as the uglobian paradigm Schumacher began to work out. Although frugality and responsibility are contrary to consumerism and excessive economic growth, it becomes more and more evident that they are not contrary to what is fundamentally regarded as economic rationality. We are back at the origins of the word frugality in Latin. *Frugalis* means useful or worthy and *frux* means productive in a fruitful way. It is promising that at the heart of all the chapters in this book we discover this frugality dimension. At least one thing becomes clear from the legacy of Schumacher. When we want economics to be more in equilibrium with our social and ecological environment, an economic paradigm based on frugality and responsibility has to be taken very seriously.

Schumacher died on 4 September 1977. Just before his death he had traveled extensively through Australia, Asia, America and Europe. During his travels, which left him exhausted, he had given countless lectures to various audiences composed of academics, politicians, and the general public. He obviously lived a life of great intensity. On the professional level he was able to link theory with practice in various fields. The last paragraph of Schumacher's *Small is Beautiful* contains the core of this legacy:

> Everywhere people ask: 'What can I actually *do?*' The answer is as simple as it is disconcerting: we can, each of us, work to put our own inner house in order. The guidance we need for this work cannot be found in science or technology, the value of which utterly depends on the ends they serve; but it can still be found in the traditional wisdom of mankind.

References

Bergson, H. (1932). *Les deux sources de la morale et de la religion*. Paris: P.U.F.

Botkin, J. (ed.) (1979). *No Limits to Learning*. Oxford: Pergamon.

Bouckaert, L. (2004). 'De begrensde economie'. In J. Graafland & F. van Peperstraeten (eds), *De omheining doorbroken, Economie en filosofie in beweging*, pp. 33–4. Budel: Damon.

Bouckaert, L., Opdebeeck, H. & Zsolnai, L. (2008). *Frugality. Rebalancing Material and Spiritual Values in Economic Life.* Oxford: Peter Lang.

Colander, D. (2005). 'Economics as an ideologically challenged science', *Revue de Philosophie économique,* 11, 9–30.

Coolsaet, W. (1980). 'Fritz Schumacher', *Tijdschrift voor diplomatie,* 6 (February), 426–34.

Daniels, P. (2005). 'Economic Systems and the Buddhist World View', *Journal of Socio-Economics,* 34 (2), 245–68.

Ekins, P. & Max-Neef, M. (1992). *Real Life Economics.* London: Routledge.

Friedman, M. & Boni, P. (1996). *Martin Buber and the Human Sciences.* New York: State University of New York Press.

Fullbrook, E. (2003). *The Crisis in Economics.* London: Routledge.

George, S. (2003). *The Lugano Report. On preserving Capitalism in the 21st Century.* London: Pluto Press.

Goderez, C. (1976). *The World Bank in Small Business Development.* Washington D.C.: The World Bank.

Goudzwaard, B. (1978). *Kapitalisme en vooruitgang.* Assen and Amsterdam: Van Gorcum.

Irvine, K. & Kaplan, S. (2001). 'Coping with Change: The Small Experiment as a Strategic Approach to Environmental Sustainability', *Environmental Management,* 28 (6), 713–25.

Johnson, W. (1978). *Muddling toward Frugality.* San Francisco: Sierra Club Books.

Kuhn, T. (1970). *The Structure of Scientific Revolutions.* Chicago: University of Chicago Press.

Langenberg, S. & Vandekerckhove, W. (eds) (2005). *Hoe vrij is de markt zonder (spirituele) grenzen?* Antwerpen and Apeldoorn: Garant.

Leeman, W. (1977). *Centralized and Decentralized Economic Systems.* Chicago: The Rand McNally College Publication Company.

Lekachman, R. (1979). 'Between the Hoe and Tractor', *New York Times Book Review,* May 20, 12.

Lutz, M. & Lux K. (1979). *The Challenge of Humanistic Economics.* London and Menlo: The Benjamin Cummings Publishing Company.

Manuel, F. (1979). *Utopian Thought in the Western World.* Oxford: Blackwell.

Nussbaum, M. (2010). *Not for Profit.* Princeton: Princeton University Press.

Olson, M. (1974). *The Logic of Collective Action.* Cambridge, Mass.: Mancur Olson.

Opdebeeck, H. (1986). *Schumacher is Beautiful.* Antwerp: DNB.

Opdebeeck, H. (2002). *Building Towers, Perspectives on Globalisation.* Leuven: Ethical Perspectives Monographs Series Peeters.

Opdebeeck, H. (2012). 'Responsibility in a globalised environment: a charter of human responsibilities', *Journal of Global Responsibility*, 3 (1), 111–20.

Perrotta, C. (2003). 'The legacy of the past: ancient economic thought on wealth and development', *European Journal of the History of Economic Thought*, 10 (2), 177–229.

Rich, A. (2006). *Business and Economic Ethics: the Ethics of Economic Systems*. Leuven: Peeters.

Schumacher, E. (1973). *Small is Beautiful*. London: Blond and Briggs.

Schumacher, E. (1977). *Guide for the Perplexed*. London: Jonathan Cape.

Schumacher, E. (1979). *Good Work*. London: Jonathan Cape.

Sloterdijk, P. (2009). *Du musst dein Leben ändern*. Frankfurt am Main: Suhrkamp Verlag.

Stern, P. (2000). 'New Environmental Theories: Toward a Coherent Theory of Environmentally Significant Behavior', *Journal of Social Issues*, 56 (3), 407–24.

Tawney, R. (1962, first edn 1921). *The Acquisitive Society*. London: Collins.

Tyrrell, G. (1930). *Grades of Significance*. London: Rider and Comp.

Vandenbroeck, G. (ed.) (1978). *Less is more*. New York: Harper.

Van Parijs, Ph. (2003). 'Frugal tastes and frugal conduct', *Ethical Perspectives*, 10 (2), 151–5.

Varma, R. (2003). 'E.F. Schumacher: Changing the Paradigm of Bigger is Better', *Bulletin of Science, Technology & Society*, 23 (2), 114–24.

Zsolnai, L. & Ims, K. (eds) (2006). *Business Within Limits*. Oxford: Peter Lang.

PROPOSAL for a Charter of Universal Responsibilities presented at the Rio+20 Conference June 2012

Preamble

We, Representatives of the Member States of the United Nations, gathered in Rio de Janeiro for the Earth Summit, June 2012

Recognizing

1. that the scope and irreversibility of the *interdependences* that have been generated among human beings, among societies, and between humankind and the biosphere constitute a radically new situation in the history of humankind, changing it irrevocably into a community of destiny;
2. that indefinite pursuit of *current lifestyles and development*, together with a trend to *limit one's responsibilities*, is *incompatible* with harmony amongst societies, with preservation of the integrity of the planet, and with safekeeping the interests of future generations;
3. that the scope of today's *necessary changes* is out of range of individuals and implies that all people and all public or private institutions become involved in them;
4. that the currently existing *legal, political and financial procedures designed to steer and monitor* public and private institutions, in particular those that have an impact worldwide, do not motivate these latter to assume their full responsibilities, and may even encourage their *irresponsibility*;

5. that *awareness of our shared responsibilities* to the planet is a condition for the survival and progress of humankind;

6. that our *shared responsibility, beyond the legitimate interests of our peoples*, is to preserve our only, fragile planet by preventing major unbalances from bringing about ecological and social disasters that will affect all the peoples of the Earth,

7. that *consideration of the interests of others and of the community*, and reciprocity among its members are the foundations of mutual trust, a sense of security, and respect of each person's dignity and of justice;

8. that the proclamation and *pursuit of universal rights* are *not sufficient to adjust our behaviour*, as rights are inoperative when there is no single institution able to guarantee the conditions of their application;

9. that these facts require the adoption of *common ethical principles* as inspiration for our behaviour and our rules as well as those of our peoples

We adopt, in the name of our peoples, the present Charter of Universal Responsibilities and we commit:

- to make it the foundation for our behaviour and our relations,
- to promote it among all sectors of society,
- to take it into account and to put it into practice in international law and in national law.

Principles of Universal Responsibility

1. The exercise of one's responsibilities is the expression of one's freedom and dignity as a citizen of the world community.

2. Individual human beings and everyone together have a shared responsibility to others, to close and distant communities, and to the planet, proportionately to their assets, power and knowledge.

3. Such responsibility involves taking into account the immediate or deferred effects of all acts, preventing or offsetting their damages, whether or not they were perpetrated voluntarily and whether or not they affect subjects of law. It applies to all fields of human activity and to all scales of time and space.

4. Such responsibility is imprescriptible from the moment damage is irreversible.

5. The responsibility of institutions, public and private ones alike, whatever their governing rules, does not exonerate the responsibility of their leaders and vice versa.

6. The possession or enjoyment of a natural resource induces responsibility to manage it to the best of the common good.

7. The exercise of power, whatever the rules through which it is acquired, is legitimate only if it accounts for its acts to those over whom it is exercised and if it comes with rules of responsibility that measure up to the power of influence being exercised.

8. No one is exempt from his or her responsibility for reasons of helplessness if he or she did not make the effort of uniting with others, nor for reasons of ignorance if he or she did not make the effort of becoming informed.

Notes on Contributors

LUDO ABICHT is emeritus professor of ethics and Middle Eastern studies at the universities of Ghent and Antwerp. He was professor of European Studies at the University of New Brunswick (Fredericton, NB, Canada), Antioch University (Ohio, US) and UC Berkeley (US). He is the author of many articles in *New German Critique*, *Monthly Review*, *Athenäum*, *Civis Mundi*, *Etcetera* and *Mores*. He has published many books, among which *Paul Adler, ein Dichter aus Prag* (1973).

CHRISTIAN ARNSPERGER is professor of economics at the Université catholique de Louvain in Louvain-la-Neuve, Belgium. He is also a senior research fellow with the Belgian National Science Foundation (F.R.S.-FNRS). His research and teaching work takes place at the juncture between economics, ethics and ecology. His main current research topic is the transition towards a 'green economy' and its implications in terms of banking and finance. He is also active in the area of monetary economics and within the paradigm of ecological economics. He is the author of numerous articles in peer-reviewed scientific journals and has published many books, among which most recently *Money and Sustainability: The Missing Link* (Triarchy Press 2012, with Bernard Lietaer, Sally Goerner and Stefan Brunnhuber); *L'homme économique et le sens de la vie: Petit traité d'alter-économie* (Textuel 2011); and *Full-Spectrum Economics: Toward an Inclusive and Emancipatory Social Science* (Routledge 2010).

LUK BOUCKAERT is emeritus professor of ethics at the Catholic University of Leuven (K.U. Leuven, Belgium). He is a philosopher and an economist by training. His research and publications fall within the fields of business ethics and spirituality. In 1987 he founded with some colleagues the interdisciplinary Centre for Economics and Ethics at Leuven. In 2000 he started the SPES Forum (Spirituality in Economics and Society) and some years later the international European SPES Forum. He wrote several books in Dutch. Recent publications in English include: *Spirituality as a Public Good* (co-edited with Laszlo Zsolnai, 2007), *Frugality. Rebalancing Material and Spiritual Values in Economic Life* (co-edited with H. Opdebeeck and L. Zsolnai, 2008), *Imagine Europe* (co-edited with J. Eynikel, 2009), *Respect and Economic Democracy* (co-edited with Pasquale Arena, 2010) and *The Palgrave Handbook of Spirituality and Business* (co-edited with Laszlo Zsolnai, 2011).

PHILIP BRUCE graduated in chemistry from Aberdeen University, attended a senior management course at INSEAD and worked for 23 years with ICI where he held a variety of roles from operations, sales, marketing, purchasing and business to general management. Philip Bruce has been the Group Managing Director of Scott Bader Group since March 2005. Scott Bader is a Trustee owned company headquartered in Northamptonshire with five key manufacturing locations around the world, producing different chemicals.

LUIGINO BRUNI is professor of economics at the Lumsa University in Rome and at the Sophia University Institute at Loppiano (Florence). For the last fifteen years his research has covered many areas including microeconomics, ethics and economics, history of economic thought, methodology of economics, sociality and happiness in economics. Recently, he has taken a great interest in the civil economy and economics-related categories, such as reciprocity and gratuitousness. Luigino's current research focuses on the role of intrinsic motivation in economic and civil life.

BERNHARD CALLEBAUT is professor at the Sophia University Institute at Loppiano (Florence). He did studies in law and philosophy and graduated in sociology at the Catholic University of Louvain. He took his PhD in social sciences at the Pontifical University of Saint Thomas Aquinas in Rome, where he also taught. His main interests are in the fields of sociology of religion and sociology of cultural processes. He has published on the role of religious movements, charisma and modernity, the sociology of science and technology and the European unification process.

GERRIT DE VYLDER obtained his PhD in economics from Tilburg University (UvT) in the Netherlands. He is presently teaching economic history and international political economy at Lessius University College (subfaculty of Business Studies), Antwerp, Belgium, and is connected to the Centre for Economics and Ethics at Leuven University. He also has been guest-lecturing on the topic of India and the ethical and philosophical aspects of globalization and economic growth in a number of institutions in different countries. He has written articles and books on development projects, the history of the publishing and printing sectors in Belgium, the colonial trade of Antwerp, the international textile trade and the economic history of India and Turkey. He is currently working on the history of globalization (from an Asian and Indian point of view), and on the relationship between religion (Hinduism, Buddhism, Confucianism/ Taoism, Islam, Christianity) and economics, and between Orientalist literature and economics.

CARLOS HOEVEL is professor of history of economic and political ideas, business ethics and philosophy of economics at the departments of Economics and Business of the Catholic University of Argentina (UCA). He is also director of that university's Center of Studies for Economy and Culture and of the journal *Cultura Económica*. He is a doctor in philosophy (UCA) and a master of arts in the social sciences (University of Chicago). Some recent publications: *La filosofia dell'economia di Antonio Rosmini*; *Bag and Life: the University under the Sway of Global Market*; *Mann's Buddenbrooks, Adorno's & Horkheimer's Odysseus and the Tragedy of Business Leadership*; *Rosmini's Economic Personalism and the Soul of Europe*; and most recently *The Economy of Recognition: Person, Market and Society in Antonio Rosmini*.

KNUT J. IMS is professor in business ethics at the Department of Strategy and Management at the Norwegian School of Economics. He has a PhD from The School of Economics and Legal Science, Gothenburg University, Sweden, and teaches business ethics at bachelor, master and PhD levels. He is a member of the business ethics faculty of the CEMS. He is the co-editor (with L. Zsolnai) of *Business within Limits: Deep Ecology and*

Buddhist Economy (2006). His recent publications include 'Consumerism and Frugality: Contradictory Principles in Economics?' (with O. Jakobsen) in L. Bouckaert, H. Opdebeeck and L. Zsolnai (eds) *Frugality. Rebalancing Material and Spiritual Values in Economic Life* (2008), 'Holistic Problem Solving' (with L. Zsolnai) in L. Zsolnai, and A. Tencati (eds), *The Future International Manager: A Vision of the Roles and Duties of Management* (2009), 'From the Art of Reading to the Art of Leading' (with L.J. Pedersen) in *Spiritual Humanism and Economic Wisdom. Essays in Honour of Luk Bouckaert's 70th Anniversary* (eds H. Opdebeeck & L. Zsolnai, 2011), and 'Deep Authenticity – An Essential Phenomenon in the Web of Life' (with O. Jakobsen) in *Business Ethics and Corporate Sustainability* (eds A. Tencati and F. Perrini, 2011).

OVE JAKOBSEN is professor in ecological economics at Bodø Graduate School of Business, University of Nordland (Norway). He is co-founder and leader of the Centre for Ecological Economics and Ethics at HHB. He is a member of the National Committee for Research Ethics in the Social Sciences and the Humanities (NESH). In addition to holding a PhD in economics from the Norwegian School of Economics and Business Administration, Jakobsen holds three master degrees; in philosophy, marketing, and administration and leadership. In 2000, Jakobsen received the SAS and the Norwegian Economics Association prize for the the the best integration of environmental and societal responsibility in lectures at Norwegian Business Schools. His major research interests are ecological economics/circulation economics, business ethics/CSR, holistic science and development based on sustainability, resilience and quality of life. He has published a number of scientific articles and books both nationally and internationally.

PAUL JORION is professor at the Free University of Brussels where he obtained a PhD in the social sciences and MA degrees in sociology and social anthropology. He was a lecturer at the universities of Cambridge, Paris VIII and at the University of California at Irvine. He worked as a United Nations Officer (FAO), on development projects in Africa. Jorion was active in the American financial world as a pricing specialist from 1998 to 2007. Prior to this he was a trader on the futures markets in a French investment bank. He wrote a book on the consequences of the bankruptcy of Enron for the stock market: *Investing in a Post-Enron World* (McGraw-Hill 2003). In a book published in 2007, *La crise du capitalisme américain* (La Découverte 2007; Le Croquant 2009), Jorion predicted in detail the subprime crisis. His most recent books include *Le capitalisme à l'agonie* (Fayard 2011) and *La guerre civile numérique* (Textuel 2011).

GÁBOR KOVÁCS is affiliated with the Corvinus University of Budapest. He received his bachelor degree at the Budapest Technical College in the field of technical management and his master's degree at The Dharma Gate Buddhist College, Budapest. His thesis was about the theory and practice of Buddhist economics. From the fall of 2010 he has been working as a PhD student at the Business Ethics Center of the Corvinus University of Budapest. He has been taking part in research in the field of business ethics since 2005. His research areas encompass Buddhist economics and spiritual value-orientations in entrepreneurship. Currently he is working in a research project in the field of ecological sustainability.

MICHAŁ ADAM MICHALSKI is assistant professor in the Department of Business Ethics, Institute of Cultural Studies, Faculty of Social Sciences at Adam Mickiewicz University (AMU) in Poznań, Poland. He is a graduate of Management and Marketing at AMU Poznań, and wrote a doctoral thesis on the *Cultural Dimension of Human Labour* (2003). He published the book: *Człowiek, kultura, praca. O kulturowym wymiarze pracy ludzkiej (Man, Culture, Labour. On the Cultural Dimension of Human Labour)*, Wydawnictwo Poznańskie, Poznań, 2005.

WALTER G. MOSS is emeritus professor of history at Eastern Michigan University (EMU). He was born in Cincinnati, Ohio and received a B.S. from that city's Xavier University in 1960, as well as a PhD in Russian area studies and history from Georgetown University in 1968. From 1960 to 1962, he served as an officer in the U.S. Army, including a six-month service in France. While in graduate school at Georgetown, he also worked briefly for the Defense Intelligence Agency. From 1967 until 2010, he taught Russian and global history, at Wheeling Jesuit College. During the 1980s and 1990s he often took student groups to the USSR/Russia and Eastern Europe.

ZUBIN R. MULLA is an assistant professor at the School of Management and Labour Studies at the Tata Institute of Social Sciences (www.tiss.edu). He has a degree in mechanical engineering, a post-graduate diploma in business management, and a doctorate in management. Prior to moving to the Tata Institute in 2005, he had eight years' experience in working in engineering and management consulting in large-scale change management interventions. His current research interests include transformational leadership, Karma-Yoga (the Indian philosophy of work motivation), and strategic human resource management. One of his most notable contributions is a conceptualization of the concept of Karma-Yoga and the development of some measurement techniques for Karma-Yoga.

HENDRIK OPDEBEECK is professor of philosophy at the University of Antwerp where he is affiliated with the Centre for Ethics. He studied philosophy and economics at the universities of Leuven and Ghent where he obtained a PhD with a dissertation on E.F. Schumacher (1911–77). His research is focused on the cultural-philosophical backgrounds and effects of globalization. His publications in English include *The Foundation and Application of Moral Philosophy* (Peeters, 2000), *Building Towers, Perspectives on Globalisation* (Ethical Perspectives Monographs Series, Peeters, 2002), *Frugality. Rebalancing Material and Spiritual Values in Economic Life* (Peter Lang, 2008, with L. Bouckaert and L. Zsolnai) and *Spiritual Humanism and Economic Wisdom* (Garant, 2011, with L. Zsolnai). Hendrik Opdebeeck is president of the Belgian SPES-forum (Spirituality in Economics and Society).

JOEL THOMPSON is director of Africurrency Ltd. Africurrency designs and implements socially inclusive exchange systems built upon traditional African socioeconomic norms for the benefit of local economics. Africurrency is currently implementing an electronic complementary currency system for NGOs in Kenya, called the NGO Credit Circuit (NCC).

SIMON TRACE is the Chief Executive of Practical Action (formerly the Intermediate Technology Development Group, founded by E.F. Schumacher in 1965). He has nearly thirty years' experience in international development and took up his current post with Practical Action in 2005. Simon Trace is a chartered civil engineer with an MA in the anthropology of development from the School of Oriental and African Studies and his career has focused on the practice of technology in sustainable development. Prior to joining Practical Action he spent 20 years working for the NGO WaterAid, firstly on soil and water management, drinking water and sanitation in South Asia and then on a series of posts at its headquarters, including six years as international operations director. His career at WaterAid included a number of years seconded as an advisor to other organizations, including CARE and Unicef. He has worked across East, West and Southern Africa, South Asia and Latin America.

ROY VARGHESE, born in Kerala, India, is affiliated with the centre for Ethics, Social and Political Philosophy at the Higher Institute of Philosophy of the Catholic University of Leuven. His PhD research consisted in a comparison of Amartya Sen's and Ronald Dworkin's political theories. He has done a master's and M.Phil. in commerce at the Mahatma Gandhi University, Kerala, India and is a licentiate in philosophy from Dharmaram Vidya Kshetram, Bangalore, India. He taught business ethics and philosophy for two years. He recently did his M.Phil. at KU, Leuven. His research interests include ethics, spirituality and political philosophy. He is working as the general editor of *Sunday Shalom*, a Christian weekly newspaper from India, and is a regular contributor to Indian newspapers and magazines. Among his books is *Cathedrals of Development: A Critique on the Developmental Model of Amartya Sen*. His articles include: 'Economic Life and Human Transcendence: A Paradigm for Everyday Spirituality', 'Prodigal Freedom and Asymmetric Violence: A Development Audit', and 'Permanent Revolution and Perpetual Peace: Revisiting Kantian Cosmopolitanism'. He has written four books in the local Indian language of Malayalam.

ALEXIS VERSELE is an architect and works with Barbara Wauman and Hilde Breesch as an affiliated researcher on sustainable building at the Department of Industrial Engineering of the Catholic University College Ghent and K.U. Leuven. He is chairman of the social-profit organization Domus Mundi. Its mission consists in enabling vulnerable groups to build in an ecological and a sustainable way. He has a master's degree in architecture from Ghent and in industrial design from Milan. His research interest is focused on cost-effective commissioning of low-energy buildings, green building certification, sustainable building in developing countries, and urban renewal for vulnerable groups.

STEWART WALLIS graduated in natural sciences from Cambridge University. His career began in marketing and sales with Rio Tinto Zinc followed by a master's degree in business and economics at London Business School. He spent seven years with the World Bank in Washington DC working on industrial and financial development in East Asia. He then worked for Robinson Packaging in Derbyshire for nine years, the last five as Managing Director, leading a successful business turnaround. He joined Oxfam in 1992 as International Director with responsibility, latterly, for 2,500 staff in 70 countries and for all Oxfam's policy, research, development and emergency work worldwide. He was awarded the OBE for services to Oxfam in 2002. Stewart joined the NEF (New Economics Foundation) as Executive Director on 1 November 2003. His interests include: global governance, functioning of markets, links between development and environmental agendas, the future of capitalism and the moral economy.

BARBARA WOOD is E.F. Schumacher's eldest daughter and biographer. She has degrees in economics and history, theology, and a master's in Christianity Interreligious Dialogue. She is a writer and is active in the Catholic Church in England, particularly in the areas of ecumenism and dialogue between the religions.

LASZLO ZSOLNAI is professor and director of the Business Ethics Center at the Corvinus University of Budapest. He is chairman of the Business Ethics Faculty Group of the CEMS (Community of European Management Schools–The Global Alliance in Management Education). He serves as editor of the 'Frontiers of Business Ethics' book series at Peter Lang Publishers in Oxford. With Luk Bouckaert he founded the European SPES Forum in Leuven, Belgium. Laszlo Zsolnai's most recent books include *Spirituality as a Public Good* (2007), *Frugality. Rebalancing Material and Spiritual Values in Economic Life* (2008), *Europe-Asia Dialogue on Business Spirituality* (2008), *Responsible Decision Making* (2008), *The Future International Manager: A Vision of the Roles and Duties of Management* (2009) and *The Collaborative Enterprise: Creating Values for a Sustainable World* (2010).

Index

Frontiers of Business Ethics

Series Editor

LASZLO ZSOLNAI

Business Ethics Center
Corvinus University of Budapest

This series is dedicated to alternative approaches that go beyond the literature of conventional business ethics and corporate social responsibility. It aims to promote a new ethical model for transforming business into humanistic, sustainable and peaceful forms. The series publishes monographs and edited volumes with fresh ideas and breakthrough conceptions relevant for scholars and practitioners alike.